London, July 2010

To Michael,
... not childhood
hopefully *est*
live for moment ... 'Robert

CELEBRITY AND THE LAW

CELEBRITY AND THE LAW

Patricia Loughlan
Barbara McDonald
Robert van Krieken

THE FEDERATION PRESS
2010

Published in Sydney by:
    The Federation Press
    PO Box 45, Annandale, NSW, 2038
    71 John St, Leichhardt, NSW, 2040
    Ph (02) 9552 2200 Fax (02) 9552 1681
    E-mail: info@federationpress.com.au
    Website: http://www.federationpress.com.au

National Library of Australia
Cataloguing-in-Publication entry

    Loughlan, Patricia L
    Celebrity and the law / Patricia Loughlan, Barbara McDonald, Robert van Krieken

    Includes index.
    .
    ISBN 978 186287 738 2 (pbk)

    Celebrities – Legal status, laws, etc – Celebrities in mass media.
    Libel and slander – Australia.
    Privacy, right of – Australia.

346.94033

Typeset by The Federation Press, Leichhardt, NSW.
        Printed Ligare Pty Ltd, Riverwood, NSW.

FOREWORD

The Honourable Murray Gleeson AC,
Former Chief Justice of the High Court of Australia

People become celebrities in many different circumstances. Some are born to celebrity status, and others have it thrust upon them. Some work hard to acquire, cultivate and exploit it. Others seek to avoid it. A celebrity may be a victim of a widely publicised crime or disaster. The capacity for commercial exploitation of fame, either by the famous person, or by some third party, is not an essential aspect of this status, but it is the sort of thing that is likely to lead to legal disputes. At least in the past, a large part of the law has been concerned with protecting commercial interests and enforcing rights of, or in the nature of, property. It is not surprising that the kind of celebrity that is often before the courts, and the kind of conduct about which celebrities often complain, involves commerce on one side of the record, and perhaps on both sides.

The law's concerns are widening. A glance at the law reports in Australia, and the United Kingdom, of 100 years ago will confirm the past emphasis on rights of property and commercial interests. A glance at the current law reports will confirm a trend towards a concern with rights of personality and dignity. Both kinds of concern are relevant to this book. Celebrities, even those who are market-oriented, are not interested only in money. Questions of personal security, for themselves or their families, may be important. They can be threatened, or ridiculed, or humiliated; in some cases they may be unusually vulnerable to such injury. And not all who fail to respect the private and family lives of others do so for their own commercial purposes.

The authors of this informative and stimulating work have made plaintiff-celebrities the focus of their attention. In explaining various aspects of the law of tort and of equity, and considering possible future developments, they demonstrate that established principles of passing-off, defamation, and private nuisance, expanding principles of confidentiality and privacy, and statutory prohibition of misleading or deceptive conduct such as is found in s 52 of the *Trade Practices Act* of the Commonwealth, all protect legal rights and interests of celebrities. Yet these are not special rights and interests. They belong to all citizens.

In the developing legal areas, there has been some difficulty in reaching agreement about the nature of the interests which the law protects. Privacy is an example. As a legal concept, it is now enshrined in human rights instruments that have influenced the common law, especially in the United Kingdom. It has long had an established place in the law in the United States. Yet, as a rubric for legal analysis, it is not entirely satisfactory. The fourth category of invasion of privacy famously identified by Dean Prosser, (i.e. appropriation, for a defendant's advantage, of a plaintiff's image), is more commonly associated with what most people would identify as a right of publicity rather than a right of privacy. If two film stars, who live by publicity, sell, for a large sum of money, the exclusive rights to photograph their wedding, they are exploiting legitimately, and licensing some third party to exploit, their fame and their images. If a third party undermines that enterprise by unauthorized publication of photographs of the wedding, it seems incongruous to describe what is going on as an intrusion upon privacy. It is a diversion of the benefits of profitable publicity. The problem is not that the personal dignity of the film stars has been affronted; it is that their earning capacity has been unfairly compromised. Their complaint is essentially commercial; and the law should deal with it on a frankly commercial basis. On the other hand, in other circumstances, intrusive conduct by a photographer may damage interests associated with human dignity, whether or not the plaintiff is a celebrity. The interest protected in the case of a celebrity who sells the exclusive right to take and publish her photograph in a certain setting, or in a certain attire, is not easily recognized either as confidentiality or as privacy. Yet it is not difficult to see why the law of commerce would seek to protect it. At the same time photographs of the same celebrity and her children taken in some family or recreational setting may involve clear disrespect for her private or family life. This seems to accord with the approach of the European Court of Human Rights. The conduct of a stalker, whether his motives are personal or commercial, may be damaging to any victim, and the law's protection understandably may be based on the concept of human dignity. Confusing the two kinds of legal protection is unproductive, and may devalue the currency of important concepts. United States law, which recognizes a distinct right to publicity, covering a person's right to the exclusive use of name and image, appears also to recognize a right that is not confined to people who exploit their fame for commercial purposes (it found such a right in Dr Martin Luther King) and that subsists after death (it was enforced by Dr King's legal personal representatives). If the Australian law were to recognize such a right of publicity, it would need to address the issue of potential inheritance of the right.

Judges and commentators often refer to the impact, in these areas of the law, of technological change. There is no better example than photography. Many of us can remember when cameras were fairly large objects. A lot of people owned cameras, but few carried them around all day. Today, most people walking through the city streets carry pocket-sized electronic devices which are capable, not only of taking photographs, but also of transmitting the images over the Internet. This can be a force for good. The death of a young woman during a political rally in the Middle East could be seen almost immediately in Australia, because bystanders were equipped with mobile phones that took and transmitted photographic images. Equally, it can be an instrument of harassment or menace. When we walk into a shop, an office building, a railway station, or a courthouse, we are under photographic surveillance. We seem quietly to accept this; but the capacity for disrespect of human dignity is plain.

There may be a danger that, in responding to the evident pressures caused by such changes, courts will stretch concepts of confidentiality, privacy, intrusion and exploitation beyond their proper limits. Australian lawyers are sometimes surprised at what Americans have managed to gather within the idea of privacy. In our own law, confidentiality no longer depends upon the terms upon which information is imparted, and can be found in the nature of particular information and the circumstances in which it is obtained or published. Even so, some caution is necessary. Different people, or different generations within the community, may have different ideas about the kind of information which should not be made public. The dictates of self-respect are not understood in the same way by everybody. A judge's standards as to the offensiveness of disclosure of a certain kind of personal information may be different from those of a Facebook contributor; although the judiciary itself is not without diversity in that regard. There is also such a thing as too much information. When President LB Johnson showed his surgical scar to a television audience, he started a trend in public life. We now have forced upon us a great deal of information that is offensive to those of us who would prefer not to know the intimate medical concerns of our political leaders or our entertainers. Perhaps there should be a new category of nuisance to protect us from people who want to tell us things about themselves that we would rather not know. Perhaps we need to be more aware of the importance that many people attach to freedom from information. Offensive disclosure of personal information nowadays is often made voluntarily, even enthusiastically, by the subject of the information.

The case of *Australian Broadcasting Corporation v Lenah Game Meats Pty Ltd* has been referred to in later cases about privacy, but an interesting issue was that raised by the intervener, the Australian Government. The Government argued that, because a film of the respondent's meat processing operation, to the respondent's knowledge, had been made by a trespasser, that in itself was a sufficient basis for an injunction to restrain the appellant (the Australian government broadcaster) from broadcasting the film. The implications of that proposition for a case about leaked government documents are obvious, as was the Government's interest in intervening. The reasons for judgement refer to certain concessions that had been made in the Tasmanian courts about the matter of confidentiality. The respondent's problem, bearing in mind these concessions, was to identify a viable cause of action against the broadcaster. The Government raised a question that went far beyond any of Dean Prosser's categories of privacy, and that had wide implications for freedom of speech.

It is interesting to note the observation, supported by the authors, that although the United States has developed an elaborate theoretical basis for the law of privacy, in practice many of the actions that have succeeded in the United Kingdom or Australia in recent years, and that have been described as involving privacy, would have failed in the United States because of the First Amendment. The case of *Dow Jones & Co Inc v Gutnick* exemplified some problems of technological change, but the capacity to publish or broadcast defamatory material internationally is not new. Nor is defamation the only area of tort law where a defendant, who causes harm internationally, may be liable under laws that are stricter than those of the defendant's home base. Product liability and information liability may involve different issues, but the risk of causing harm across the globe is the same. The plaintiff in the case of *Gutnick* was not a libel tourist. He was a resident of the State of Victoria, he carried on business there, he had a reputation there, and, according to established principles of Australian law, the material that allegedly defamed him was published there. He sued in the Supreme Court of Victoria, he confined his claim to damages to his reputation in Victoria, and he undertook not to sue in any other jurisdiction. If the material of which he complained had appeared in a hard-copy issue of the Wall Street Journal sent by airmail to a Melbourne subscriber it seems unlikely that his proceedings would have caused much surprise. In giving reasons for declining to adopt the single publication rule in Australia, or to establish a special rule for Internet publications, the High Court referred to practical considerations both for and against such a change. For example, it would be easy for an Internet publisher to organize its business so that its publications originated in India. If that meant that anyone defamed by such a publication could sue only in India, then Australian public policy would be unlikely to be satisfied.

Celebrities, and their concerns, have given the authors much to explore, but one of the most informative features of this book is the way in which those concerns relate to rights and interests which are common to all citizens.

CONTENTS

ACKNOWLEDGEMENTS

Front cover image by Michael Fitzjames

John Jewel (1522-1571) Bishop of Salisbury
National Portrait Gallery London

Jean-Jacques Rousseau (1712–1778)
Reproduced with permission of Réunion des Musées Nationaux Agence Photographique

Campaign button showing images of Democratic presidential candidate Sen Barack Obama, and the Rev Martin Luther King Jr
AAP Image/Jae C Hong

Diana, Princess of Wales, sprints back to her car after leaving a gym in Earl's Court
Reproduced with permission, Press Association Images

Hello! Magazine's publisher outside the High Court in London
Nicolas Asfouri/AFP/Getty Images

JK Rowling Testifies on Harry Potter Lexicon Battle
Daniel Barry/Getty Images News/Getty Images

Max Mosley Wins Damages Against News of the World
Peter Macdiarmid/Getty Images News/Getty Images

Prince Charles' Diaries
Reproduced with permission, News International

INTRODUCTION

> [T]he elevation of appearance over substance, celebrity over character, short-term gain over lasting achievement is precisely what your generation needs to help end.
>
> *Commencement Address at Arizona State University*
> *by President Barack Obama, 13 May 2009*

At Arizona State University, a great leader aligns celebrity with appearance and short-term gain and calls upon a generation to repudiate it so that a virtuous society can emerge. But as we write this Introduction, celebrities are arriving in Cannes and a CNN reporter standing on some pretty ordinary steps has just said wildly, 'celebrities will be walking up *these* stairs'. The CNN Weather Reporter has just *apologised* to the celebrities because rain is expected for the weekend. At Cannes, celebrity is, well, celebrated.

The three of us, two legal academics and a sociologist, have been for some time intrigued both by celebrity itself and even more by our society's highly ambivalent responses, legal and otherwise, to celebrity. We began our own conversations about celebrity, appropriately enough, in the Society Café. This book is the outcome of our interest in, our conversations about and our legal and sociological analyses of the celebrity phenomenon which has characterised our modernity. We take Paris Hilton seriously here. Celebrities are not the opposite of heroes. After all, President Obama is the first sitting head of state to make the Forbes Celebrity 100 Power List.

This book recognises that celebrities are not just people; they are much more than that, constituting a strategically important part of the fabric of society, politics, law and economics. The book looks beyond celebrities as unique individuals to see the circuits of power which produce celebrity as a social phenomenon, one which has its root in aristocracy but which has become democratised. It also views celebrities as cultural, expressive and communicative resources which are potentially immensely valuable to the societies in which they function.

The book has a simple three-part structure. The first defines celebrity and outlines how it is distinct from 'fame'. It traces the historical and conceptual underpinnings of the contemporary celebrity phenomenon and its links with power, illuminates the relationship of celebrity, individualism and meritocracy and draws out the importance of court society and the theatre in laying the foundations for contemporary celebrity.

The second and third parts are legal in focus.[1] The second part draws upon the laws of passing-off and defamation to explore the legal implications – particularly the protection or lack of protection – of a celebrity's reputation and identity. Celebrities, unsurprisingly, value their reputations and their public identities. They demand, and to some extent receive, legal protection in the form of control over at least the commercial use of their identities and, through the law of defamation, over what can be said or implied about them. The problem lies in the fact that all sorts of people for all sorts of reasons want to talk and write about celebrities. They want to comment on and criticise their conduct and appearance and make various commercial and cultural uses of celebrity identities. Each expansion in the legal protection and control granted to celebrities over their identities and reputations therefore also potentially reduces the freedom of others (photographers, impersonators, cultural critics, clothing manufacturers, magazine proprietors, car dealers, fans ...) to make communicative and competitive use of the celebrity.

The third part draws upon the law of breach of confidence and the rapidly-developing law of privacy to illuminate the tension between the celebrity's desire for privacy, or at least for exclusive control over what aspects of their private lives are made public, and the demands of the media and others for freedom to obtain and reveal to whomever they choose whatever information they choose, however intimate, about that celebrity.

The areas of law under consideration in this book are dynamic and evolving, reflecting as they do both the complicated, worldly demands of the celebrity and, in the background, an abiding public interest in fairness, free competition and a big, buzzing communicative sphere. We have in this book provided both a legal and a sociological analysis in our attempt to understand how the legal order has responded and ought further to respond to the phenomenon of celebrity. We have addressed and hoped to engage the interest of both media professionals and the legal profession in what is rapidly developing into an area of distinct and specialised interest, the law of celebrity.

---

1   A disclaimer: the legal analysis presented in this book focuses on how each of the areas of law under consideration (passing-off, defamation, and privacy) is relevant to celebrities qua celebrities. It does not purport to provide a comprehensive statement of the general law in these areas and the reader is accordingly directed to the many available excellent specific texts. In particular, the reader is directed, for a general work on passing off and the law of registered trade marks, to M Davison, K Johnston, P Kennedy, *Shanahan's Australian Law of Trade Marks & Passing-Off,* 3rd edn (Thomson/LawBook Co, 2003). There are many excellent, detailed and informative studies of general defamation law and of its effect on the media and freedom of speech. For the former, see P Milno and WHV Rogers, *Gatley on Libel and Slander,* 11th edn (Sweet & Maxwell, 2008); RP Balkin and JLR Davis, *Law of Tort,* 4th edn, (LexisNexis Butterworths, 2009); DN Butler and S Rodrick, *Media Law in Australia,* 3rd edn (LawBook Co, 2007); P George, *Defamation Law in Australia* (Cambridge University Press, 2006). For the latter, see E Barendt, *Freedom of Speech,* 2nd edn (Oxford University Press, 2005); R Weaver, A Kenyon, D Partlett and C Walker, *The Right To Speak Ill: Defamation, Reputation & Free Speech* (Carolina Academic Press, 2006); M Chesterman *Freedom of Speech in Australian Law: A Delicate Plant* (Ashgate, 2000). On privacy, see Butler and Rodrick, op cit, and Barendt, op cit.

Chapter 1
UNDERSTANDING CELEBRITY

Introduction

Celebrity is a serious business. It has enormous economic impact, generating spectacular incomes and stimulating both production and consumption. It plays an important role as an organising principle in politics as well as in everyday life. Queen Elizabeth I was not the first to understand the extent to which sovereign authority draws from its performance,[1] but she certainly gave considerable impetus to the linkage between celebrity and power. Those wishing to be significant players in the world of politics neglect that connection at their cost. Some, like Charles I and Louis XVI, lost their heads, others merely lose elections. Usually it is celebrities in the field of politics who get assassinated, but John Lennon's shooting in 1980 by a fan, imagining himself to be the 'real' John Lennon,[2] is a reminder that all celebrities are exposed to similar dynamics resulting from being the object of their audience's hopes, fears, desires and obsessions.

In contrast, then, to the usual inclination to treat celebrity as a frothy and insubstantial topic, in this book we will sketch its changing social, economic, political and particularly legal dimensions, and draw out the ways in which it has become a central dimension of contemporary social life. For example, at first glance the 18th French philosopher, Jean-Jacques Rousseau (1712–1778) and Diana, Princess of Wales (1961–1997) would seem to fall into entirely different social categories. Rousseau was the serious thinker who made a real difference to society, Diana was the flighty media junkie, the 'people's princess' loved by many, for reasons they may have found difficult to explain. But, in fact, Rousseau was the European celebrity of his day, constantly being gossiped about in newspapers and cafés, as recognised a face on the streets as Diana. Antoine Lilti quotes Rousseau's complaints about the visitors plaguing him:

---

1   As Ian Ward observes, 'Erasmus's *Education of a Christian Prince* was an instruction manual for the performance of good governance. In their different ways, Thomas Elyot's Book Named the Governor and George Puttenham's *The Arte of English Poesie* argued that only a magistrate aware that government was a matter of aesthetic harmony could hope to govern wisely or promote virtue. Performance was everything.' Ward I, 'Fairyland and its Fairy Kings and Queens' (2001) 14(1) *Journal of Historical Sociology* 1 at 7.

2   Elliott, A, 'Celebrity and Political Psychology: Remembering Lennon' (1998) 19(4) *Political Psychology* 833.

> Celebrity, like its older half-sister, fame, is essentially about relatively high public *visibility* and *recognition*.

They were officers and other people who had absolutely no taste in literature. In fact the majority of them had never read my work. And yet this did not prevent them, based on what they told me, from trekking thirty, forty, even sixty leagues to come and admire an 'illustrious man, a celebrity, quite celebrated, a great gentleman, and so forth'.[3]

It was not Rousseau's philosophy which was attracting this kind of attention, notes Lilti: 'No longer were there readers who wanted to see the author, but instead curious minds looking to glimpse a famous figure whose name had become recognized'.[4]

Alongside all the differences between them, then, Rousseau and Diana also shared the experience of celebrity – of being highly visible to a broader public and possessing the capacity to attract relatively large amounts of attention. This attention can in turn be transformed into other kinds of 'capital' – esteem, status, wealth, influence, perhaps even power. Celebrity, like its older half-sister, fame, is essentially about relatively high public *visibility* and *recognition*. Rousseau and Diana both had 'fame' in sense of being well-known, just as large numbers of people knew of Alexander the Great, Abelard and Heloise, and Henry VIII. But their fame also had other characteristics, not shared by earlier generations of the famous, which made it particularly modern and deserving of a distinct concept: celebrity, by which we mean fame – being visible, recognised and well-known – plugged into networks of mass communication, themselves circuits of desire and commerce.

This book reflects on the social, economic, political and particularly legal dimensions of celebrity's creation of specific kinds of value – status, esteem, recognition, wealth, influence, authority and even power. It will focus on three particularly important arenas of the law of celebrity: the use of trade mark and passing-off law to provide commercial protection for the celebrity persona, the use of the law of defamation, and the use of the law of privacy and breach of confidence. There are other areas of law where celebrity status raises special issues, such as the treatment of celebrities in family law,[5] the management of celebrities' affairs, and the criminology of celebrity, dealing with the crime directed at,[6] or committed by, celebrities, but they are beyond the scope of this book.

To set the scene for our discussion of these legal aspects of celebrity, we will begin in this chapter with an outline of the most important ways in which celebrity can be understood as part and parcel of modern society,[7]

---

3   Lilti, A, 'The writing of paranoia: Jean-Jacques Rousseau and the paradoxes of celebrity' (2008) 103(1) *Representations* 53 at 69.

4   Ibid at 69.

5   Kessler, RM and McCormack, S, 'Representing 'high profile' clients in family law cases' (2005) 19(1) *American Journal of Family Law* 12; Penfold, R, 'The star's image, victimization and celebrity culture' (2004) 6(3) *Punishment & Society* 289.

6   Penfold, above n 5 at 289.

7   Elliott, above n 2 at 836-37.

and as providing an 'index' to the character, but also the underlying logic, of contemporary social life.

What is celebrity?

The characteristics of celebrity which Rousseau and Diana shared included the capacity to communicate with relatively large audiences relatively quickly, a fascination with social mobility, meritocracy and the possibilities of 'democratic aristocracy', a split between the private and the public self and a need to manage the relation between the two.[8] In both the 18th and 20th centuries, 'being well-known' was an autonomous form of capital or surplus-value, independent of whatever achievement or social position one was well-known for. At both times it was and remains capable of being exchanged for, and transformed into, other kinds of capital: power, wealth, esteem, status. In both cases, the power relations between celebrities and their audiences were or are entirely symbolic, as opposed to political, military or economic power. Of course, the differences are also important. Diana could reach a much larger audience much more rapidly, Rousseau's network of peer-celebrities was tiny compared to Diana's, she could draw on much more sophisticated forms of visual representation that generated new types of relationship between celebrities and their audiences, which were far more intimate than was possible in the 18th century. Rousseau's public-relations technology was in its infancy, whereas Diana was bound up with a highly complex and independent industry of celebrity-production.

We will examine the similarities and differences between the worlds of Rousseau and Diana in more detail shortly, but first we need to sketch our position on some of the more central conceptual issues. To begin with, celebrity is by definition about individuals, and this poses a problem for analysis. It makes it difficult to look beyond an endless string of particular examples – Monroe, Elvis, Madonna, Diana, and so on – to see what social position all these individuals occupy, how they are constituted as a group, and what underpins celebrity as a changing social, political, economic and legal phenomenon.

It is possible, then, to look beyond celebrities as unique individuals and see how celebrity is produced as a social phenomenon. One can also tease out the various aspects of the logic underpinning the production of celebrity, a certain kind of 'celebrity function' or role, independently from the specific individuals who become celebrities at any particular time and place. The identification of a relatively small group of people as celebrities helps to reduce social complexity, and provides dense bundles of symbolic and cultural capital around which social life can be organised. Celebrities also provide a means of cognitive orientation, as 'expressive elites',[9] and constitute the

---

8   Lilti, above n 3 at 53; Ward, above n 1.

9   Keller, S, *Beyond the Ruling Class: Strategic Elites in Modern Society* (Random House, 1963).

> It is possible to look beyond celebrities as unique individuals and see how celebrity is produced as a social phenomenon.

embodiment and reference points for both social stability and processes of social change, representing emerging as well as established social 'characters'. As a stimulus and focus for gossip, they make a significant contribution to social integration, establishing and reproducing a particular moral grammar of recognition and esteem.

The analysis of celebrity tends to be dominated by an opposition between the 'hero' and the 'celebrity'.[10] This contrast is usually bundled up with a critique of contemporary social life as being overly 'obsessed' with the 'cult' of celebrity, an obsession which is by definition a distraction from more 'real' and virtuous concerns. By the 18th century the word had come to be accompanied by a critique of the possible, indeed often probable, 'falseness' of the attention generated by celebrity, and this idea is central to what is possibly the most frequently-cited definition of celebrity, Daniel Boorstin's observation that '[t]he celebrity is a person who is known for his well-knownness'.[11] Today one would say 'famous for being famous', the circularity of the formulation indicating the superficiality of celebrity.

Celebrities were 'human pseudo-events', entirely manufactured creations to be contrasted with genuine 'heroes' – someone (apparently always a man) who did 'great' things or displayed 'great' qualities. 'The hero,' wrote Boorstin, 'was distinguished by his achievement; the celebrity by his image or trademark. The hero created himself; the celebrity is created by the media. The hero was a big man; the celebrity is a big name'.[12] The logic is one of historical decline, where authentic fame and greatness has been replaced by synthetic and empty celebrity – well-knownness – with no basis in accomplishment, talent, moral capacity, or skill.

This account leaves us, however, with not much more than a sense of moral outrage and pessimism about cultural decline. It is important, we believe, to reject this opposition between authentic heroes and synthetic celebrities. It is in the nature of 'heroism' that it be communicated to a public, and there will always be some technique to how the available media are used to that effect. It simply is not true that a real hero requires no public relations; there is no such thing as an 'unsung hero', only anonymous individuals who have done unrecognised heroic things. Integral to heroism is precisely its 'celebration' – achievement and merit need to be communicated to exist as social realities.

One can take any of the heroes that Boorstin celebrates (!) and identify the public-relations machinery that was associated with the achievement of their status *as* heroes. Abraham Lincoln was adept at using the new technology of

---

10   Bauman, Z, *Liquid Lives* (Polity, 2005), pp 47-51.
11   Boorstin, DJ, *The Image, or What Happened to the American Dream* (Penguin, 1962), p 67.
12   Ibid, p 61.

photography to imprint his image on the public mind and Samuel Johnson was similarly concerned with how his reputation could be systematically enhanced. Indeed, it is precisely an element of the hero's 'presentation of self' to deny that there is any strategy, that *their* heroism is entirely 'natural' and requires no synthetic support from the organisation of their public perception. 'All the world's a stage,' wrote Shakespeare, 'and all the men and women merely players': this is as true of heroes as it is of movie stars and television chat-show hosts.

Problems also emerge on the other side of the distinction – Charles Lindbergh made various deliberate efforts to establish his celebrity status, but he was also actually the first to fly solo across the Atlantic; Michael Jordan might be attached to the most sophisticated public relations and marketing machinery known to human history, but his basketball skills are also pretty impressive. Was Einstein a hero or a celebrity? Rousseau? Darwin? Babe Ruth? Churchill? John F Kennedy? The strategic communication of one's claims to attention and visibility is an aspect of every public figure, varying only according to the technology available, and Boorstin mistakes this part of public identity for the whole, seeing celebrities as *nothing more* than their public relations. In reality, celebrity consists of varying combinations of some contribution to human existence, which can be either negative or positive, and the communication and marketing of that contribution in the public sphere, organised around various techniques of attracting public attention.

Celebrity should not be understood as distinct from 'real' achievement, so that one is *either* a hero *or* a celebrity. In reality the two are combined in some way, so that every celebrity lies somewhere on a spectrum of combining achievement or talent, and what can be called the 'surplus value' of celebrity, or the 'celebrity effect' – that is, the independent value of 'well-knownness'. Some celebrities, it is true, are shooting stars, lying more at the marketing end of the spectrum, with very little to give to the world beyond youth or novelty, others lie somewhere in the middle with their basically mediocre skills being inflated by the wonders of public relations, others will be making significant contributions to human existence almost despite their marketing, and still others have a constitutional dislike of the publicity apparatus and will make some more or less successful attempts to hide their genuine talents under a bushel.

To understand the basic principles and logic driving and underpinning celebrity as a social, political and economic phenomenon, we think it is useful to identify the ways in which we can see the world we live in today as having its own, constantly changing, social practices and structures, moral grammar, construction of self and identity, legal order and political economy organised around the distribution of visibility, attention and recognition. Rousseau and Diana can then be seen as occupying different positions in a process by which social institutions, social interaction, and the individual sense of self are increasingly organised around an ever-more differentiated network of more highly visible and recognised individuals.

There are many definitions of celebrity: Boorstin's 'known for being well-known', the Celebrity Register's 'a celebrity is a name which, once made by news, now makes news by itself',[13] Rein et al's 'a person whose name has attention-getting, interest-riveting and profit-generating value',[14] Richard Brookhiser's 'a famous person to whom one feels attached',[15] Chris Rojek's 'the attribution of glamorous or notorious status to an individual within the public sphere',[16] or 'nothing more than cultural impact on a public'.[17] Perhaps a good-enough rule of thumb would be that a celebrity is a person whose photograph or life story has any commercial value. But it is difficult to reduce it to a single line, so we would prefer to offer the following, admittedly more convoluted, break-down of the elements of celebrity:

Celebrity

- is a quality or status characterised by a capacity to attract attention,
- generates some 'surplus value' or benefit derived from being well-known
- is attached to individuals who are highly visible and well-known in at least one public arena
- can be either positive or negative, for example, notoriety
- is heightened by some degree of 'ordinariness' – a movement from humble origins to higher status allowing for affinity with non-celebrities
- requires a person to be interesting, although not necessarily powerful, with a distinctive narrative
- attracts constant scrutiny of private lives and public roles

The development of celebrity is tied to that of modernity itself, but this does not mean, as some observers believe, that 'there was no such thing as celebrity prior to the beginning of the 20th century'.[18] We need to begin, then, with a closer look at the history of celebrity.[19]

---

13   Rein, IJ, Kotler, P and Stoller, MR, *High Visibility: the making and marketing of profes- sionals into celebrities* (NTC Publishing Group, 1997), p 14.

14   Ibid, p 15.

15   Brookhiser, R, 'Celebrity conquers America' (1998) 49(4) American Heritage Magazine, at <www.americanheritage.com/articles/magazine/ah/1998/4/1998_4_30.shtml>.

16   Rojek, C, *Celebrity*, (Reaktion Books, London, 2001), p 10.

17   Rojek, C, 'Celebrity' in Ritzer G (ed) *Encyclopedia of Social Theory* (Sage, London, 2005), p 86.

18   Schickel, R, *Intimate Strangers: The Culture of Celebrity* (Doubleday, 1985), p 23.

19   The core text here is Braudy, L, *The Frenzy of Renown: Fame and its History* (Oxford University Press, 1986); also important are Ponce de Leon, CL, *Self-Exposure: Human- Interest Journalism and the Emergence of Celebrity in America, 1890-1940* (University of North Carolina Press, 2002); Gamson, J, *Claims to Fame: Celebrity in Contemporary America* (University of California Press, 1994); Sentilles, RM, *Performing Menken: Adah Isaacs Menken and the Birth of American Celebrity* (Cambridge University Press, 2003); Tillyard, S, 'Paths of glory: fame and the public in eighteenth-century London', in Postle, M, (ed), *Joshua Reynolds: The Creation of Celebrity* (Tate Publishing, 2005), pp 61-69; Brock, C, *The Feminization of Fame, 1750–1830* (Palgrave Macmillan, 2006).

From fame to celebrity

The Oxford English Dictionary identifies Richard Hooker's reference in 1600 to 'the dignity and celebrity of mother cities' as the earliest use of the word, but 'celebretie' first appears in English in 1565, in the commentary by the leading Protestant reformer John Jewel (1522–1571), Bishop of Salisbury,[20] on the baptism practices of the Apostles, remarking that 'whereas he [Jesus] commanded them to baptize in the name of the Father, and of the Sonne, and of the Holy Ghost, they [the Apostles] baptized in the name of Iesus Chiste Onely, intending thereby to make that be of more fame and celebritie'.[21] A little later in 1587, John Bridges, Dean of Sarum, explained that the Apostle John preached at the Church of Ephesus, which he saw as a key site, 'because for the multitude of beleeuers, and the celebritie of the place'.[22] It was used, then, to refer to the condition of being well-known, in forms such as 'the celebrity of his name' or 'the celebrity of his writings'.

John Jewel (1522-1571) Bishop of Salisbury
National Portrait Gallery London

Despite being defined in dictionaries simply as 'famousness', celebrity was used alongside or instead of fame to capture something additional, a degree of *currency* and *activity*. The derivation from the Latin *celebritus* is usually described as 'famous or thronged',[23] but a more accurate rendition would be to say 'famous *and* thronged'; the Latin word also means 'much spoken of', and this is an important slant on the meaning – one can be famous without being 'thronged' or very much spoken of. Celebrity was attributed to individuals who were famous for particular reasons, and with specific effects, linked to its original meaning as noun, indicating a celebration, or festivity. One could be respectably and quietly 'famous', whereas to have 'celebrity'

---

20   Himself, in a sense, a 'celebrity' of the Anglican Reformation – there is a collective portrait of Jewel, Hugh Latimer, Sir Nicholas Bacon, Sir Francis Walsingham, and William Cecil.

21   Jewel, Iohn (Bishoppe of Sarisburie), *A replie vnto M Hardinges ansvveare by perusinge whereof the discrete, and diligent reader may easily see, the weake, and vnstable groundes of the Romaine religion, whiche of late hath beene accompted Catholique.* Imprinted at London : In Fleetestreate, at the signe of the Blacke Oliphante, by Henry VVykes, 1565, p 114.

22   Bridges, J, *A defence of the gouernment established in the Church of Englande for ecclesiasticall matters.* London: Printed by Iohn VVindet [and T Orwin], for Thomas Chard, 1587, p 343.

23   *The Oxford English Dictionary* (2nd edn,1989).

had different quality, a certain buzz in everyday social life. Alexander the Great, Charlemagne and King Arthur were famous, to be sure, but not exactly notorious topics of everyday conversation, unlike what Nell Gwynn – the 17th century English actress and Charles II's mistress – got up to with the king. Fame was something stored safely in a display cabinet, framed, or cast in stone, marble or bronze – and thus tending to be posthumous, although not exclusively – whereas celebrity was a current topic passed around the table, inspected, fondled, turned over and tapped – which also meant a more fragile life-span.

The first use of the word as a noun to refer to individuals appears to be in the mid-19th century, in Ralph Waldo Emerson's commentary on the English aristocracy, where he notes that the English nobility included 'the celebrities of wealth and fashion' among those to be kept firmly in their place.[24] It is probably only in the early 20th century that the word starts to be used with a frequency and breadth that approximates its contemporary meaning, with the spread of film and radio. However, the word was lagging behind its referent, the history of which is more complex, and which does not lend itself easily to neat categorisations, identifications of 'origins', or sequences.

In every human group, at the point where power, status and wealth is unevenly distributed, certain individuals will become more publicly visible than others – emperors, kings, queens, princes, aristocrats, prophets, popes, saints, martyrs, philosophers, warriors and heroes – become eligible to be considered as worthy of distinctive attention. Given its family connection to 'fame', one obvious place to begin any history is with Alexander the Great, who made sure that the populations of the enormous areas of Europe and Asia Minor that he conquered kept him at the forefront of their minds by having his image imprinted on the coinage used in those territories. As Leo Braudy observes, Alexander 'remains the earliest example of that paradoxical fame in which the spiritual authority of the hero is yet a model for a support of ordinary human nature'.[25]

But Alexander's fame is not yet Rousseau's celebrity, and like the concept 'modernity' itself, from the European Middle Ages onwards, there are various turning points, watersheds and revolutions that one could choose to identify the beginnings of a specifically 'modern' form of fame which constitutes the core of celebrity. In the history of the West – the increasing value placed on individualism, rise of the public sphere and then the mass media, democratisation, increasing social differentiation and social density – have all turned fame into something requiring another word – celebrity – to capture its distinctive and ever-changing features. The 'landscape of renown' changed along with society itself,[26] and in many respects the history of celebrity runs alongside that of whatever we choose to conceive of as 'modernity'.

---

24   Emerson, RW, *English Traits* (BiblioBytes, Hoboken, NJ, 1999), p 56.
25   Braudy, above n 19, p 43.
26   Ibid, p 588.

State-formation and court society

The best way to grasp the modernisation and democratisation of fame, and the corresponding production of celebrity, is to see it as lying at the intersection of a number of different historical developments, with changing configurations of those distinct transformations producing differing kinds of celebrity. The first of these is the concentration of political and military power in the state within the context of urbanisation and the development of capitalist economic activity, beginning with Absolutist monarchies and then developing into the modern, democratic nation-state. This state formation was accompanied by the formation and evolution of a 'court society' characterised by theatricality and performativity – the competitive organisation of power and social mobility around the strategic projection of symbolically-constituted identity. The period in European history described as the 'Renaissance' (between the 14th and 17th centuries), did not only see changes in ideas and culture, the emergence of humanist philosophy, new forms of artistic expression, painting and architecture, and new approaches to knowledge. It was also a period of the consolidation of political and military power in absolutist national monarchies, fuelled by European colonisation of Africa, the Americas, the Middle East, India and East Asia, as well as increased extraction from the population.

Political power and authority became concentrated in court society, heavily dependent on lines of patronage flowing around the monarch which were both volatile and relatively 'open' and competitive, given the ever-present need for sources of income to finance the expanding needs, some legitimate and some merely profligate, of the 16th century courts. Increasing wealth among the merchant class made it possible for them to purchase noble titles, which the Crown was happy to supply in order to meet its own financial requirements,[27] as well the education required to serve in the state's administration. The European absolutist monarchies of the 16th century can also usefully be seen as 'theatre states, in which the dramatic effect of ceremonial actions was at least as important as the reality of power',[28] with Elizabeth I and Louis XIV only among the more prominent examples of such anchorage of power in its performative, charismatic projection on the realm of symbol and ceremony.

In court society there is only a weak division between public and private life – one's public position is heavily dependent on all aspects of one's relation with others. Behaviour at any time and place can decide a person's place in society, could mean social success or failure', and 'society encompassed the whole being of its members'.[29] The operation of this type of power relationship demanded continuous *observation* both of others and of oneself, and the constantly fluctuating relations between various members of court society.

---

27   Stone, L, 'The inflation of honours 1558-1641' (1958) 14 *Past & Present* 45.
28   Asch, RG, *Nobilities in Transition, 1550-1700: courtiers and rebels in Britain and Europe* (Arnold, 2003), p 93.
29   Ibid, p 115.

'We princes, I tell you,' declared Elizabeth I, 'are set on stages, in sight and view of all the world',[30] and how she was viewed mattered enough for Elizabeth to attempt to control her portraiture, issuing a draft proclamation 'Prohibiting Portraits of the Queen' (1563) which:

> commandeth all manner of persons ... to forbear from painting, graving, printing, or making of any portrait of her majesty until some special person, that shall be by her allowed, shall have first finished a portraiture thereof; after which finished, her majesty will be content that all other painters of gravers ... shall and may at their pleasures follow that said patron or first portrayer.[31]

The basic elements of court rationality can be seen, then, as constituting the core of a nascent 'celebrity rationality'. Court society established a particular psychological disposition, a certain *habitus*, organised around a constitutive theatricality and heightened visibility to everyday life, a perpetually performative self, intense and constant competition according to ever-shifting rules and norms leading to a blurring of the boundary between public and private life, and the production of every-changing 'favourites' surrounded by their own networks of patronage and favouritism, but also constantly renewed patterns of competition. The figure of the 17th century courtier then became differentiated into a number of different social types – the public servant, the politician's advisor, the manager, but also the celebrity, the witty, beautiful and talented focus of public scrutiny and attention with access to power, constituting a living lesson in how to achieve such access.

Individualism and meritocracy

The second line of development was the changing social and political construction of human beings as *individuals* with particular rights, possibilities and opportunities. Modern celebrity is by definition individualistic and meritocratic: it attaches to individuals not to collectives. Even celebrity couples need each to be celebrities in their own right. It presumes the possibility of the attainment of higher visibility and greater recognition through individual attributes and talents, and there are meant to be no ascribed restrictions to the possible movement from obscurity to celebrity. The idea that celebrities are 'ordinary folk', 'just like us' has become a central if contradictory theme in contemporary approaches to celebrity.

Celebrity and individualism are joined at the hip, and the processes of individualisation and celebrification can be seen as interdependent, mutual indexes of each other. The origins, nature and development of the idea of 'the individual' as a self-actualising entity constituting the foundational principle

---

30   Levin, C, '"We Princes, I tell you, are set on stages": Elizabeth I and dramatic self-representation' in SP Cerasano and M Wynne-Davies (eds), *Readings in Renaissance Women's Drama: Criticism, History, and Performance, 1594-1998* (Routledge, 2002), pp 113-24.

31   Hughes, PL and Larkin, JF (eds), *Tudor Royal Proclamations*, Vol 2 (Yale University Press, 1969), p 241.

for the allocation and distribution of esteem and regard, then, have important implications for the structure and dynamics of celebrity itself.

The most influential account of the historical emergence of an individualistic consciousness is Jacob Burckhardt's *The Civilization of the Renaissance in Italy* (2004 [1860]).[32] Burckhardt drew attention to the significance of the Italian Renaissance as a transformation of society, culture and experience that was itself anchored in the specifics of northern Italian political conditions, in releasing people from the medieval conception of the self as a communally defined entity to allow for a recognition of identity and self-interest apart from the collectivities to which people belonged. He argued that in the Middle Ages, both the way in which people regarded each other and the way they observed their interior life 'lay dreaming or half awake beneath a common veil', a veil 'woven of faith, illusion, and childish prepossession, through which the world and history were seen clad in strange hues'. Individuals were only conscious of themselves as members of 'a race, people, party, family, or corporation only through some general category'.[33] But towards the end of the 13th century, observed Burckhardt, 'Italy began to swarm with individuality', with Dante only the most prominent example. 'The Italians of the 14th century,' wrote Burckhardt, 'knew little of false modesty or of hypocrisy in any shape; not one of them was afraid of singularity, of being and seeming unlike his neighbours'.[34]

For Burckhardt, Renaissance individualism was associated from the beginning with the idea of celebrity – one achieved and sustained one's individuality precisely through distinction, prominence and public recognition. This was why Burckhardt went on to argue that the new forms of individuality were accompanied by 'a new sort of outward distinction – the modern form of glory'.[35] Again Dante was exemplary – although he also had his reservations about the transience of this-worldly fame, Burckhardt felt that 'he laid stress on the fact that what he did was new, and that he wished not only to be, but to be esteemed the first in his own walks'.[36] Individuality was expressed through the constant production of novelty and innovation, and the organisation of individual striving around the high points, the landmarks and reference points of these creative production processes. He highlights the 'cultus' of the birthplace, death and burial sites of famous men such as Dante, Petrarch and Boccaccio. It became 'a point of honour for the different cities to possess the bones of their own and foreign celebrities',[37] so that '[h]istory and the new topography were now careful to leave no local celebrity unnoticed'.[38]

---

32   Burckhardt, J, *The Civilization of the Renaissance in Italy, 1860* (Penguin, 2004).
33   Ibid, p 98.
34   Ibid, p 99.
35   Ibid, p 104.
36   Ibid, p 104.
37   Ibid, p 106.
38   Ibid, p 107.

Jean-Jacques Rousseau (1712–1778)

The 'boundless ambition and thirst after greatness'[39] in this 'age of overstrained and despairing passions and forces'[40] in Northern Italy was indeed powerful enough for people to commit murder in order to achieve celebrity; he quotes Machievelli's critique, in his *History of Florence*, of his predecessors, who had 'erred greatly and showed that they understood little the ambition of men and the desire to perpetuate a name. How many who could distinguish themselves by nothing praiseworthy, strove to do so by infamous deeds!'[41] These crimes included, for example, the assassination of Alessandro de' Medici, Duke of Florence, by Lorenzino de' Medici in 1537, which the historian Paolo Giovio attributed to Lorenzino's desire, after a public disgrace, for 'a deed whose novelty shall make his disgrace forgotten'.[42]

Thinking in terms of an 'emergence' or 'discovery' of 'the individual' is not without its problems. Peter Burke, for example, argues that Burckhardt's contrast with the Middle Ages was too sharply drawn, underestimating the significance of individuality in the Middle Ages, particularly from the 12th century onwards,[43] and exaggerating the concern with the self in the 15th and 16th centuries, with people continuing to identify with 'family, guild,

---

39   Ibid, p 109.
40   Ibid, p 110.
41   Ibid, p 109.
42   Ibid, p 110.
43   Morris, C, *The Discovery of the Individual, 1050-1200* (University of Toronto Press, 1987).

faction or city'.[44] The Renaissance concern with celebrity was not a universal passion, there were equally strong countervailing currents, and the evidence on portraiture is contradictory, showing a concern for *both* the collective and institutional aspects of identity *as well* as individual distinctiveness. Although Burke agrees that one can observe 'a changing sense of self between Petrarch and Descartes, both more unified than before and more sharply distinguished from the outside world of family and community',[45] his own preferred account is a multi-layered one, drawing attention to the effects of increased travel, the spread of print, urbanisation, Protestantism, and the return to classical Greek and Roman thought.

Burke does mention an alternative to thinking in terms of a change in 'spirit', but only in passing, noting that '[T]he parallel between these developments and the rise of the centralised nationstate is an intriguing one'.[46] This idea is developed in more detail by Aaron Gurevich, who suggests that it is important to see shifts in individual self-awareness as interdependent with changing structure and dynamics of the social groups of which individuals were part, and more generally 'the emergence of the individual' as interlinked with broader social transformations.[47] In other words, to understand the nature of individualism, one has to look simultaneously at the social forms and institutions within which people are able to express or manifest their individuality. As soon as one looks beyond the worlds of art, literature and philosophy, there is no shortage of evidence concerning the institutional dimensions of early modern European society, politics, administration and law which did probably more than the emergence of a 'spirit' of individualism systematically to turn 'peasants into Frenchmen'[48] and all levels of social life an ensemble of factories of individualism.

There were two central elements of the intensified concern with the self which are useful to highlight in relation to the question of celebrity. The first was an increase in attention to an obvious corollary question, that of authenticity and sincerity, of what distinctions could or should be made between the 'real' self as opposed to its theatrical presentation. This was a question which was possibly most acute in court society given its stress on performativity, but it had also become a more general issue throughout 16th century social life. The opposition which emerged was between 'prudence' – the conscious tailoring of the presentation of self to particular ends divorced from any particular relationship to ethics (Machiavelli) – and 'sincerity' – the insistence that exterior presentation and interior psychic life should more or less correspond. Montaigne expressed the second position when he wrote

---

44   Burke, P, 'Representations of the self from Petrarch to Descartes' in R Porter (ed), *Rewriting the Self: Histories from the Renaissance to the Present* (Routledge, 1997), pp 17-28 at 18.

45   Ibid, p 27.

46   Ibid, p 27.

47   Gurevich, AJ, *The Origins of European Individualism* (Blackwell, 1995), pp 10-14.

48   Weber, E, *Peasants into Frenchmen: The Modernization of Rural France, 1870-1914* (Stanford University Press, 1976).

'It is enough to make up our face, without making up our heart'.[49] This contrast between 'political prudence' and 'beautiful souls'[50] often took the form of a tension between aristocratic and bourgeois or republican rationality, as well as a bourgeois critique in the name of authenticity, of aristocratic deceitfulness, and this can be explained in terms of the distinct structures of their differing situations.[51]

The second important aspect of the logic of early modern individualism worth pausing beside, itself tied to the expansion of court society and state administration, was the close association with the related ideas of democracy and meritocracy. If one allowed for some degree of detachment of individual identity from its social origins and context, it followed that social status was increasingly to be understood in terms of individual attributes, talent and effort rather than social location, as *achieved* rather than *ascribed*. Individualistic cognitive structures, institutional forms and social practices opened the doors to the idea the distribution of esteem and recognition becoming increasingly democratic – accessible to everyone regardless of their lineage or social location – and meritocratic – its outcomes explainable in terms of individual merit – skill, aptitude, expertise, knowledgeability, effort, application, stamina, wisdom, charisma, and so on – rather than character- istics such as background, class, racial or ethnic identity. Such a distribution of recognition need be no less hierarchical and no less productive of elites and aristocracies, it was simply that its logic and foundations had shifted to questions of merit.

The idea that the king had two bodies, a public persona or office as well as his physical body, had characterised theories of politics since the 12th century. In *Willion v Berkley*,[52] the court argued as follows:

> [T]he King has two Capacities, for he has two Bodies, the one whereof is a Body natural, consisting of natural Members as every other Man has, and in this he is subject to Passions and to Death as other Men are: the other is a Body politic, and the Members thereof are his Subjects, and he and his Subjects together compose the corporation, as Southcote said, and he is incorporated with them, and they with him, and he is the Head, and they are the Members, and he has sole Government of them: and this Body is not subject to Passions as the other is, nor to Death, for as to this Body the King never dies, and his natural Death is not called in our Law (as Harper said) the Death of the King, but the Demise of the King, not signifying by the Word (Demise) that the Body politic of the King is dead, but that there is a Separation of the two Bodies, and that the Body politic is transferred and conveyed over from the Body natural now dead, or now removed from the Dignity royal, to another Body natural.[53]

49   Montaigne, M de, *The Complete Essays of Montaigne* (Stanford University Press,1958), pp 773-74.

50   Vowinckel, G, *Von politischen köpfen und schönen Seelen. Ein soziologischer Versuch über die Zivilisationsformen der Affekte und ihres Ausdrucks* (Juventa, 1983).

51   Vowinckel, G, 'Command or Refine? Cultural Patterns of Cognitively Organizing Emotions' (1987) 4 *Theory, Culture & Society* 489 at 490.

52   (1561) Plowden 223; (1562) 75 ER 339.

53   *Willion v Berkley* (1561) Plowden 223 at 233a.

However, in the course of the 16th and 17th centuries, as court society and absolutist state administration expanded, the king's 'Body politic' became an increasingly complex beast, and under influences such as the utilitarian concerns of neo-stoicist approaches to politics and society, kings like Louis XIV expanded the conception of personal service by the nobility to include and become consistent with more impersonal conceptions of service to state and society driven by more pragmatic and goal-directed criteria of value, worth and nobility. By the late 18th century, the shift had run most of its course and Chaussinand-Nogaret goes as far as to argue that 'there was no longer any significant difference between the nobility and the bourgeoisie'.[54]

Transformations of communication

Thirdly, celebrity clearly depends on its communication. This means that the nature of the means of communication has a defining impact on the structure and dynamics of celebrity, and the communication revolution that took place with the advent of the printing press in the 15th and 16th centuries was a key element of the foundations of modern celebrity. In a sense every age produces its celebrities, its famous and prominent individuals, but the nature of the modes of communication supporting celebrity in the ancient and medieval worlds were slow and cumbersome, and as soon as information was to flow beyond their immediate context, it was delayed in time and tended to be about events and personalities in the past, rather than in the present. This was to change with the invention of movable type and the printing press, many say by Gutenberg in the German town of Mainz around 1450, and the spread of printing workshops and presses from that point onwards.

The impact of printing on European culture, society, politics and law is difficult to overestimate. Elizabeth Eisenstein, for example, argues that we might as well dispense with concepts like the Renaissance which are difficult to pin down and define, and simply speak of the transition from a scribal to a typographical culture and society. It is hard to imagine the transformations wrought by the Reformation, for example, without print – AG Dickens estimates that Luther's 30 publications sold more than 300,000 copies between 1517 and 1520, and Protestant reformers were keenly aware of the power of the printed work in liberating them, as they saw it, from the Roman bondage. As Dickens observes:

> Unlike the Wycliffite and Waldensian heresies, Lutheranism was from the first the child of the printed book, and through this vehicle Luther was able to make exact, standardized and ineradicable impressions on the mind of Europe. For the first time in human history a great reading public judged the validity of revolutionary ideas through a mass-medium which used the vernacular language together with the arts of the journalist and the cartoonist.[55]

---

54   Chaussinand-Nogaret, G, *The French Nobility in the Eighteenth Century: from Feudalism to Enlightenment* (Cambridge University Press, 1985), p 53.

55   Dickens, AG, *Reformation and Society in Sixteenth-century Europe* (Thames and Hudson, 1966), p 51.

The impact of printing on European culture, society, politics and law is difficult to overestimate ... we might as well dispense with concepts like the Renaissance which are difficult to pin down and define, and simply speak of the transition from a scribal to a typographical culture and society.

The spread of the printed word and the creation of a reading public contributed to an increasing individualism, because every reader had their own, individual and anonymous, relationship with the imagined community created by books, newspapers, and pamphlets. Printed text became a tool of the powerful and those who resisted them alike, an arena which struggles over power had henceforth to enter sooner or later. From this point onwards, the mobilisation of any effective number of people was organised around printed materials. The bourgeoisie was by definition a republic composed of 'men of letters', their ideas spread as effectively and widely as they were only by virtue of the printing press. Even if literacy was slower to spread, up until the end of the 19th century hearing publics were listening to written materials (Eisenstein 1968: 30). Everything that ordinary people knew about themselves, their lives and their social roles was transformed, henceforth informed to a far greater extent than was even possible before printing, whether directly or indirectly, by the thoughts of Erasmus, Luther, Calvin, Dante, Shakespeare, Castiglione, even Aristotle, Plato, and the neo-stoicists.

The emergence of 'typographical man' was to open up an enormous new, and infinitely expandable, social space in which a growing number of individuals could use the greater circulation of stories and images to carve out novel ways of attracting attention, recognition and esteem – novelists, philosophers, diarists, playwrights, biographers and autobiographers, and then actors and actresses, through the publicity which surrounded their performance. A public sphere organised around the printed word created both new foundations and a new vehicle for celebrity. As Eisenstein pointed out, print made literature hugely more attractive and effective as a means of achieving celebrity, and Juvenal's *insanabile scribendi cacoethes* – incurable passion for writing – was transformed into something quite different when it became an 'itch to publish':[56]

> The wish to see one's work in print (fixed forever with one's name, in card files and anthologies) is different from the urge to pen lines that could never get fixed in a permanent form, might be lost forever, altered by copying, or – if truly memorable – carried by oral transmission and assigned ultimately to 'anon'.[57]

---

56   Merton, RK, *On The Shoulders of Giants: A Shandean Postscript* (Free Press, 1965), pp 83-85; Merton, RK, 'The Matthew Effect in Science' (1968) 159(3810) *Science* 56 at 61.

57   Eisenstein, EL, 'Some conjectures about the impact of printing on Western society and thought: a preliminary report' (1968) 40(1) *Journal of Modern History* 1 at 23.

One of the many ways in which the nature of the radical transformation of social life has been captured has been to speak of the emergence of a 'public sphere', a realm of on-going debate of current political and social issues which the German sociologist Jurgen Habermas sees as consisting of books, pamphlets, newspapers, journals as well as locations and events such as literary salons, coffee houses, meeting halls, reading clubs, public assemblies.[58]

> 'By the 1750s, all sorts of people who wanted notoriety were leaking to or placing in the press intimate or scandalous details of their own lives. Celebrity was born at the moment private life became a tradeable public commodity'.
> *Stella Tillyard, historian*

In England, in addition to print becoming cheaper and the audience larger, wealthier, and increasingly hungry for books and printed materials of various sorts, an important shift in the production process of all aspects of the public sphere was the expiry of the Licensing Act in 1694. Up until then, the two 'players' in relation to the control of the expanding market for printed materials were printers and publishers on the one hand, and the Crown on the other, seeking 'to prevent printing seditious and treasonable Book, Pamphlets, and Papers' (*Licensing of the Press Act* 1662), which was achieved by granting a monopoly over printing to the Company of Stationers. The Commons' refused to renew the Licensing Act in 1694 – they felt it was bad legislation for a number of reasons, including that it gave the Company of Stationers disproportionate monopoly rights, placed too many restrictions on the importation of books, and its penalties were far too draconian for the offences it identified.[59] In response to lobbying from both authors seeking another form of protection, and publishers (who shielded their own interests behind those of authors in relation to the Crown,) the *Statute of Anne* (1710)[60] granted copyright to authors (for 28 years). The growing audience for books, magazine, journals and newspapers – there were 60 weekly newspapers being printed in London by 1770[61] – meant that authors joined their publishers in having a greater financial interest all types of literary production, and private patronage had given way to the public market as the primary source of economic support for authors. The effect of this was to give the public even greater control over what was to constitute celebrity, and weak libel laws meant that scandal, gossip and innuendo dominated the public sphere.

The proliferation of the means by which celebrity could be generated, in newspapers, coffee-houses, salons, and reading clubs, meant that it became possible for celebrity producers to become celebrities themselves at the same

---

58   Habermas, J, *The Structural Transformation of the Public Sphere* (Polity Press, 1989).

59   Auchter, D, *Dictionary of Literary and Dramatic Censorship in Tudor and Stuart England* (Greenwood Press, 2001), pp 389-90.

60   An Act for the Encouragement of Learning, by vesting the Copies of Printed Books in the Authors or purchasers of such Copies, during the Times therein mentioned.

61   Tillyard, S, above n 19, p 63. Also, highlighted quote, ibid, p 64.

time. It had been possible for historians and philosophers to become celebrated themselves by writing about other famous people, but projected into the past, hardly ever while they were still alive. It was after the production of printed materials had reached a certain degree of efficiency and range of distribution that it was possible for celebrity producers to become contemporaneous with their celebrities, and for individuals seeking celebrity to work with increasing efficiency on the production of their own celebrity.

The mechanics of celebrity production and its particularly modern, democratic logic of establishing an intimate relationship of identification with the audience are now clearly visible, as Braudy notes, in the figures of Rousseau and Benjamin Franklin, a 'living emblem of the self-created and self-described for the 18th century'.[62] What Braudy refers to as 'modern' fame is by now distinctive enough to be understood as 'celebrity':

> Both Franklin and Rousseau practice an assertiveness, a willingness to take the stage, that is justified not by blood or money but by a paradoxical uniqueness: Praise me because I am unique, but praise me as well because my uniqueness is only a more intense and more public version of your own ... Rousseau strikes a wholly modern note in the history of fame by his preoccupation with the expectation of being recognized for what he 'really' is. He seeks a fame for naturalness, a fame for inner qualities, for what one is without the overlay of social forms. It is a fame of feeling, a 'natural fame' that is held personally, without forebears or tradition, and rejects any honor or virtue that must be validated by social position and social visibility.[63]

The concept of 'puffing' – 'the giving of extravagant or unwarranted praise or commendation; promotion or advertisement through the writing or publication of puffs'[64] – had emerged to capture what would today be called public relations or publicity, a manufacturing of public opinion, the systematic and goal-direction organisation of the presentation of self in public which was increasingly to become the norm. Authors, for example, would arrange for their friends to write favorable reviews; when the Scottish writer James Beattie asked a colleague to write a favourable review of his forthcoming book, he observed that '[p]uffing is so constantly used on these occasions that the omission of it would seem to bespeak either total unconcern about public approbation or that the production is altogether unsupported or friendless'.[65]

Producing celebrity

During the course of the 19th century, celebrity was industrialised along with the rest of social life. Populations grew and urbanised enormously, in the United States, the population grew from 7 million to 64 million between 1810

---

62   Braudy, above n 19, p 366.

63   Ibid, pp 371-72; for Rousseau, see also Lilti, above n 3 and Brock, above n 19, pp 15-45.

64   *The Oxford English Dictionary* (2nd edn, 1989).

65   Cited in Sher, RB, *The Enlightenment and the Book: Scottish Authors and their Publishers in Eighteenth-century Britain, Ireland, and America* (University of Chicago Press, 2006), p 138.

and 1890, in England it went from 8 million to 27 million. As populations grew and towns and cities expanded, so too did audiences for all forms of entertainment – advances in stage technology made theatre more spectacular, better costuming, new generation of actor-managers (the Kembles, Eliza Vestris, Charles Kean, Henry Irving, and Herbert Beerbohm Tree.) The development of railways, steamships, and the telegraph made the rapid transfer of information and news possible[66] and the demand for news was insatiable. Printing presses became faster and more productive to match the growing size of the readership – *The Times* was first printed with steam-driven printing presses in 1814, and in 1833 the rotary printing press was introduced in the United States, capable of printing millions of copies of newspapers per day. The growth of newspapers was spectacular: the *New York Sun* was founded in 1833 and sold 3000 copies that year, by 1838 it was selling 30,000.[67]

The introduction and spread of photography from 1840 made an enormous difference to the democratisation of the production of celebrity, taking, as Braudy puts it, 'the art of imaging out of the hands of those skilled enough to paint or engrave as well as those rich enough to buy and place it at the disposal of virtually everyone'.[68] The photograph made it possible for the aspiring celebrity to establish a far more intimate relationship with their audience, spontaneous, adaptable and with the aura of 'reality'. By mid-19th century, it was becoming compulsory for anyone wishing to have a public profile to have their photos taken and distributed as their *carte de visite*. Around the turn of the century photography became even more convenient and widespread with the advent of the Brownie camera, as well as advances in focusing and motorised film.

Alongside the technology of mass communication, the organisational technology of celebrity-production was also developing. Reynolds and Brady were still what Rein et all call a cottage industry as public relations outfits, but publicity entrepreneurs like PT Barnum (1810–1891) were to push the boundaries of that cottage industry to its outer limits, and pioneer techniques and strategies which laid the foundations for the expansion of the celebrity industry in the 20th century. Barnum's genius [as a promoter of events and shows that captured the public's attention] was not that he was good at fakery, fraud, and hyperbolic invention, it was that he tricked his audiences but also revealed the nature of the trick.[69]

The 19th and early 20th century is populated by an expanding network of celebrities in a variety of fields – politics, theatre, literature – who draw on increasingly sophisticated techniques of celebrity production. William 'Buffalo Bill' Cody (1846–1917) was an important example, responding to the demand for tales and representations of the Wild West, first with the

---

66   Mathieson, T, 'The viewer society: Michel Foucault's "Panopticon" revisited' (1997) 1(2) *Theoretical Criminology* 215 at 220.

67   Ibid at 220.

68   Braudy, above n 19, p 492.

69   Ibid, p 501.

reporting of his actual exploits as a buffalo hunter and Indian scout, but then, with the frontier more or less conquered, and with more significant impact, as a showman endlessly portraying and re-creating the frontier world and the ideal American carving out the New World in an image of his own choosing. Buffalo Bill was the perfect example of the hero turned celebrity, in which heroic deeds take on an extended symbolic life as they are endlessly mimicked, and the skill of the representation becomes as important as the heroic act itself, indeed, it becomes more important, and reality turns into hyperreality and a simulacrum of itself.

There were numerous women in public life achieving celebrity status, as singers, poets, lecturers and of course as actresses and dancers.[70] In the United States, the Civil War actress Adah Isaacs Menken (1835-1868) was inspired by Lola Montez's (1821-1861) career, a 19th century Madonna,[71] constantly reinventing herself and flirting with scandal, playing male parts on stage, presenting herself as both respectable and challenging convention, crossing the boundaries of different kinds of celebrity, writing poetry and essays and maintaining friendships with members of the literary elite like Walt Whitman, Mark Twain and Alexander Dumas (Sentilles 2003). Sarah Bernhardt (1844–1923) was referred to as 'Sarah Barnum' because of her Barnumesque skill in self-promotion,[72] and she was only one of a network of actresses who all extended the 18th century theatrical practice of flirting around the boundary between public and private lives, with the effect, regardless of whether it was the intention, of enhancing their capacity to attract and hold public attention.[73]

In what Rein et al call the 'industrializing stage' of celebrity production, the growth of the movie industry in Hollywood led in the 1920s to the development of a variety of specialists – 'talent agents, personal managers, publicists, professional coaches, and financial managers',[74] who assess and develop individuals' talents, generate interest from venues, negotiate salaries and fees. The organisational structure was still relatively loose and unintegrated, and this was to change from the 1950s onwards, in the 'factory stage', with a greater concentration and denser networks of specialists setting up barriers to entry and organising to protect and promote their interests. Control shifted more clearly to the managers, backed by larger budgets, with a larger proportion of celebrities' earnings going to the costs of management. Celebrity production characterises more and more sectors – from movies to music, but then also say Rein et al, 'sports, politics, art, business, and religion'. These techniques are now used to produce a wide variety of 'products'

---

70   Sentilles, above n 19.

71   Ibid, p 8.

72   Eltis, S, 'Private lives and public spaces: reputation, celebrity and the late Victorian actress' in M Luckhurst and J Moody (eds) *Theatre and Celebrity in Britain, 1660-2000* (Palgrave Macmillan, 2005), pp 169-88 at 169.

73   Ibid.

74   Rein, Kotler and Stoller, above n 13, p 39.

– politicians, sports stars, artists, writers, business leaders. The basic elements are the selection of a potential audience, the positioning and refinement of the aspirant's 'concept and story', and their clothing, appearance and behaviour reworked to fit the required image. There is more planning and research, and greater integration of research, product development, pricing, advertising, and distribution.[75]

Rein et al see the period after the 1980s as a 'late-factory stage', characterised by greater decentralisation as celebrity production shifts from key centres like Hollywood, New York and Detroit – to a greater number of smaller centres. The various sites of celebrity production have also become more closely interconnected, and as markets expand and become more differentiated, the profits to be made have grown, as have the amounts that celebrities themselves are capable of earning. The take-off of sports celebrity since the 1970s is an important example here, tied to the increasing televising of sport, its impact on fashion, and its relationship to conceptions of fitness and health.[76]

The economics of attention – the Matthew effect

In his studies of the sociology of science, Robert K Merton (1968; 1988) once observed that status and recognition in scientific endeavour is often characterised by what he called 'the Matthew effect', after the Gospel according to Matthew 25:29: 'For unto every one that hath shall be given, and he shall have abundance: but from him that hath not shall be taken away even that which he hath'.[77] Merton argued that 'this is the form, it seems, that the distribution of psychic income and cognitive wealth in science also takes'.[78] He drew attention to the way in which the Nobel Laureates interviewed by Harriet Zuckerman[79] consistently observed that researchers who already had a 'name' in the field received disproportionately greater attention for work that was comparable to that done by lesser-known researchers, and that initial advantages of location and resources tend simply to accumulate over time. Those who achieved recognition earlier in their career were more productive later on, the impact of a scientific contribution was greater the more established the reputation of the researcher, and in contests over the attribution of new discoveries, the established name general wins out. Name-recognition plays

---

75   Ibid, p 44.
76   Turner, G, 'The economy of celebrity' in Redmond S and Holmes S (eds), *Stardom and Celebrity: a reader* (Sage, 2007), pp 193-205 at 197.
77   Merton, RK, 'The Matthew Effect in Science' (1968) 159(3810) *Science* 56. Merton later noted the various arguments that can be mounted about designating it the Matthew effect: Matthew probably did not write the Gospel according the St Matthew, Mark and Luke probably said it first, if Jesus was being quoted then one might as well call it the Jesus effect, and it was probably a folk saying in general circulation in any case, but nonetheless stuck with Matthew: Merton, RK, 'The Matthew Effect in Science II' (1988) 79 *Isis* 606 at 609.
78   Merton, 'The Matthew Effect in Science II', above n 77, p 609.
79   Zuckerman H, *Scientific Elite: Nobel Laureates in the United States* (Free Press, 1977).

an important role in the selection of journal articles considered worth reading, and generally reputation – of the researcher themselves and the university where they work – operates as an important cue for selecting the publications worthy of attention from an ever-expanding array of possibilities.

The Matthew effect was what Boorstin was observing with his 'well-known for their well-knownness' comment, but he got it the wrong way around. It is not so much that celebrities are well-known (simply) because of their well-knownness, it is that being well-known tends to *generate* greater well-knownness, much like scientific reputation tends to produce still more reputation. The concept of the Matthew effect underlines a central element of the logic of celebrity production, that the capacity to attract attention – demanding expressive and communicative skills that we tend to see as 'superficial' – is itself a self-reproducing form of capital. As Georg Franck observes in his analysis of what he calls 'the attention economy', celebrity can be regarded as a form of risk-capital, where risk taking can lead to massive windfalls which can then be converted with new projects into even more celebrity (attention) capital. Celebrity, suggests Franck, 'is simply the status of being a major earner of attention'.[80] The logic underpinning celebrity is that of the difference in dynamics between a dyad and a triad: in a dyad, the attention that A and B pay to each other can only be determined by the inherent attention-attracting characteristics of each of their attributes or action. However, in a triad, the fact that C pays attention to B will itself tend to increase the attention A also pays to B, and once C becomes a group, the larger the group, the stronger B's 'pull' on A's attention will be.[81]

Celebrity attention capital plays an important role in any 'production', be it a play, a film, a radio program, an advertising campaign, a university course of study, a conference, a public lecture, a political party or campaign, a social movement, or even a state. In a post-industrial world where the supply of knowledge and information threatens to engulf everyone, what is in short supply is the means to discriminate between what is on offer, and the capacity to attract attention – of consumers, voters, students, job applicants, readers, and audiences.[82] As Herbert Simon put it:

> in an information-rich world, the wealth of information means a dearth of something else: a scarcity of whatever it is that information consumes. What information consumes is rather obvious: it consumes the attention of its recipients. Hence a wealth of information creates a poverty of attention and a need to allocate that attention efficiently among the overabundance of information sources that might consume it.[83]

---

80   Franck G, 'Ökonomie der Aufmerksamkeit' (1993) 47(9/10) Merkur 748 at 748.

81   Franck, G, *Ökonomie der Aufmerksamkeit. Ein Entwurf* (Carl Hanser, 1998), pp 98-100.

82   Davenport, TH and Beck, JC, *The Attention Economy: Understanding the New Currency of Business* (Harvard Business School Press, 2001); Lanham, RA, *The Economics of Attention: Style and Substance in the Age of Information* (University of Chicago Press, 2006); Franck, G, above n 81.

83   Simon, HA, 'Designing Organizations for an Information-Rich World' in M Greenberger (ed), *Computers, Communication, and the Public Interest* (Johns Hopkins University Press, 1971), pp 40-41.

We have seen how central 'stars' were to the theatre already in the 18th century, and the motion picture industry quickly realised that the principle remained a sound one and that stars had important economic effects. They more clearly differentiated between film industry products, improved the capacity to predict success, and enabled prices to be stabilised and, ideally, increased over time.[84] Celebrity, properly managed, creates profit, driven by 'the attention paid by distant, dispersed, heterogeneous but nonetheless numerous third parties, a corresponding "network of weak ties"'.[85] As Rein et al put it, a celebrity can be defined as anyone 'whose name has attention-getting, interest-riveting and profit-generating value,[86] and a great deal of economic activity revolves around high visibility attaching to particular individuals.[87] Celebrities are what Richard Lanham calls 'attention-traps',[88] like Marcel Ducham's urinal and bicycle wheel, or Warhol's Campbell's soup can and Monroe silkscreen portraits.

In the 'name economy', celebrities mediate the relationship between economy and culture, and go beyond organising attention and consumption in any particular field, turning products into a recognised face, name and body, to acting as the linchpins between different fields of cultural production: television, radio, film, literature, theatre, music, fashion, and politics. Celebrities stand, argues Moeran, at the centre of the intersection between commerce and culture, mediating between the public's desires, needs, wishes and aspirations, and the patterns of economic production and consumption which both respond to and help creates those desires and needs. The list of examples of the richly-rewarded individuals at the top of the celebrity hierarchy, because of their high visibility across all celebrity sectors – models, actors, sports stars, fashion designers – is long and growing: just to pick one, Tiger Woods (does one need to explain that he is highly successful American golfer?) is reported as having become, in 2006, the first athlete to earn more than US$100 million in one year, of which $90 million was earned in endorsements and appearances, as opposed to US$10 million for playing golf.[89] The economic network surrounding celebrities is extensive, restricted only by the imagination of the celebrity and their management, although there is a tendency not to travel too far from base: models starts cosmetic or jewellery lines, swimwear brands or lingerie stores, actors and pop stars establish production and recording companies.

---

84   Klaprat, C, 'The Star as Market Strategy: Bette Davis in Another Light' in T Balio (ed), *The American Film Industry* (University of Wisconsin Press, 1985), pp 351-76.

85   Wenzel, H, 'Obertanen. Zur soziologischen Bedeutung von Prominenz' (2000) 28(4) *Leviathan* 452 at 462.

86   Rein, Kotler and Stoller, above n 13, p 15.

87   Ibid, p 27.

88   Lanham, above n 82.

89   Lind, E, 'What About ... (earnings of celebrities)' *Forbes Global* (2007) 3(17) (15 October 2007) at 52.

Celebrities stand at the intersection between commerce and culture, mediating between the public's desires, needs, wishes and aspirations, and the patterns of economic production and consumption

The value of the coupling of celebrity identity to particular products is not always certain, but it can be gold-plated: when it became known that Michael Jordan was returning to playing basketball for the Chicago Bulls in 1995, the value of the stocks of the companies he was associated with – Nike, McDonalds, Quaker Oats, Sara Lee – increased by around 2 per cent, or roughly US$1 billion.[90]

Celebrity's futures

Most of the current critical analysis of celebrity is based on Boorstin's distinction between celebrities and heroes, and revolves around the possibility that celebrity is an unfortunate affliction that might somehow just go away. In 1968 Andy Warhol observed that: 'In the future everyone will be world famous for fifteen minutes'. In 1979, he added: 'I'm bored with that line. I never use it anymore. My new line is, "In fifteen minutes everybody will be famous"'.[91] Warhol may here have been making a perceptive observation on the overall direction that celebrity is moving – towards a greater distribution among a larger number of people, but for shorter periods of time, taking up a larger proportion of our attention. It is also equally likely that he was simply saying what he knew would attract our attention. Either way, it is true that the most recent development in the production of celebrity has been the proliferation of what Chris Rojek calls 'celetoids', the individuals promoted in the media who happen to have participated in a *Big Brother* or the various types of *Idol* programs, or gained short-term media attention for innumerable other reasons,[92] becoming, as Boorstin observed, well-known simply for being well-known. As one observer noted in relation to the 'Pop Idol' phenomenon, it is 'a diamond-studded annuity that generates in excess of $1 billion a year worldwide through advertising, license fees, sponsorships, merchandising, telephone voting, record sales and touring'.[93] This then tends to be bemoaned as the 'cult of celebrity', a debasement of the public sphere, and an 'obsession' that distracts people from more noble and virtuous concerns.

---

90   Mathur, LK, Mathur, I and Rangan, N, 'The wealth effects associated with a celebrity endorser: The Michael Jordan phenomenon' (1997) 37(3) *Journal of Advertising Research* 67.

91   Warhol, A and Colacello, B, *Andy Warhol's Exposures* (Hutchinson, 1979), p 48.

92   Rojek, above n 16, p 21; see also Turner, G, 'The Mass Production of Celebrity: "Celetoids", Reality TV and the "Demotic Turn"' (2006) 9(2) *International Journal of Cultural Studies* 153; Collins, S, 'Making the Most out of 15 Minutes: Reality TV's Dispensable Celebrity' (2008) 9(2) *Television & New Media* 87; Holmes, S and Jermyn, D (eds), *Understanding Reality Television* (Routledge, 2004); Franck, E and Nuesch, S, 'Avoiding 'Star Wars' – Celebrity Creation as Media Strategy' (2007) 60(2) *Kyklos* 211.

93   Learmonth, M, 'The show's big winners' *Variety* (8-14 May 2006) 98 at 99.

However, this type of cultural pessimism about celebrity betrays a poor sense of the social, political, economic and technological underpinnings of celebrity. We can no more do without celebrity in contemporary society than we can dispense with electricity, or democracy. The 'celebritisation of society' has been a long-term process tied to the increased differentiation of the division of labour, the emergence of mass society and its globalisation, generated ever-longer and more complex 'chains of interdependence'.[94] As social life becomes denser, more competitive, more highly differentiated, and more dependent on a variety of means of indirect communication, visibility beyond one's immediate circle of face-to-face contacts becomes increasingly significant and also increasingly lucrative, with the rewards attached to the accumulation of attention capital expanding as the economic significance of attention-capital increases in a post-industrial knowledge and information society.

> 'I saw how hard it was to work your way up [in the media]. The work was badly paid … But I saw a short cut. If I become famous, I will never have a problem getting my work published'. *Julia Allison, journalist**

Ever since the emergence of the 'Gutenberg galaxy',[95] the historical tendency has been towards a 'city' organised not just around physical relations, but also around intangible relationships based on the flow of information and on the structuring of human attention. The rise of post-industrial society, focusing on the production and distribution of knowledge and information, and the shift in communicative infrastructure brought about by the Internet, have accelerated this tendency to the point where some observers will claim that the significance of the intangible circulation of information now outweighs that of tangible, real objects, and that the virtual community has a similar status to the real community. This increases the significance of the gatekeepers and switching points for the distribution of attention, 'the subway stations attention must pass through to get where it ultimately goes'.[96] Celebrities of all sorts – movie stars, outstanding sports men and women, television chat show, *Big Brother* and *Idol* participants, anyone who can get a large audience for their blog or website – are primary examples of such 'attention traps'.

The social, economic and legal significance of celebrity is both as intellectual property in itself and also as a central element of the circulation of all forms of cultural and intellectual property, as a reference point and gateway for their distribution. The economic value of attention is of such importance today that there is clearly a need for the legal regulation of celebrity identities.

---

94   Elias, N, *The Civilizing Process*, Blackwell (Basil Blackwell, 2000).

95   McLuhan, M, *The Gutenberg Galaxy: the Making of Typographic Man* (Routledge & Kegan Paul, 1962).

96   Rötzer, F and Goldhaber, MH, 'The attention economy will change everything: an e-mail interview with Michael H Goldhaber' (1998), at <www.heise.de/tp/r4/artikel/1/1419/1.html>.

*   Wilson, S, 'Gossip girls', *Good Weekend*, 22 November 2008, p 28. Allison's website is <www.juliaallison.com/bio.html>

This is especially so when there is an interest in asserting ownership of that identity as a form of property, but also when there is a need to adjudicate between that legal claim to ownership of celebrity identity and other rights and interests, especially those of free speech and freedom of communication. However, not all aspects of celebrity are entirely reducible to property and commercial value. As Rosemary Coombe argues, 'the definition of celebrity images as personalised property fails to address their social and cultural significance ... [and] ... reinforces an impoverished understanding of freedom of expression, and, consequently, of democracy'.[97] The next chapter turns, then, to an outline of the ways in which celebrity identity has been legally defined and protected against such competing interests.

---

97   Coombe, R, 'Publicity rights and political aspiration: mass culture, gender identity, and democracy' (1992) 26(4) New England Law Review 1221 at 1223.

Chapter 2
COMMERCIAL USE OF THE
CELEBRITY IDENTITY

We're not trying to stop anyone from legitimately supporting themselves but we cannot allow our brand to be abused[1]

Isaac Farris, (nephew of the Rev Martin Luther King Jr),

I have a brand ...[2]   *Anonymous*

Introduction

The identity of Martin Luther King Jr., in so far as it 'is' anywhere, must be, one would perhaps think, in the public domain as an exemplar to us all of the good and the great. But it is not in the public domain. King's identity is largely in private hands.

In the quotation above, Martin Luther King Jrs' nephew, on behalf of his family, is asserting an ownership of King's identity and a legal claim to a share of proceeds from the unauthorised sale of T-shirts, badges and other merchandise depicting King with Barack Obama. Notably, Farris is not criticising or attempting to prohibit the production of such merchandise on any ground of indignity or lack of respect to the memory of his celebrated uncle. It is not the commercialisation of identity as such that is the issue, but rather, the unauthorised use of a celebrity identity with a consequent diversion of profit from the legal owners of the 'brand'.

Celebrities are fun but they are also, frequently, commercially-minded brokers of their personae and traders in their own identities. Celebrities have a commercial interest in turning their identities into assets with a money value. Celebrities demand and, to some extent, receive special legal 'protection' for the commercial, trading interest that they have in their identities.

This chapter outlines the parameters of that legal protection. It states and analyses Australian regulation of those contemporary commercial and

---

1   'Family Has A Dream – Royalties', *The Daily Telegraph*, 15 November 2008.
2   An anonymous commentator remarking on the attempts by the family of Martin Luther King Jr to establish King as a brand. See <www.likelihoodofconfusion.com> (accessed 24 November 2008).

marketing practices which make use of the names, images or other aspects of the identity of celebrities in the promotion of goods and services. In particular, the chapter will outline the two dominant legal responses to the problem of providing protection to the celebrity interest in controlling the commercial use of identity, that is, the *misrepresentation* model as exemplified by the passing-off action in the United Kingdom and Australia and the *misappropriation model* as exemplified by the right of publicity action in the United States.

We enjoy celebrities. Perhaps we even consume celebrities. Celebrities are cultural, expressive and communicative resources for all of us, objects of fascination, subjects of song and targets for beloved comic practices like impersonation. As such, celebrities are potentially immensely valuable to the societies in which they function. The problem, as identified in the Introduction, is that each expansion in the legal and commercial control over the identities afforded to celebrities also potentially reduces the freedom of others to make reasonable communicative and competitive use of the celebrity identity.

This can be illustrated by a case involving Olivia Newton-John's attempt to stop publication of a cosmetics advertisement which used a look-alike of her, with the words, 'Olivia? No. Maybelline' below the picture.

Newton-John was attempting to assert control over the commercial use of her identity. But the cosmetics trader was also, in effect, asserting something, namely, its rights to harness, for a commercial end, the undoubted cultural energy created by Newton-John's identity.[3] Newton-John lost her case, but consider the similar case of Chuck Yeager, a famous test pilot, World War II war hero and former Air Force General, who recently brought successful legal proceedings to stop a cell phone service company from using the following statements in a press release announcing its new service:[4]

> Nearly 60 years ago, the legendary test pilot Chuck Yeager broke the sound barrier and achieved Mach 1. Today, Cingular is breaking another kind of barrier with our MACH 1 and MACH 2 mobile command centers.

The defendant cell phone service company argued that Yeager's achievements were in the public domain and ought to be available, as a factual and cultural matter, for anyone to reference. Yeager retorted that the company's use of his name falsely implied that he endorsed the company's service and thereby violated his legal right to control the commercial use of his own identity. Yeager won his case, but a dispassionate observer might well think that Yeager did, after all, break the sound barrier and that that achievement was

---

3   *Newton-John v Scholl-Plough (Aust) Ltd* (1986) 11 FCR 233. The cosmetics trader was successful against the celebrity in this case on the legal ground that while the viewer of the advertisement would undoubtedly think of Newton-John and summon her identity to mind, the viewer would not, so the court found, falsely believe that Newton-John was associated with or endorsing the product.

4   *Yeager v Cingular Wireless LLC* (unreported, US District Court for the Eastern District of California, 12 June 2008).

something that anyone ought to be able to talk about in any way that they might want to. Commercial speech is speech too.

There are no blindingly obvious rights and wrongs in this area of law and dispassionate observers can find themselves perplexed. Certainly, more is at stake than just a struggle for control by profit-minded traders.

The Siren Song Of The Celebrity: Eat. Drink. Wear. Drive. See. Consume.

[T]he toll levied on distinction for the delectation of vulgarity

Tolley v JS Fry & Sons Ltd [1931] AC 333 at 347,
per Lord Blanesburgh

With these words, an English court interpreted the commercial use, without consent, of a celebrity identity, wherein a chocolate trader had used the name and image of a well-known amateur golfer of the day. The golfer sued for that unauthorised use.[5] The commercial practice was relatively novel then. Neither traders nor celebrities nor judges knew quite what to do or what the possibilities were. Distinction and vulgarity were thought to be qualities which attached to different kinds (or classes) of people and commercial matters were associated, at least by judges in English superior courts, with vulgarity.

It has been estimated that close to one-third of all advertising on television now involves a celebrity.[6] It seems to be an indisputable fact of marketing that products sell better with a celebrity endorsement or even just a celebrity shown in an advertisement for the product. Studies have shown that when a person whom the viewer can specifically identify, such as a celebrity, as opposed to just an actor or model (no matter how attractive) appears in an advertisement, the information contained in the advertisement is better retained by the consumer.[7]

Pepsi paid Michael Jackson several million dollars just to sing one of his own songs for a Pepsi advertisement and 'allow' Pepsi to sponsor his Victory Tour. At no point was Jackson required even to have a Pepsi in his hand.[8] It seems that a celebrity could be standing 50 metres away from a product and yet the presence of the celebrity would still have a positive effect on the marketing of the product. The celebrity presence is part of what is known as

---

5   *Tolley v JS Fry & Sons Ltd* [1931] AC 333. The plaintiff golfer alleged that the defendant's advertisement implied that he had received payment for the advertisement, which would damage his reputation as an amateur player. It was held both at trial and on appeal to the House of Lords that the advertisement did imply that the plaintiff had received payment for the advertisement and this implication was found to be capable of being defamatory.

6   McCarthy, JT, *The Rights of Publicity and Privacy* (Thomson West, Eagan MN, 2nd edn, 2005), s 4:8 pp 185-196.

7   Ibid, pp 185-196.

8   See Madow, M, 'Private Ownership of Public Image' (1993) 81 *California Law Review* 125 at 129.

One study estimated that the corporations whose products had been marketed with the endorsement of Tiger Woods lost a collective $5-$12 billion after the sex scandal.

'atmospheric advertising', a type of advertising which neither conveys information about the product nor compares it with competing products, but rather creates an invented 'atmosphere' around the product, a kind of mist of images and values and associations.[9]

The process of creating celebrity marketing enchantment can of course also work in reverse. The marketing destinies of products and their associated celebrities become closely connected and that connection is not always positive for the marketability of the product. If a celebrity who has endorsed a product misbehaves in some public way, the positive associations between the celebrity and the product deteriorate and sales of the product can accordingly sharply decrease. One economic study estimated that the shareholders of those corporations whose products had been marketed with the endorsement of Tiger Woods lost a collective $5-$12 billion after the sex scandal.[10] Advertisers in such circumstances then usually rush to drop the celebrity's association with the product. Although if a celebrity's deviation from wholesome and mainstream norms were in fact to have the effect of increasing the endorsed product's attractiveness to a particular target market, the celebrity association might well be permitted to continue, regardless of the outrage of the right-minded.

Product endorsement contracts have 'morality clauses', but drafting such clauses is beset with difficulty, as the sorts of situations which can befall celebrities and cause them to lose favour with the public are so various. Whoopi Goldberg, for example, was quickly and ruthlessly dumped from the Slim-Life advertising campaign after public reports that she had made a crude joke about George W Bush's name.[11] Michael Vick, an NFL megastar, lost millions of dollars in endorsements with Nike and others, when he was indicted for his involvement in an interstate dog-fighting ring.[12] The latter fiasco, in particular, would have been hard to predict.

As was explored in depth in Chapter 1, the phenomenon of celebrity worship and the 'culture of celebrity' have received considerable academic attention and have generated an extensive and learned analytical literature which attempts to describe and explain the phenomenon. Our adoration of the celebrity has been, for example, described as a substitute for real and authentic social interactions with family, friends and community, which are apparently a lot better for us than the pseudo, meta-interactions we have

---

9   Heymann, LA, 'Metabranding And Intermediation: A Response To Professor Fleischer' (2007) 12 *Harvard Negotiation Law Review* 201 at 206.

10   Knittel, Christopher R and Stango, Victor 'Shareholder Value Destruction following the Tiger Woods Scandal' (2010). This paper, written by two economists from the University of California, Davis is available online at <http://faculty.gsm.ucdavis.edu/~vstango>.

11   Chiappinelli, E, 'The Corporatization Of Communication' (2007) 30 *Seattle University Law Review* 959 at 974.

12   <http://sports.espn.go.com/nfl/news/story?id=2941489> (accessed 27 May 2009).

with celebrities.[13] Some think that celebrity now replaces both monarchy and deity.[14] What Queen Elizabeth and Apollo were, Paris Hilton and Brad Pitt are. Celebrities have been headily described by cultural theorists as being, 'a location for the interrogation and elaboration of cultural identity'[15] and as 'cultural texts – floating signifiers that are continually invested with libidinal energies, social longings, and political aspirations'.[16] The celebrity image has been described as, 'a cultural lode of multiple meanings, mined for its symbolic resources'.[17] Insights such as these – stimulating, accurate and beautiful though they may be – are not, however, particularly helpful in directly explaining the commercial effectiveness of celebrity endorsements of products.

A major and even dominant element in the contemporary public fascination with celebrity has been analytically traced down to a particular, quasi-obsessional interest in the celebrity's private life. Celebrity increased in significance and potency and magnetism when private life became a tradeable commodity and interest in the private life of the public person is viewed by some theorists as central to the very definition of 'celebrity' or, put another way, to the construction of the concept of 'celebrity':[18]

> We can map the precise moment a public figure becomes a celebrity. It occurs at the point at which media interest in their activities is transferred from reporting on their public role (such as their specific achievement in politics or sport) to investigating the details of their private lives.

If what we really want to know is 'what the celebrity is *really* like,'[19] (behind the performance on the public stage), then it is not unduly speculative to think that one way in which our curiosity might be satisfied is if we know

---

13   Turner, G, *Understanding Celebrity* (Sage Publications, London, 2004), pp 6, 23: 'The celebrity generates para-social interactions that operate as a means of compensating for changes in the social construction of the communities within which many of us live'. See also Rojek C, *Celebrity* (Reaktion Books, London, 2001), p 52: 'The term "para-social interaction" is used to refer to relations of intimacy constructed through the mass-media rather than direct experience and face-to-face meetings'.

14   Rojek, above n 13, p 14 and see above, Chapter 1.

15   Turner, above n 13, p 24.

16   Coombe, R, 'Publicity Rights and Political Aspiration: Mass Culture, Gender Identity and Democracy' (1992) 26 *New England Law Review* 1221 at 1223.

17   Coombe, R 'Author(iz)ing The Celebrity: Engendering Alternative Identities' in Marshall, PD, *The Celebrity Culture Reader* (Routledge, New York, 2006), p 722.

18   Turner, above n 13, p 8; see also Madow, above n 8, p 131, 'The strategic deployment of information and images about the *private life of celebrities* is central to constructing celebrity'. The historical analysis of celebrity and its origins contained in Chapter 1 above interrogates and challenges the relative simplicity of analyses such as that of Turner. Further, the exposure of the private lives of celebrities, while it may be central to the construction of celebrity itself, is increasingly a controversial matter and one over which celebrities are asserting greater control through the development of a tort of privacy. See Chapter 4 below.

19   Lumby, C, *Gotcha: Life In A Tabloid World* (Allen & Unwin, Sydney, 1999), p 91. See also p 110, 'the contemporary media encourages consumers to identify directly with the person behind the performance'. See also Turner, G, above n 13, p 106, 'the desire for the authentic, to reach the core of the personality, to find out what they are really like'.

(or think we know) which consumer products the celebrity uses. For example by knowing what shampoo a celebrity like Shane Warne uses, what brand of watch he wears, what type of car he drives, we have at least an illusion of knowing the private world of the celebrity. Celebrity product endorsement, in short, seems to fit neatly into celebrity worship and *vice versa*.

One thing in all this is clear(ish). The process is not particularly rational or logical or even sensible. and people are not exactly acting as mature and rational citizens when they impulsively rush out to purchase something because they have been enchanted by the vision of a celebrity associated with the product. In a case where Paul Hogan successfully brought an action to stop a television advertisement for shoes, which was a 'take-off' on a scene from a scene in the movie *Crocodile Dundee* – 'That's not a shoe. *This* is a shoe' – one judge explained his understanding of how and why the marketing practice of using a celebrity identity in association with a product works:[20]

> Character merchandising through television advertisements should not be seen as setting off a logical train of thought in the minds of television viewers. Its appeal is nothing like the insistence of a logical argument on behalf of a product which may persuade but also may repel. An association of some desirable character with the product proceeds more subtly to foster favourable inclination towards it, a good feeling about it, an emotional attachment. No logic tells the cameras that boots are better because Crocodile Dundee wears them for a few seconds on the screen … but the boots are better in his eyes, worn by his idol.

It may be the very absence of rationality that is built into the marketing practice of celebrity endorsement that explains the apparent irrelevance of truth to the whole process. Although there is some evidence that the effectiveness of celebrity endorsements declined slightly as the knowledge became more widespread in the general public during the 1990s that celebrities were doing product endorsements purely for the money and not because they actually believed in or used the products,[21] it does not appear to be the case that the public actually believes that or cares as much as one might expect it would care, whether the endorsing celebrity does in fact use the product.

The case of *Paul Hogan v Koala Dundee Pty Limited*[22] involved two small souvenir shops using the name 'Dundee' and some visual references to the well-known film character of 'Crocodile Dundee'. Pincus J, though finding the defendant traders liable for passing-off, discounted the relevance of truth and genuine belief in the area of celebrity associations and endorsements. He hypothesised that in a case where a sporting celebrity, for example, wore advertising logos on his outfits, 'nobody really thinks that he is expressing a view about the particular brands of products thus publicised'.[23]

---

20   *Pacific Dunlop Ltd v Hogan* (1989) 23 FCR 553 at 583 per Burchett J.
21   Schaffer, SE, 'Reading Our Lips: The History Of Lipstick Regulation In Western Seats Of Power' (2007) 62 *Food & Drug Law Journal* 165 at 207.
22   (1988) 12 IPR 508.
23   Ibid at [53].

However, perhaps the public *does* care about whether celebrities really do use the product. Or maybe it is just that the public is believed by traders to care. Product endorsement contracts frequently contain clauses which require the celebrity actually to use the endorsed product in public or at least refrain from using competing products. Charlize Theron, for example, was recently sued in the United States for wearing a Dior watch at a Texas film festival news conference, in breach of her endorsement contract with Raymond Weil watches.[24] In a case which settled before trial, Nicole Kidman sued a British newspaper for defamation after it ran an article which alleged that Kidman's favourite scent was not in fact Chanel No 5 but another named perfume and that Kidman had been seen publicly dabbing on the other perfume while on the red carpet. The newspaper article stated that Chanel was unhappy with the actress' conduct and that Kidman was, by using the other perfume in public, in breach of her contract with Chanel. Kidman's solicitors declared the article 'grossly defamatory' and issued a writ.[25] A finding that Kidman's reputation was lowered in the community by an allegation that she uses a different perfume from the one which she endorses for money would be most interesting and would give us, perhaps not the truth exactly, but at least a judicial holding on the question of what people think about the truth or otherwise of celebrity product endorsements.

The Law

There are various ways in which the law could regulate and balance the desire of celebrities for full control of the commercial use of their identities with the corresponding desire of others to use also those identities for their own commercial or cultural purposes. An entirely plausible legal regime could, for example, simply not directly govern the area at all, leaving the celebrity to the mercy of the laws of defamation, (to cover those uses of the identity which lowered the celebrity's reputation in the eyes of the community), and to the laws of privacy and trespass which are available to all of us, celebrity or not. There might even be much to be said for such an approach. It certainly has a sense of wild freedom about it.

Such an approach would, however, have to contend with another view, as reflected in the statement by a respected American treatise writer, that celebrity identity control flows from, 'the inherent right of every human being to control the commercial use of his or her identity'.[26] While such a statement, (which gives a huge rhetorical boost to a proposed and controversial right), should probably be viewed more as a partisan assertion than as a legal or moral fact, it does reflect a strong and probably widely-held belief that some form of legal control over use of the celebrity identity is appropriate.

---

24   <www.telegraph.co.uk/news/worldnews/1541998/Charlize-Theron-sued-for-wearing-Dior-watch/html> (accessed 26 May 2009).

25   Defamation claims by Nicole Kidman are further discussed in Chapter 3, below.

26   McCarthy, above n 6, s 1:3, p 3 and s 4:8, pp 195-196.

In any event, wild freedom does not appear to have widespread appeal as a regulatory model in the area of celebrity identity, and the law, both in Australia and elsewhere, does, in fact, govern the area quite closely. Given the staggering amounts of money which are at stake in the control of the celebrity persona, it would perhaps be very surprising not to find legal regulation present. In 2000, for example, Tiger Woods signed a five-year endorsement contract with Nike for $100 million[27] and it is inconceivable that Nike would enter into such a contractual arrangement were it not reasonably legally certain that no other sportswear manufacturer could legally use Woods' identity without authorisation during that time.

There are, broadly speaking, two lines of legal approach to the matter, or, put another way, two regulatory models which have been adopted to regulate the use of celebrity identity. If each model is named after its dominant legal idea, one can be called the 'misappropriation model'. The misappropriation model, which is legally known as the tort of 'right of publicity,' can be found in various forms in the United States and Canada. The other regulatory approach can be called the 'misrepresentation model', legally known as the tort of passing-off, is found in Australia and the United Kingdom. These models, or regulatory approaches, frequently generate similar judicial outcomes on similar facts, but they follow significantly different analytical pathways to those outcomes.

The Misappropriation Model

This model is based both on legal ideas of turning the celebrity identity into property which the celebrity actually 'owns', and on further ideas of misappropriation and unfair competition. The legal cause of action is known as the 'right of publicity'.

To understand it, let us return to the case of Olivia Newton-John and the Maybelline advertisement for cosmetics.[28]

To look at it one way, Maybelline's use of a look-alike of Olivia Newton-John and its use of her name, meant Newton-John's identity was used (or 'taken') without payment and without her consent for a commercial end and that is wrong and unfair. Newton-John had invested considerable resources into the building up of her celebrity identity (that buzz, that aura) and another trader was getting the benefit of that investment without the costs. In short, the other trader was free-riding on the buzz and the aura surrounding Newton-John's identity to sell its products. Her identity was misappropriated as surely as if her money had been siphoned from her bank account.

To take another example, Johnny Carson, the celebrity host of a popular television talk-show called the 'Tonight Show', had been introduced for

---

27   For an account of the Nike advertising campaign with Woods' identity, see Cole, CL and Andrews, DL, 'America's New Son; Tiger Woods and America's Multiculturalism' in Marshall, above n 17, p 345.

28   *Newton-John* (1986) 11 FCR 233 and see above, p 28.

many years with a voice-over intoning the words, 'Here's Johnny'. The defendant, a trader in portable toilets, adopted the phrase in the promotion of its toilets and Carson sued. Although no other indicium of Carson's identity was used by the defendant, it was held by a court in the United States that the use of the phrase alone was sufficient to evoke Carson's identity, and that his identity had been intentionally appropriated by the defendant for commercial exploitation without consent. That was enough for legal liability.[29]

The Misrepresentation Model

This model is based on legal ideas about prohibiting marketplace misrepresentations to the public and preventing consumer confusion. The legal cause of action is known as the tort of passing-off.

To continue with the analysis of the Maybelline-Newton-John case, a trader was able to use the identity of a public figure in such a way that the public was not deceived or confused. No cosmetics customer would think that Newton-John was actually posing in the advertisement or endorsing or otherwise associated with the product.[30] Accordingly, no misrepresentation was made and no misleading or deceptive conduct was engaged in by the defendant. There was therefore, in a free culture and a competitive economy, no legal ground for prohibiting the practice. Nor, on the moral, social and economic reasoning underlying this model, should there be.

In Australia, which grounds legal liability on finding a misrepresentation to the public, the Carson complaint would be unlikely to succeed. An Australian court would, most likely, not find that customers of portable toilets were led to believe that Carson had in fact consented to the use of his identity to advertise the toilets or that he was in fact endorsing the product. It is more likely to be found that it was a playful use by the defendant of a phrase which merely evoked a celebrity identity which formed part of the popular culture of the day, with no resulting consumer confusion and therefore no legal liability.

The fundamental policy issue in this area of celebrity law is whether the socially and legally optimal approach to the 'protection' of the celebrity persona is achieved through making the celebrity's identity to be, in effect, a property right, as has been done in the United States under the misappropriation model, and through the development of a 'right of publicity'; or whether it is better, as in Australia and the United Kingdom, to utilise the traditional

---

29   *Carson v Here's Johnny Portable Toilets, Inc* 698 F 2d 831 at 835 (6th Cir 1983).

30   This was in fact the finding in the case and the outcome was a win by the defendant cosmetics company. See *Newton-John* (1986) 11 FCR 233 at 235 per Burchett J, 'the casual reader would get the impression that indeed the advertiser had made use of Olivia Newton-John's reputation to the extent of gaining attention, but not to the extent of making any suggestion of an association'.

law of passing-off, with its requirement of finding a misrepresentation that the celebrity has approved of or licensed or endorsed the product.

The Misappropriation Model: The right of publicity

> [T]he inherent right of every human being to control the commercial use of his or her identity.
>
> *J Thomas McCarthy, The Rights of Publicity and Privacy s 4:8, pp 195-96*
> *(2005, 2nd edn), s.1:3, p 3.*

A brief look at the workings of the misappropriation model, as it functions in the United States, in particular, is in order here. Although the focus of this book is generally on Australian law, it is also clear that there are also possibly increasingly strong elements of the American 'misappropriation model' in both Australian case-law and Australian commentary. The misappropriation model haunts the Australian jurisprudence on the use of the celebrity identity like a pushy ghost. Many judges and academics seem to like it and certainly it is admired by many lawyers and others who act in the interests of celebrities. That is perhaps not surprising. Celebrities are a global phenomenon and many if not most of the same concerns, values, pressures and arguments that are found in the North American jurisdictions can be and are found here. There are frequent calls, especially from commentators in the United States, for 'global harmonisation' of the area of protection of the celebrity persona. The proposed 'harmonisation' is usually to be based on imitation of the American misappropriation model and is motivated by the 'tremendous value world-wide' of American celebrities.[31]

The name given to the right of action granted to celebrities in the United States under the misappropriation model is the 'right of publicity'. The right is a property right and the celebrity's identity is, in principle, to be treated in the same way as any other form of property:

> If you see someone taking your coat from a hook in a restaurant, the natural impulse is to say 'Excuse me, but you are taking something that belongs to me'. In the same way, a plaintiff who asserts the right of publicity says to the defendant, 'Excuse me, but you are using my identity to draw attention to your commercial advertisement. That belongs to me'.[32]

The essential elements of the action for infringement of the right of publicity are that the defendant must, without consent and to the injury of the celebrity,

---

31   See, for example, Lapter, AJ Esq, 'How The Other Half Lives (Revisited): Twenty Years Since *Midler v Ford*: Global Perspective On The Right Of Publicity' (2007) 15 *Texas Intellectual Property Law Journal* 239 at 278, 320-324.

32   McCarthy, above n 6, s 4:8, pp 83-84. Note that McCarthy's analogy, linking a person's identity to the person's coat, is marvellously vivid and persuasive. But the reader is here advised to stay cool and to remember the rhetorical and manipulative power of analogy and metaphor to focus attention on some aspect of similarity between things, while casting differences, sometimes important differences, into the shadows. For more on this, see Loughlan, P, 'Pirates, Parasites, Reapers, Sowers, Fruits, Foxes ... The Metaphors of Intellectual Property' (2006) 28 *Sydney Law Review* 211.

have made use of the celebrity's identity for the defendant's own commercial gain and for the purposes of trade.[33] For example, these elements of legal liability were all found to exist when Bette Midler sued Ford Motors and an advertising agency for an infringement of her right of publicity. The car company had used, without Midler's consent, a 'sound-alike' in imitation of Midler's voice in an advertisement for Ford cars. The court said: 'A voice is as distinctive and personal as a face. The human voice is one of the most palpable ways identity is manifested'.[34] Neither Midler's name nor her picture nor any other indicium of her identity besides the sound-alike voice was used in the advertisement and the advertisement did not otherwise imply that she was endorsing the product. It was nonetheless held that, 'the sellers have appropriated what is not theirs and have committed a tort in California'.[35]

Similarly, the musician, Donald Henley, founder and member of the band 'The Eagles,' successfully brought action against the defendant department store for infringement of his right of publicity when the defendant ran an advertisement with a picture of a man wearing a shirt, known as a 'henley', and containing the words, 'This is Don's henley,' with an arrow pointing at the advertised shirt and other lines like 'Don loves his henley; you will too'. It was held that the musician could be identified from the advertisement and that the advertisement had appropriated the plaintiff's identity and 'used the value associated with Don Henley's identity and personality in order to attract consumers' attention'.[36]

Liability was imposed in the *Henley* case, as in the *Midler* case, not because consumers would be confused or misled, but on the ground that the defendant had, 'received a benefit by getting to use a celebrity's name for free in its advertising'.[37] This is a long way away from the use of Olivia Newton-John's identity in the Maybelline advertisement, where the defendant had indeed used Newton-John's name and likeness for free and received from that use the benefit of increased attention to its advertisement and presumably

---

33 The existence and legal basis for the right of publicity varies from State to State in the United States. Many States recognise it as a common law right while other states provide for the right through statute. The following is the relevant provision in a California statute, *California Civil Code* s 3344 which makes it unlawful to:
> knowingly use another's name, voice, signature, photograph, or likeness, in any manner, on or in products, merchandise, or goods, or for purposes of advertising or selling, or soliciting purchases of, products, merchandise, goods or services, without such person's prior consent.

The right is described in the *Restatement (Third) of Unfair Competition* s 46, cmt c (2006) as a right which exists to 'secure for plaintiffs the commercial value of their fame and prevent unjust enrichment of others seeking to appropriate that value for themselves'. The right is also found in s 652C of the *Restatement (Second) of Torts* (1977) which reads, 'One who appropriates to his own use or benefit the name or likeness of another is subject to liability to the other for invasion of his privacy'.

34 *Midler v Ford Motor Co* 849 F 2d 460 at 463 (1988).

35 Ibid at 463.

36 *Henley v Dillard Dept Stores* 46 F Supp 2d 587 at 593 (1999).

37 Ibid at 597.

increased sales of its product, but had not done so in a way that amounted to a misrepresentation or resulted in consumer confusion.[38]

American case-law in the area of the right of publicity is quite replete and among those many cases are many which may appear, to the Australian legal eye, to be quite extreme and, to a conservative Australian legal eye, almost bizarre in their protection of the celebrity. The *Henley* and *Midler* cases themselves, though described above in a calm manner, could on one view be seen as extreme, given that a celebrity trader is in each case given a legal remedy and a defendant trader's freedom is inhibited despite no consumer confusion and no use of the celebrity's name or image or likeness. The concept of 'use of a celebrity identity' does appear, in the exercise of the right of publicity, to stretch to cover a trader's use of anything which evokes the celebrity in the mind of the target consumer.

This 'stretch' was vigorously criticised by a judge of the United States Court of Appeals, Ninth Circuit in *White v Samsung Electronics America, Inc,*[39] a case which involved the defendant's television advertisement using a robot dressed in a particular configuration of wig, gown and jewellery which would call to the mind of viewers a celebrity of the time, Vanna White, an actor in a popular game show called 'Wheel of Fortune'. The robot was held by the majority of the court to constitute a use of Vanna White's identity and a breach of her right of publicity was therefore established. Justice Kozinsky dissented:[40]

> Under the majority's opinion, it's now a tort for advertisers to remind the public of a celebrity. Not to use a celebrity's name, voice, signature or likeness; not to imply the celebrity endorses a product; but simply to evoke the celebrity's image in the public's mind. This Orwellian notion withdraws far more from the public domain than prudence and common sense allow. It conflicts with the Copyright Act and the Copyright Clause. It raises serious First Amendment problems. It's bad law, and it deserves a long, hard second look.

Justice Kozinsky's dissent, though famous in legal circles, has not held the day and the right of publicity has, in the United States, carried on with its established trajectory of, arguably, extreme celebrity identity protection.

The assignability and, in particular, the inheritability of the property right in the celebrity identity in the United States may again, at least to the conservative Australian legal eye, appear to take the concept of celebrity identity protection to an extreme. Surely you cannot leave your identity, your persona, who you are, to someone else in your will? Haven't you left this

---

38   *Newton-John* (1986) 11 FCR 233 and see above, p 28.

39   *White v Samsung Electronics America, Inc* 989 F 2d 1512 (1993).

40   Ibid at 1514. Lindsay Lohan has recently brought a legal action for breach of her right to privacy and unauthorised commercial use of her 'name charcterization and personality'. The action is based on an advertisement featuring no overt reference to the actress, but with a 'milkaholic' baby named 'Lindsay': *Lindsay Lohan v E*Trade Securities LLC* (Index No 10-004579) March 2010, Supreme Court of the State of New York.

world for a better one? Can this be for real?[41] It is in fact a relatively common legal principle in many American States. It was recently held, for example, that the use of a brief, 13-second sound recording of a deceased celebrity's voice without the consent of the celebrity identity's new, post-mortem owner was a 'misappropriation of identity' and the using trader was accordingly liable, despite the fact that such a use was not an infringement of any *copyright* laws.[42]

> The advent of various new forms of digital media and Internet technology is raising new issues, creating new ways of using a celebrity identity and forcing new developments in the right of publicity.

Many States have no limitation on the duration of such post-mortem celebrity identity rights. This is true, for example, of the law of Tennessee, which governs the rights of publicity of Elvis Presley,[43] and so, on one way of looking at it, 'The King' really is not entirely dead after all. Marilyn Monroe, despite a post-mortem cultural presence at least as potent as that of Elvis Presley, does not have post-mortem rights of publicity because at the time of her domicile and death in New York and California in 1962, neither State granted post-mortem rights and statutes which purport to grant such rights do not operate retrospectively.[44]

The advent of various new forms of digital media and Internet technology is raising new issues, creating new ways of using a celebrity identity and forcing new developments in the right of publicity. One contemporary issue absorbing an American appeal court and many academic commentators, as similar cases will undoubtedly absorb other courts deeply into the future, is the decision in *CBC Distribution & Marketing, Inc v Major League Baseball Advanced Media, LP*.[45] In that case, a fantasy sports provider used the names

---

41   It can be somewhat odd to read Australian judges and commentators complaining that it is 'fictional' or 'artificial' to have to find a misrepresentation in order to engage the law governing celebrity protection in Australia when the 'real mischief' is, in their view, misappropriation of identity (see below, p 46). The oddity flows from the fact that the misappropriation model, which these same judges and commentators appear to admire, is based on a principle that human beings have property in their identities which they can assign to others while they are alive and leave to their heirs when they are dead. 'Artificiality' is, it seems, in the eye of the legal beholder.

42   *Facenda v NFL Films Inc*, 488 F Supp 2d 491 at 501-503 (2007).

43   *Tennessee Code Annotated* §47-25-1104 (2005) and see Dowd, RJ, 'Rights Of Publicity: Elvis, Marilyn, And The Federal Courts' (2007) 54-SEP *Federal Lawyer* 12 at 13.

44   See Dowd, above n 43 at 13 and *Shaw Family Archives Ltd v CMG Worldwide Inc* 486 F Supp 2d 309 (2007).

45   443 F Supp 2d 1077 (2006) cert denied by the Supreme Court: Order List – 2 June 2008. For commentaries, see Howells D 'Log Me In To The Old Ballgame: CBC Distribution & Marketing, Inc v Major League Baseball Advanced Media, LP' (2007) 22 *Berkeley Technology Law Journal* 477; Grossman G, 'Switch Hitting: How CBC V Mlb Advanced Media Redefined The Right Of Publicity' (2007) 14 *UCLA Entertainment Law Review* 285; Mead, D 'CBC Distribution And Marketing, Inc v Major League Baseball Advanced Media, LP: Why Major League Baseball Struck Out And Won't Have Better Luck In Its Next Trip To The Plate' (2007) 8 *Minnesota Journal of Law, Science and Technology* 715.

and performance statistics of real, Major League baseball players in its Internet-based fantasy baseball league and was sued by the Major League Baseball Players' Association for violation of the baseball players' rights of publicity. The decision of the District Court of Missouri was against the Players' Association on the ground, among others, that what was important was *how* the names were used by the defendant, not the simple fact that they were used, and that the defendant did not use the names and performance statistics as symbols of the players identities, but as 'historical facts' about the players.[46] That appears to be quite a disturbingly difficult distinction to have to make when contemplating the use of a celebrity identity in this context and an appeal court may clarify the matter.

In other recent developments in the right of publicity in the United States, the marketing practice of digital product placement in television programs and films is raising significant concerns about celebrity rights to control the use of their identities. The legal right of publicity developed in a cultural and technological context where the distinction between an advertisement and a cultural product like a television program or a film was stronger and more easily made than it is in an era when technology permits the seamless and undetectable insertion of a branded product into any existing program or film, after and sometimes long after, filming has ended.[47] Although there is as yet no decided case, concerns have now been expressed that an actor's appearance in a film using a branded product can create an implied endorsement of the product, but without the consent of and without any additional payment to the actor beyond the amount already paid for the acting role.[48] Further, even where an implied endorsement cannot be found, the view has been expressed that digital product placement can infringe an actor's right of publicity, which does not require the finding of an implied endorsement but, more simply, under the California Civil Code, for example, a finding that a person's identity has been knowingly used on a product or in relation to advertising a product without that person's prior consent.[49] The celebrity can argue, possibly persuasively, that the defendant has infringed his or her right of publicity by using, 'his underlying persona within that captured medium [of film] to draw attention to a product without his consent'.[50]

---

46   *CBC Distribution & Marketing* 443 F Supp 2d 1077 at 1089 (2006), cert denied by the Supreme Court: Order List – 2 June 2008. The court noted (at 1084-1085) that Missouri law follows the right of publicity as in the *Restatement (Third) of Unfair Competition*, which requires for liability that the defendant has used the plaintiff's name as a 'symbol of his identity'.

47   Almond, BD, 'Lose The Illusion: Why Advertisers' Use Of Digital Product Placement Violates Actors' Right Of Publicity' (2007) 64 *Washington & Lee Law Review* 625 at 627.

48   See ibid at 642-43; Savare, M, 'Comment, Where Madison Avenue Meets Hollywood and Vine: The Business, Legal, and Creative Ramifications of Product Placements' (2004) 11*UCLA Entertainment Law Review* 33 at 356 (quoting a partner in a product placement company, asserting that product placements benefit advertisers and manufacturers by creating 'indirect celebrity endorsement[s]').

49   See above, n 17.

50   Almond, above n 47 at 661.

This brief overview of the elements and some of the more extreme and the more recent contextual applications of the American right of publicity has provided an illustration and explication of the misappropriation model of regulation of the commercial use of a celebrity identity. It is property-based and highly protective of the celebrity identity. It rewards the investment made by the celebrity in creating his or her public identity and inhibits free-riding by others on that investment. The corresponding Canadian regulatory model, called the tort of appropriation of personality,[51] also provides a remedy for 'the appropriation for commercial purposes of another's likeness, voice, or personality'.[52] While the Canadian tort is weaker and somewhat less protective of the celebrity identity than the American right of publicity, it is nevertheless the same sort of a property-based right of action which focuses on the appropriation of an identity rather than on demonstrating misrepresentation and consumer confusion.[53]

The Misrepresentation Model: The tort of passing-off

> There should be no a priori assumption that only a celebrity or his successors may ever market (or license the marketing of) his own character. Monopolies should not be so readily created.

> *Elvis Presley Enterprises Inc v Sid Shaw Elvisly Yours (1999) 47 IPR 441*

The right of publicity in the United States is a 'purpose-built' cause of action, directly responding to the needs and demands of celebrities for protection against unauthorised commercial use of their identities and designed specifically for that end. Protection of the celebrity identity is handled in the Anglo-Australian jurisdictions through a misrepresentation model and, more specifically, through the ancient tort of passing-off and by the newer statutory cause of action given by s 52 of the *Trade Practices Act 1974*[54] against misleading and deceptive conduct by traders. Both the tort of passing-off and the s 52 action are abstract and general and, importantly, they cover vast

---

51   *Krouse v Chrysler Canada Ltd* [1973] 1 OR 2d 225 (Can); Howell RG, 'Publicity Rights in the Common Law Provinces of Canada' (1998) 18 *Loyola of Los Angeles Entertainment Law Review* 487. Japan also has a property-based right which gives celebrities an exclusive right to commercial exploitation of their identities. See the *Oniyanko Club* case, Hanrei Jihl (No 1400) Tokyo High Court judgment, September 26 1999, as described in Tessensohn JA and Yamamoto S 'Supreme Court Of Japan Brings Racehorses' Publicity Rights To Heel' [2005] *EIPR* 187 at 189.

52   *Krouse* [1973] 1 OR 2d 225 at 225.

53   Lapter, above n 31 at 301.

54   Section 52 of the *Trade Practices Act 1974* (Cth), and each corresponding statutory provision in each of the States and Territories, prohibits 'conduct that is misleading or deceptive or is likely to mislead or deceive' and it provides an alternative but essentially co-extensive action where facts exist which would also give rise to an action for passing-off. Actions are, in such cases, almost always based on both passing-off and on s 52. For a specialised account of the differences between the tort of passing-off and s 52, see Davison M, Johnston K and Kennedy P, *Shanahan's Australian Law of Trade Marks & Passing-off* (Lawbook Co, 3rd edn, 2003), pp 611-618.

areas of market-place conduct which have nothing to do with celebrities or the commercial use of their identities. Cases involving problems of celebrity identity are therefore dealt with, in the law of passing-off, by specific application of broad legal principles which were developed without heed to celebrity needs or demands.

Passing-off is a tort and, like most of the existing torts, we more or less instinctively feel it to be a properly actionable wrong. If you are assaulted or defamed by someone, we feel that you ought to have a cause of action against the assaulter or defamer. If your real property is rendered uninhabitable by the actions of your neighbour, then you ought to be able to sue your neighbour. The tort of passing-off, with a moral idea at its heart about rectitude and decent behaviour on the part of traders in the market-place, also feels instinctively right.

The basic form of the tort was articulated in the 19th century case of *Perry v Truefitt* and holds good to this day, '[a] man is not to sell his own goods under the pretence that they are the goods of another'.[55] Passing-off has grown considerably from the time of *Perry*, however, and the next statement, which describes the modern and extended form of the tort, is broader and now more accurate: Passing-off both prevents one trader from misrepresenting his or her goods or services as being the goods or services of the plaintiff trader and also prevents one trader from holding out his or her goods or services as having some association or connection with the plaintiff trader when that is not true.

False commercial information distorts consumer choice in a competitive economy and thereby reduces efficiency. Consumers are entitled to accurate information in order to make their choices without confusion. A trader is entitled to trade in a market and attempt to persuade consumers that they can obtain the best value for their money with that trader, without other traders lying to those consumers and diverting their trade. Passing-off prohibits particular kinds of lies and marketplace miscommunications, namely, false representations about trade source which harm or are likely to harm the goodwill of another trader. Trade source is, in law, a special fact. It is viewed by the law as something that people in trade should tell the truth about and so not telling the truth about trade source and trade source connection among traders is an actionable wrong.

The sort of association or connection between traders which the defendant in a passing-off action is alleged to have made a representation about is not a precise thing. The law here is analysing what is being explicitly or impliedly being said by traders who are not, except coincidentally, lawyers, to consumers who are also not, except coincidentally, lawyers. Precision is not required for liability:[56]

---

55   *Perry v Truefitt* (1842) 6 Beav 66; 49 ER 749. See also the more recent statement by Lord Oliver in *Reckitt & Colman Ltd v Bordern* (1990) 17 IPR 1 at 7, '[t]he law of passing-off can be summarised in one short, general proposition, that no man may pass off his goods as those of another'.

56   Wadlow C, *The Law Of Passing-off* (Sweet & Maxwell, London, 1995), p 280.

> If there is damaging confusion between the businesses of the defendant and the plaintiff as a result of the misrepresentation by the defendant, then it is immaterial that the misrepresentation may not imply the existence of any particular connection between the parties. It is unreasonable to expect those confused to have any precise opinion as to the legal nature of the connection they suppose to exist … [E]ven if the public would know that the plaintiff and the defendant are different legal persons, it may believe that in dealing with the defendant it is dealing with a part of the plaintiff's enterprise in the broadest sense and therefore it can rely on the plaintiff being ultimately responsible for the defendant's integrity… In the typical case the question is best approached without attempting to analyse precisely what connection with the plaintiff's business is claimed by the defendant.

The way in which issues concerning the protection of the celebrity identity fit into and are governed by this broad and flexible old tort is roughly this: when a trader uses the identity of a celebrity in its advertisement without the consent of the celebrity, the celebrity's legal argument is that the trader is thereby misrepresenting its goods as having some association or connection with the celebrity, in particular, misrepresenting that the celebrity is endorsing the trader's goods, when that is not true. In these circumstances, the trader may be liable in passing-off. Because a celebrity endorsement is, in the ordinary course of trade, handled as a commercial relationship between the celebrity and the trader with a signed contract between them, when the public sees a celebrity endorsement of a product, it tends to believe (or, at least, the law thinks that the public tends to believe) that such a commercial relationship exists here too, and that a licensing agreement has been entered into between celebrity and trader. So, if the image of Angelina Jolie were to be used without her consent in an advertisement for Chanel No 5 perfume the person viewing the advertisement would be likely to think that Jolie had in fact consented to the use of her image and was endorsing or in some way associating herself with the product. In effect, a legally significant lie would have been told. It would be a misrepresentation by the trader that would be legally actionable by Jolie on the ground of passing-off.

An important point of difference between the right of publicity as it exists in the Untied States and the Australian action for passing-off relates to the property status in the celebrity identity in the case of the right of publicity, and the absence of such a status in the case of the action in passing-off. Whereas the celebrity in the United States actually 'owns' his or her identity, that is not the case in Australia. The celebrity here does not own his or her identity. All that the celebrity owns here is a right to go into court and stop a defendant from making use of the celebrity's identity in a way that constitutes a misrepresentation about commercial association and misleads the public.

The leading formulation of the tort of passing-off can be pithily described as requiring 'the classical trinity' of elements: reputation, misrepresentation and damage.[57] Here is the classical trinity as formulated by the House of Lords:[58]

---

57   *ConAgra Inc v McCain Foods (Australian) Pty Ltd* (1992) 23 IPR 193 at 247.

58   *Reckitt & Colman Ltd v Bordern Inc* (1990) 17 IPR 1 at 7.

> The leading formulation of the tort of passing-off can be pithily described as requiring 'the classical trinity' of elements: reputation, misrepresentation and damage.

First he [the plaintiff] must establish a goodwill or reputation attached to the goods or services ... Secondly he must demonstrate a misrepresentation by the defendant to the public (whether or not intentional) leading or likely to lead the public to believe that the goods or services offered by him are the goods or services of the plaintiff ... Thirdly, he must demonstrate that he suffers ...

In other words, *first*, prove that your product has an established reputation in the marketplace. (If your product is not known, then no one is likely to mistake another product as being yours.) *Second*, prove that the defendant has said or done something, overtly or covertly, expressly or impliedly, to lead people to think that his product actually is your product or has some connection with you or your product. (If the defendant is 'passing-off its product as being yours, then there must be a lie in it somewhere) The lie that is being told by the defendant is rarely a direct or express lie. It is more subtle than that.[59]

If, for example, Chanel, without consent, used the words 'Angelina Jolie loves Chanel No 5 and recommends it to you' in an advertisement, that would be an express and misleading representation and dealt with easily by the law of passing-off. Misrepresentations, however, can be and usually are considerably more subtle than that, although they have and are intended to have the same effect. Consider, for example, an advertisement for Chanel No 5 with the name of the product stated in the advertisement over a background photo of Jolie walking off into the distance and apparently not relating with the product in any way. Here the endorsement (and therefore a connection between Chanel and Jolie) is merely implied, but the trader is equally legally liable, so long as the public still reads the advertisement as containing an endorsement by Jolie or at least as based on a consensual use of her identity in association with the product. If, however, Jolie has in fact consented to the use of her identity in the advertisement and has entered into a commercial licensing arrangement with Chanel by which Chanel can use her identity and pay royalties for each such use, then no misrepresentation has taken place and no consumer has been misled as to the nature of the arrangement. People think she is getting paid for it and she is.

Third, prove that some damage has occurred to you as a result of the defendant's activities or that such damage is likely to occur if the defendant does not stop doing what it is doing.

It should be noted that there is also an alternative formulation of the elements of the tort of passing-off required for liability, namely, that of Lord

---

59   See *Spalding Bros v Gammage Ltd* (1915) 32 RPC 273 at 284:

> [T]he basis of a passing-off action being a false representation by the defendant, it must be proved in each case as a fact that the false representation was made. It may of course have been made in express words, but cases of express misrepresentation are rare.

Diplock in *Erven Warnink Besloten Vennootschap v J Townend & Sons (Hull) Ltd*, finding that a case of passing-off requires:[60]

> (1) a misrepresentation (2) made by a trader in the course of trade, (3) to prospective customers of his or ultimate consumers of goods or services supplied by him, (4) which is calculated to injure the business or goodwill of another trader (in the sense that this is a reasonably foreseeable consequence) and (5) which causes actual damage to a business or goodwill of the trader by whom the action is brought or (in a quia timet action) will probably do so.

This test, while it has been criticised and has probably now been surpassed in application by the 'classical trinity' as described above, has also been applied in Australian celebrity endorsement cases.

The first Australian case squarely in the area of commercial use without consent of a celebrity identity was *Henderson v Radio Corporation*, where a well-known pair of ballroom dancers sued on the basis that a photograph of them dancing had been placed, without their consent, on the cover of a gramophone record of dance music.[61] The equivocal reasoning in the judgment, which swung between support for a misappropriation model and support for a misrepresentation model for regulating the area of celebrity endorsement in Australia, was reflective of both Australian adherence to the English tradition of passing-off and, undoubtedly, an awareness of dynamic developments in the United States with respect to the right of publicity. That right had been judicially recognised for the first time as the 'right of publicity' only a few years before, in 1953 in the United States, with an express acceptance of the right as being property-based and, 'in addition to and independent of that right of privacy'.[62]

The *Henderson* case has been extraordinarily potent, not only in its immediate aftermath and in Australian jurisprudence, but even, in a reverse of the usual legal cultural cringe, in recent English law.[63] The *Henderson* court found that the use of the image of the two celebrity dancers on the cover of the record would be understood by consumers as implying that the dancers had recommended the record and it therefore found that the use of the dancers' identities was a misrepresentation which gave rise to passing-off liability. But the court also, when examining the issue of injury to the plaintiffs, one of the required elements for liability in passing-off, took the opportunity to draw upon the language of appropriation of property and even, in its presumably rhetorical use of the word 'robbed', the inflammatory language of the criminal law:[64]

---

60   *Erven Warnink Besloten Vennootschap v J Townend & Sons (Hull) Ltd* [1979] AC 731 at 742.

61   *Henderson v Radio Corporation* (1958) 1A IPR 620.

62   *Haelan Laboratories, Inc v Topps Chewing Gum, Inc* 202 F 2d 866 at 868 (2d Cir, 1953).

63   *Henderson* was cited with approval and relied on in the recent English case of *Irvine v Talksport Ltd* [2002] EWHC 367 (Ch) at [26], a landmark decision which removed the former 'common field of activity' requirement as an element of liability in celebrity endorsement cases in the United Kingdom. See also the Court of Appeal decision on damages in the case at *Irvine v Talksport Ltd* (2003) 57 IPR 651.

64   *Henderson* (1958) 1A IPR 620 at 638 per Evatt CJ and Myers J.

[T]he wrongful appropriation of another's professional or business reputation is an injury in itself, no less, in our opinion, than the appropriation of his goods or money. The professional recommendation of the respondents was and still is theirs, to withhold or bestow at will, but the appellant has wrongfully deprived them of their right to do so and of the payment or reward on which, if they had been minded to give their approval to the appellant's record, they could have insisted. In our opinion it is idle to contend that this wrongful appropriation is not an injury to the respondents. It is as much an injury as if the appellant had paid the respondents for their recommendation and then robbed them of the money.

On the surface of the case, the *Henderson* judgments appear to have set Australian celebrity endorsement law on a path of incremental development of the tort of passing-off and to have encouraged a fairly traditional trajectory of misrepresentation liability. That is indeed a reasonable and appropriate and accurate interpretation of the case, in light of the specific finding of the existence of an endorsement misrepresentation, the emphasis in the case on finding passing-off precedents in the area and the fact that in the oft-cited passage above, the statements about misappropriation were made in the context of deciding about damages, not about over-all liability. On this view, the case is merely an interesting and important passing-off case, applying established principles to novel facts, and little more.

Many learned commentators, however, and many even more learned judges have thought otherwise. One commentator put it indirectly:[65]

Subsequent Australian decisions have revealed an increasing recognition that 'celebrity' may indeed be protectable as property capable of commercial exploitation'. *Significant progress* was made in Henderson's case.[66]

The language of 'progress', of course, gives a rhetorical boost to the point being made, since one tends to view 'progress' considerably more favourably than one views simple 'change', let alone, 'derogation from principle'.

Several Australian judges have either attempted to rest a celebrity endorsement decision directly on the misappropriation ground or have found the necessary misrepresentation while complaining that such a finding is fictional or annoying to have to do. (Blast that doctrine of precedent!) Their judgments have been described as 'a covert application of a test of misappropriation in the guise of passing-off'.[67] In *Hogan v Koala Dundee*,[68] for instance, the defendant ran two small souvenir shops which he called Dundee Country and promoted his wares with a stuffed koala which used strong visual references

---

65   Davison, Johnston and Kennedy, above n 50, p 575. See also McKeough J, Stewart A and Griffith P, *Intellectual Property In Australia* (Butteworths, 3rd edn, 2004), p 434:

This decision [*Henderson*] effectively opened the way for 'appropriation of personality suits, where a famous identity sues to prevent their name or professional image being used without payment to secure their consent.

66   Emphasis added.

67   Howell R, 'Personality Rights: A Canadian Perspective: Some Comparisons With Australia' (1990) *Intellectual Property Journal* 212 at 221.

68   (1988) 12 IPR 508.

to the film character of Crocodile Dundee (a sleeveless vest, a bush hat with crocodile teeth on it and a big knife). The result sought and obtained by Paul Hogan, the plaintiff filmmaker and producer was an injunction and in his judgment, the presiding judge, Pincus J, essentially invoked the tort of misappropriation of identity, reaching back to the Henderson case for support:[69]

> The essence of the wrong done ... is not in truth a misrepresentation that there is a licensing or sponsoring agreement between the applicant and the respondent; it is in the second ground taken in the Henderson case, namely wrongful appropriation of a reputation or, more widely, wrongful association of goods with an image properly belonging to the applicant.

But, blast the doctrine of precedent as one might wish, the doctrine of precedent exists and it is not for judges of the Federal Court sitting alone at first instance to set aside established principle and precedent. Within a few short months of handing down the judgment in *Koala Dundee*, Pincus J's incursion into judicial creativity was rejected by the Full Federal Court. In *Pacific Dunlop Ltd v Hogan*,[70] where the defendant had without Paul Hogan's consent imitated a scene from the movie *Crocodile Dundee* and mutated it into a television advertisement for shoes (*'That's* not a shoe. *This* is a shoe'), the court, found the defendant liable for passing-off and for breach of s 52. It rested its analysis fully and squarely on the need for finding a misrepresentation. The question which was asked and affirmatively answered was this:[71]

> The question for the judge to decide in the present case was whether a significant section would be misled into believing, contrary to the fact, that a commercial arrangement had been concluded between [Paul Hogan]and the appellant under which [Paul Hogan]agreed to the advertising.

The public does not have to be found by the court to believe that an actual licence has been given by the celebrity, just that some kind of loose, though commercial, association exists.

In *Twentieth-Century Fox Film Corp v South Australian Brewing Co Ltd*,[72] a small brewing company used the mark DUFF on its new line of beer. The cartoon character Homer Simpson in the popular television series *The Simpsons* drinks DUFF beer. What's more, the tin in which the South Australian DUFF beer was marketed looked like the tin used for the beer in the cartoon series. There was clearly some playful cultural referencing going on here, but the law of passing-off, not known for either its clarity or its playfulness, provided the foundation for a finding that the defendant beer company had passed off its product as having a commercial association with the television series and a significant section of the public would believe that misrepresentation:

69   *Hogan* (1988) 12 IPR 508.

70   (1989) 87 ALR 14.

71   *Pacific Dunlop* (1989) 87 ALR 14 at 43. Sheppard J dissented and found as a fact, at 32, that 'viewers of the advertisement could not reasonably conclude that Mr Hogan had consented to or authorised the advertisement'.

72   (1996) 34 IPR 225.

It is true that it would be artificial to anticipate that every person buying 'Duff Beer' would take the time to analyse the subtle legal or merchandising overtones and connotations and ask specifically whether the beer is made with the licence or permission of the applicant. I consider however that the brewery's beer will produce this impression.

For liability to be imposed on the defendant user of the celebrity identity, the celebrity must be identifiable from the defendant's advertisement, which must point pretty unequivocally to the celebrity. Where, as in *10th Cantanae Pty Ltd v Shoshana Pty Ltd*, the celebrity name alleged to have been misused is a relatively common one and the image in the advertisement is not clearly one of the relevant celebrity, there is no liability.[73] In this case, the plaintiff, whose name was 'Sue Smith,' was well-known at the time for her work in television, (how fleeting is fame), but she was unable to stop the defendant's advertisement, which used only her outstandingly common name and not her likeness.

Impersonators are relatively immune from liability in passing-off in Australia because such liability, according to the basic principles of passing-off would depend upon a finding of misrepresentation, namely, that a significant section of the public would believe that the impersonator had actually had authorisation from the relevant celebrity to conduct the impersonation or that the celebrity had endorsed or way in some way associated voluntarily with the impersonation. This result is, of course, very different from the result in the United States, where, for example, Elvis Presley impersonators have been stopped from performing in stage shows[74] and where a threat by the businessman (who had purchased from the Elvis Presley estate for $US114 million the right to control Elvis' name and likeness) to sue all Elvis impersonators for breach of the right of publicity was widely reported in the press.[75] The right of publicity is yet again considerably more protective of the rights of the celebrity and less protective of the rights of others, such as impersonators, to access the celebrity identity than is the tort of passing-off.

The celebrity must not only be identifiable for liability to be engaged, the public must be led to believe in the existence of some sort of commercial association or connection between the defendant and the celebrity. Whether the public will so perceive and so believe is always a question of fact and much will depend on the particular way that the defendant has used the celebrity identity and upon the view that the trier of fact has of the robustness of consumer good sense. Celebrity identities can accordingly be used for commercial purposes by others without the consent of the celebrity, but such use carries risks and must be done with a sure hand, plenty of legal advice and an acceptance of some uncertainty of outcome should litigation occur. Details, sometimes even very minute details, of the exact way that the use

---

73   *10th Cantanae Pty Ltd v Shoshana Pty Ltd* (1987) 10 IPR 289.
74   See *Elvis Presley v Russen* 513 F Supp 1339 (1981).
75   See, for example, *The Australian* 18 April 2003.

of the identity occurs will always be important. So, for example, in *Honey v Australian Airlines Ltd*,[76] the defendant airline's use of a photo of Honey, a then well-known sporting hero, was found not to suggest any endorsement of the product by the celebrity or other commercial connection between the celebrity and the defendant and there was accordingly no liability. The defendant airline had produced a poster with the photo of Honey taking up the bulk of the viewing space on the poster, but with the defendant's own name and logo at the bottom of the poster. The court found that members of the public would look at the poster and think that the airline was promoting Australian sport and using the photo of Honey for that purpose. If the airline had used the same photograph of Honey, but with, say, a more pronounced referencing of its own business product and more prominent positioning of its own trade marks, so that the public would look upon the poster as an advertisement for the airline rather than as a poster promoting sport, the result would have been different.

The issue of protection for the celebrity identity through the tort of passing-off after the death of the celebrity is at present largely unresolved in Australia. As noted above, the right of publicity in several States in the United States survives the death of the celebrity,[77] but that may not be the case with passing-off actions in Australia. There are problems. The misrepresentation requirement of the tort means that the public would have to be shown to have a background belief that licensing or other commercial arrangements and associations of a legal nature between celebrities or celebrity representatives or celebrity legal entities on the one hand and product traders on the other hand do take place even after the celebrity is dead.[78] It may be that such a background belief now exists in Australia, but it is not certain. In the case of *McCorquodale v Masterson*,[79] which involved the executors of the estate of Process Diana and the Princess Diana Memorial Fund opposing a trader's registration of the trade mark 'Diana's Legacy In Roses' on the basis that it contained a confusing connotation, the court did find as follows:[80]

> There is a real likelihood that consumers would understand that goods bearing the impugned mark are in some way sponsored or approved by the Fund or the Princess' estate, even if they were ignorant about the specific details of the arrangements. The likelihood of this misunderstanding is sufficient to create a likelihood of confusion and depiction in Australia by reason of the connotation of the mark ...

---

76   (1990) 18 IPR 185.

77   See above, pp 38-39.

78   Note that at common law tort actions die with the person by whom or against whom the tort was committed, and although that has been reversed by statute, the reversal extends only to those actions subsisting at the time of the decease: *Law Reform (Miscellaneous Provisions) Act 1944* (NSW) s 2.

79   (2004) 63 IPR 582.

80   *McCorquodale* (2004) 63 IPR 582.

Disclaimers

Since liability in passing-off is founded upon a misrepresentation of commercial association and a consequent deception of the public, disclaimers of the existence of such association by the defendant should work, and they can and do. But they have to be plain and clear and appropriately positioned so that they and their disclaiming message are brought home to the eyes and mind of the public. So, for example, the cosmetics advertisement with the Olivia Newton-John look-alike and the words 'Olivia? No, Maybelline,' a case in there was held to be no relevant misrepresentation sufficient to found an action in passing-off,[81] has been explained as containing a kind of internal disclaimer.[82] The consumer is being more or less expressly told that it is not in fact Olivia but just a look-alike. Presumably the following advertisement for watches could be freely created and used without fear of passing-off liability. Suppose there were an advertisement for Rolex watches featuring a photograph of David Beckham at a restaurant, with Beckham plainly wearing a Rolex watch in the photograph and the following words appearing in large and impossible-to-miss print just under the photograph:

> The Best Endorsement Of All – He Really Wears One' Note that David Beckham has not officially endorsed our product and we have never approached him to do so. But that's our point. He really wears one!

There would, on the basis of the law of passing-off, be no liability imposed on Rolex here. No one would be deceived about a commercial endorsement or other commercial association or connection between Beckham, and Rolex and so no liability could ensure. This is especially so since watches are not the sort of product purchased casually and frequently. For such products and in such circumstances, disclaimers have been found to be more effective.[83]

Again, the drafting and positioning of a disclaimer must be done with a sure hand, plenty of legal advice and an acceptance of some uncertainty of outcome should litigation occur. There are many instances in the case law of courts refusing to accept that a disclaimer has been sufficiently brought to the attention of the public as to counter any deception or confusion brought about by a misrepresentation in the product promotion. So, for instance, in *Children's Television Workshop Inc v Woolworths NSW Ltd*,[84] the defendant sold toys which looked like popular characters from 'Sesame Street' and the 'Muppets' with no licence to do so. Despite the presence of stickers on the toys stating that the toys were not licensed by and had no legal or commercial connection with the plaintiff's television series, the defendant was successfully sued for passing-off. The stickers were held to be not prominent enough or permanent enough to come properly to the attention of the public, who

---

81 *Newton-John* (1986) 11 FCR 233.

82 *Twentieth Century Fox* (1996) 34 IPR 225 at [128].

83 See Davison, Johnston and Kennedy, above n 54, p 531, citing *Parkdale Custom Built Furniture Pty Ltd v Puxu Pty Ltd* (1982) 149 CLR 191 at 199.

84 [1981] RPC 187.

would continue to believe that the toys were being sold with some sort of licence from the plaintiff.

In *Hutchence v South Seas Bubble Co Pty Ltd*, where the defendants had been selling unauthorised INXS merchandise, T-shirts from market stalls, the court rejected the defendant's arguments that it had taken effective measures to counteract any misrepresentation of authorisation. The T-shirts were sold at a stall bearing a sign saying 'BOOTLEG T-SHIRTS', with another small handwritten sign saying that some of the garments have not been authorised and were 'genuine bootleg products'. The T-shirts also bore adhesive stickers larger than the manufacturer's label, saying, 'The manufacturer does not warrant the depiction hereon has been authorised'. The court found that many people would not know the meaning of the word 'bootleg' which was 'not in everyday parlance'[85] and would also not know the meaning of legal words like 'warrant' or 'depiction' or 'authorised'.[86] It is certainly hard here to avoid the conclusion that the court in *Hutchence* was determined not to permit a disclaimer defence, given that it rejected the efficacy of both an informal, slangy way to describe the absence of authorisation *and* a formal legal description of the absence of authorisation.

It may be that celebrities have a particular advantage in disclaimer cases, in light of the fact that a particularly distinctive mark or name (which is of course by its very nature always the case with the celebrity name) may be powerful enough in almost all circumstances to avoid the neutralising effect of a disclaimer.[87] When a mega-star is about, who could ever think straight enough to absorb the cool and rational message of a disclaimer?

With the recent decision of the Court of Appeal in the United Kingdom in *Irvine v Talksport Ltd*[88] where the photograph of a well-known sporting hero, a Formula One driver, had been used without consent in an advertisement for a radio station, the law of passing-off in the United Kingdom came to match that of Australia. Such a use of a celebrity identity was held to amount to a false endorsement and therefore to an actionable misrepresentation.[89] This has been widely viewed as a significant extension of the tort of passing-off in the United Kingdom, even though it essentially just brings English law up to where Australia law was in 1958 with the *Henderson* case (a case which was in fact relied on by the *Irvine* court) and still is.

It has frequently been noted that there is at least an apparent circularity in the reasoning that is at the heart of passing-off, namely, that you get a legal right because people think that you have the right already even if you don't, that it is the 'public's perception of licensing or endorsement that provides

---

85   *Hutchence v South Seas Bubble Co Pty Ltd* (1986) 6 IPR 473 at [27].

86   Ibid at [28].

87   Davison, Johnston and Kennedy, above n 54, p 530.

88   [2003] EWCA Civ 423.

89   See, for example, Carty, H, 'The Common Law And The Quest For The IP Effect' [2007] *Intellectual Property Quarterly* 237 at 252, calling the *Irvine* case 'the first judicial recognition that 'false endorsement' involving a celebrity could be passing-off ... this seems to be a major extension of the tort'.

the basis for the protection of the right licensed'.[90] The general public seems to expect that celebrities have extensive legal protection against unauthorised use of their identities and that expectation then forms the basis of the legal right to protection against unauthorised use of their identities. A study of this has recently been done, tracking what has been termed a 'feedback loop' that is based on the law's focus on consumer perception where, 'what consumers view as the norm becomes the norm'.[91]

The 'feedback loop,' as found in the study, is this. When the touchstone of the law is consumer perception, then if consumers think that a particular use of a trade mark (or, by extension, a celebrity likeness) requires a license from the owner, then using the mark or identity without a license creates a potential for liability. Since users of marks or licences are often risk averse, they seek licenses when none are needed and, 'as consumers encounter more and more licensed uses and fewer and fewer unlicensed uses they come to view licensing as the norm'.[92] The more that we view celebrities as having protection against unauthorised use of their identities, the more they will in fact have such protection. The study accordingly finds an inexorable shifting of rights over the use of trade marks (and, by extension, celebrity identities) from the public domain into private control, and this without an informed public debate or open legislative process.

The future

So the matter essentially rests there. The treatment of unauthorised commercial use of a celebrity identity in Australia is handled by the law of passing-off, which requires a finding that a significant section of the public would be misled into believing that a commercial connection or association of some kind exists between the celebrity whose identity has been taken and the product or business of the defendant trader. The principles have been applied in different circumstances, with different findings of fact on the facts presented to the court. But the principle has essentially remained untouched and its

---

90   Davison, Johnston and Kennedy, above n 54, p 582. See also the following remarks, which are specifically directed to the ornamental use of trade marks but which are reflective of the same sort of legal conundrum: Denicola, R, 'Freedom to Copy' (1999) 108 *Yale Law Journal* 1661 at 1663:

> There is more than a little circularity in basing a legal right to control unauthorised ornamental use on the assumptions that consumers make about the official sponsorship of the ornamented items – assumptions that rest in turn on consumers views about whether trade mark owners have the legal right to control such use. If trade mark owners win enough high-profile cases or brag loudly enough about licensing revenues from *ornamental use*, consumers will naturally think that the products they see must be licensed, which in turn will help insure that a licence is indeed required.

If the phrase 'use of a celebrity likeness' is substituted for the phrase 'ornamental use' in the passage above, the parallel is plain.

91   Gibson, J, 'Risk Aversion and Rights Accretion In Intellectual Property Law' (2007) 116 *Yale Law Journal* 882 at 907-908.

92   Ibid at 907.

future is likely to be more of the same, only more so. This gloomy (or buoyant, depending on your point of view) prognostication is based upon a general apprehension of the apparently ever-expanding social and legal enthrallment with celebrity and the fact that celebrities are an exceptionally powerful and potent social group. The legal requirement of misrepresentation will continue to exist, but the relevant misrepresentation will be more and more easily found to exist in more and more diverse circumstances. Celebrity entitlements to the use of their identities will grow.

Registered trade marks

Although the law governing the commercial use and control of the celebrity identity is primarily the tort of passing-off and the statutory cause of action under s 52 of the *Trade Practices Act*, as discussed above, the law of registered trade marks can also be for some purposes called upon by celebrities and can provide some operational advantages over passing-off. At its slickest, the law of registered trade marks can obviate the need for a plaintiff celebrity whose identity is being commercially used by another trader to have to prove any of the elements of passing-off, namely, reputation, misrepresentation and damage or injury, all of which may be difficult to prove to the satisfaction of a court even where they exist in fact. Registered trade marks can also, however, be used against the interests of a celebrity and celebrities accordingly need to be on the alert to prevent those registrations of trade marks by others which might wrongfully make use of the celebrity identity.

The *Trade Marks Act 1995* (Cth) gives to the owner of a trade mark, once registered, exclusive rights to use that mark in relation to the goods or services for which it is registered. Once the trade mark is registered, the owner can keep other similar marks from getting registered for the same or similar products[93] and can also sue anyone who uses the same or similar mark in relation to the same or similar products.[94] The law also provides particular benefits to the owner of a trade mark that is found to be 'well-known' and it allows the owner of such a mark to stop others from using the same or similar mark even in relation to entirely dissimilar products.[95]

There are very significant hurdles in the way of the law of registered trade marks becoming an effective legal instrument for celebrities pursuing commercial control over identity use, however. The underlying problem is that trade marks are essentially, in their origin and in their nature, 'badges of origin', that is signals of trade source, and they are accordingly, often simply not appropriate legal devices for celebrity identity control. Celebrities are generally not in the business of producing products apart from the public role which got them their celebrity in the first place. Registration can accordingly be difficult and even when registration is achieved, enforcement can

---

93   *Trade Marks Act 1995* (Cth), s 44.
94   *Trade Marks Act 1995*, s 120(1) and (2).
95   *Trade Marks Act 1995*, s 120(3).

be difficult. Celebrities may not only be interested in registering aspects of their identities as trade marks, however. They may also need to be aware of attempted registration by other traders of aspects of their identities.

Registration

The overall identity or persona of a celebrity cannot be registered but aspects of the celebrity identity like name, signature, or likeness are certainly 'signs', and registrable as such, within the meaning of the *Trade Marks Act 1995*, being one or more of the following: 'any letter, word, name, signature, numeral, device, brand, heading, label, ticket, aspect of packaging, shape, colour, sound or scent'.[96]

There is a presumption of registrability in relation to trade marks in the *Trade Marks Act 1995*[97] and the Registrar is instructed to register an applicant's proposed trade mark unless there is a specific ground for rejection. Of the several possible grounds for rejection, two are of particular relevance to the registration of aspects of the celebrity identity: s 41 and s 43.

Section 41

The requirement here is that the mark must be capable of distinguishing the trader's goods from the goods of other traders. The classic legal test for answering the question of whether a trade mark is capable of distinguishing a trader's goods is this:[98]

> [T]he question whether a mark is adapted to distinguish [should] be tested by reference to the likelihood that other persons, trading in goods of the relevant kind and being actuated only by proper motives – in the exercise, that is to say, of the common right of the public to make honest use of words forming part of the common heritage, for the sake of the signification which they ordinarily possess – will think of the word and want to use it in connection with similar goods in any manner which would infringe a registered trade mark granted in respect of it.

So, the issue in relation to the test for whether or not a trade mark is capable of distinguishing a trader's goods is whether other traders would think of the proposed trade mark and wish to use it in relation to their own wares. So, in

---

96   *Trade Marks Act 1995*, s 6.

97   *Trade Marks Act 1995*, s 33.

98   *Clark Equipment Co v Registrar of Trade Marks* (1964) 111 CLR 511, a test deriving from the prior English case of *Registrar of Trade Marks v W & G DuCros Ltd* [1913] AC 624 at 634-635. There is also a legislative notice following s 41 in the *Trade Marks Act 1995*, which in effect summarises the results of the application of the *Clark Equipment* test:

> Note: 'Trade marks that are not inherently adapted to distinguish goods or services are trade marks that consist wholly of a sign that is ordinarily used to indicate
>
> (a)   the kind, quality, quantity, intended purpose, value, geographical origin, or some other characteristic, of goods or services; or
>
> (b)   the time of production of goods or the rendering of services'.

United Artists Corporation v Trevor Clarke Holdings Pty Ltd,[99] an applicant attempted to register, in respect of motor vehicle sales, a trade mark with an image which was found to be deceptively similar to the opponent's famous Pink Panther cartoon character. The opponent attempted to argue that the applicant's mark was not capable of distinguishing the goods of the applicant or indeed of any trader except the opponent, but that argument was rejected on the ground that it misunderstood the nature of the *Clark Equipment* test. The right question to ask was whether other traders would think of and wish to use such an image in relation to motor vehicle sales and the answer to that was that, 'a drawing of a cat or panther has no direct reference to the service of retailing motor vehicles';[100] other traders would not think of it as it did not describe any quality or character of these services and the fact of the mark's fame was irrelevant.

On this approach, then, if Nicole Kidman were to attempt to register her name and likeness in relation to perfume, the test would require that the question be asked: would other traders in perfume think of and wish to use the name? One easy answer to the test is 'no'. Taking out the fact of fame, there is nothing inherent in the name 'Nicole Kidman' or in her likeness which makes it something that other traders would in good faith think of and wish to use. It would not be like trying to register a word like, say, 'alluring', which is arguably a term that traders in perfume would think of and want to use, as descriptive of a quality of the product.

This straightforward approach is the one adopted by the Trade Mark Office, which does not view s 41 objections as raising significant registration issues for celebrity names (and, presumably, likenesses):[101]

Section 41 objections would generally only be required in those cases where the famous name could be considered to be descriptively relevant in relation to the subject matter of goods or services to which the trade mark was being applied. This would most obviously be the case for publications in class 16 and CD ROM's in class 9.

An application for *Shane Warne* in class 16 covering publications would attract objections on the basis that the name *Shane Warne* was a reference to the subject matter of the goods and should legitimately be open for use by others in this way.

The potential difficulty in registering famous names (or presumably likenesses or other indicia of celebrity identity) in relation to publications and CD ROMS is specifically and rightly noted by the Trade Mark Office. If Nicole Kidman were to attempt to register her likeness as a trade mark in relation to posters, for example, other traders could legitimately object on the basis that they would think of and wish to use her likeness as a subject-matter for

---

99   (1998) 41 IPR 425.

100   *United Artists Corporation* (1998) 41 IPR 425 at 430.

101   *Trade Marks Manual of Practice And Procedure*, Pt 22, s 18.2.

the poster and should be able to do so without fear of an action for trade mark infringement.

This means that Nicole Kidman would therefore have a much more difficult time in registering her name or likeness in relation to posters, for example, after she became famous than she would before she became famous. But so what? That's the price of fame.

The law in England may be significantly different in relation to this problem than Australian law and English law may be or may become particularly relevant here, given the paucity of Australian law on the subject. The leading English case is *Elvis Presley Enterprises v Shaw*,[102] a decision of the Court of Appeal in which an attempt to register, inter alia, the name 'Elvis Presley' in respect of class 3 goods, comprising soaps and perfumes and so on, was rejected. The applicant was Elvis Presley Enterprises, the Tennessee-based 'legitimate' merchandiser of the Presley identity in the United States. The application was rejected on the basis that the name could not be viewed as capable of distinguishing the products in question. The court found that consumers would not think of a soap with the name Elvis Presley on it as coming from a particular trading source; it could therefore not be viewed as capable of distinguishing one trader's goods from those of another trader:[103]

> Third, the fame of Elvis Presley was as a singer. He was not a producer of soap. There is no reason why he or any organisation of his should be concerned with toiletries so as to give rise to some perceived connection between his name and the product. In these circumstances I do not accept without evidence to that effect that the mark ELVIS PRESLEY would connote to anyone a connection between [the applicant] and Elvis soap so as to distinguish their soap from that of [another trader's] soap.
>
> ... In the field of memorabilia, which I consider includes consumer items bearing the name or likeness of a famous figure, it must be for that person to ensure by whatever means may be open to him or her that the public associate his or her name with the source of the goods. In the absence of evidence of such association in my view the court should be very slow to infer it.

The name or image of a celebrity is, in short, unlikely to be perceived as signalling the trade origin of the goods and is therefore, without more, not distinctive, not capable of distinguishing one trader's goods from another. Depending on the circumstances and the level of fame, the celebrity name

---

102   *Elvis Presley Enterprises Inc v Shaw (T/As Elvisly Yours Ltd)* (1999) 47 IPR 441.

103   Ibid at 464. See also Simon Brown LJ at 466:

> The whole point of a trade mark is to distinguish the proprietor's goods from similar goods marketed by competitors. These names, the judge concluded, distinctive though undoubtedly they are by their universal association with the late great celebrity, would as registered trade marks serve to distinguish not the producers but rather the product: they would describe the essential nature of the goods being traded (Elvis Presley memorabilia in the widest sense) but say nothing as to their trade origins.

See also *Diana, Princess of Wales Trade Mark* [2001] EMTR 25.

may simply give no information to the consumer about the commercial origin of the product.

The court in *Elvis* was presented with the argument by counsel for the applicant that, '[i]t cannot be right … that the more famous the celebrity, the more difficult it becomes to register his name as a trade mark',[104] but it was not swayed by the argument. Rather, the court expressed itself to be considerably more concerned with the injustice to other traders and to the public that would flow from acceptance of the application, an acceptance which the court said would create, 'a free standing general right to character exploitation enjoyable exclusively by the celebrity'.[105]

Section 43

Section 43 of the *Trade Marks Act 1995* requires the rejection of a proposed trade mark if, because of some connotation that the trade mark has, its use in relation to the proposed goods or services, 'would be likely to deceive or cause confusion'.[106] A celebrity can make use of this section to attempt to block a registration by another trader of a trade mark which uses some aspect of the celebrity identity and which connotes the sponsorship or approval or endorsement or affiliation of the celebrity with the defendant's product, when that is not true. Whether or not a trade mark does carry such a connotation will again be a matter of fact and degree and much will often hang on the details of the proposed use. The test requires that there must be a 'real tangible danger' of deception or confusion and a mere finding that confusion would be 'more probable than not' is not sufficient.[107]

A recent significant case in the area is *McCorquodale v Masterson*,[108] where a trader applied to register the trade mark, in relation to live roses, 'Diana's Legacy In Roses' with a device of roses, doves and a big, stylised 'D'. The initial decision in the Trade Marks Office to allow the registration was based on a robust view of consumer sense and discernment. The Registrar's Delegate found that the proposed mark did indeed carry a connotation of Princess Diana and would evoke a memory of her. But that was all. It did not incorporate a connotation which would deceive or confuse people into thinking that either Princess Diana's Estate or the Princess Diana Memorial Fund had sponsored or endorsed the product.

---

104   *Elvis Presley Enterprises* (1999) 47 IPR 441 at 466.

105   Ibid (1999) 47 IPR 441 at 467.

106   It should be noted that a trade mark can be removed from the Register even long after registration if the mark has, since registration, become deceptive or confusing. See s 88 of the *Trade Marks Act 1995*.

107   *Registrar of Trade Marks v Woolworths Ltd* (1999) 93 FCR 365 at 380; *McCorquodale* (2004) 63 IPR 582 at [35]; *Southern Cross Refrigerating Co v Toowoomba Foundry Pty Ltd* (1954) 91 CLR 592 at 594-595.

108   (2004) 63 IPR 582.

Bracingly robust decisions are sometimes set aside, however, and the appeal from the Delegate's decision allowing registration of the mark to the Federal Court was successful. The court found that:

> In all the circumstances I find that the impugned mark would not only directly and immediately connote the late Princess, the impugned mark would also bespeak an association with the Fund and the estate of the Late Princess. There is a real likelihood that consumers would understand that goods bearing the impugned mark are in some way sponsored or approved by the Fund or the Princess' estate, even if they were ignorant about the specific details of the arrangements. The likelihood of this misunderstanding is sufficient to create a likelihood of confusion and depiction in Australia by reason of the connotation of the mark ...

Although robust decisions by the Trade Mark Office can be thrown out by the Federal Court of Australia, robust decisions by the High Court of Australia cannot, (although they can be explained away). In *Joseph Bancroft & Sons Co v Registrar of Trade Marks*, the trade mark in question was 'Miss America,' proposed to be registered in relation to dress fabric, and opposed on the ground that the mark carried a connotation of approval or endorsement from a real 'Miss America'. The High Court did not accept the connotation of approval argument and found that the mark would, 'at most create the impression that the fabrics were suitable to be worn by a person who desired to be dressed in the same style as' a Miss America.[109]

Although the court in *McCorquodale* explained the *Bancroft* decision as having been decided before the practice of celebrity endorsement became as widespread and as well-known as it is now,[110] it is of course also possible and right to interpret *Bancroft* as simply having made a finding about likely consumer perception on the facts, without building in an assumption which might be highly unjustified, that a different finding on the facts would be made today. The court in *McCorquodale* could have found, as the Trade Marks Office did, that the Diana mark would, like the mark in *Bancroft*, at most create the impression that the roses were suitable to be grown by a person who desired to be like Princess Diana or to provide a kind of memorial to her.

The fact that the class of goods in question in the *McCorquodale* case was live roses was also important, given that as the court found, 'the goods to which the impugned mark would apply have a real connection in the public mind with the late Princess'[111] and it is possible that if the application had been for a Diana mark in relation to a completely different sort of product like, say, motorcycle sprockets, the result would also have been different. This is the view taken by the Trade Marks Office, which gives as examples of celebrity name trade marks which would be rejected: 'Ian Thorpe' in relation to swimming costumes and 'Shane Warne' for cricket gear. The Trade Mark

---

109   *Joseph Bancroft & Sons Co v Registrar of Trade Marks* (1957) 99 CLR 453 at 459.
110   *McCorquodale* (2004) 63 IPR 582 at [55].
111   Ibid at [55].

Office suggests that there would be no s 43 issue for 'Ian Thorpe' in relation to economic forecasting or 'Shane Warne' for photocopiers[112] and has in fact expressly found, despite the opposition of Elvis Presley Enterprises, that the term 'ElvisFinance' could be registered for financial services because the name 'Elvis' next to the word 'Finance' would not be enough to cause likelihood of confusion.[113]

The matter is, in short, one of fact, and the celebrity will not always win a s 43 opposition to another trader's attempted registration of an aspect of the celebrity's identity, just as a celebrity will not always win a passing-off action based on a representation of sponsorship or affiliation. The court in *McCorquodale* found it unnecessary to decide whether the test adopted under the law of passing-off and s 52 should govern the approach to be taken in a s 43 case about implied endorsement but did state that there was 'some force' in the suggestion.[114]

Although s 43 is particularly important as a tool for celebrities to use to prevent the registering without their consent of some aspect of their identity as a trade mark for their products, it should be noted that there is also a possibility for the section to be used against celebrities' own attempted registrations of their identities for products. There is as yet no relevant case, but if, for example, a product was marketed under a trade mark which was the name of a celebrity, it might be the case that the trade mark would lead the public to think that the celebrity had something substantively to do with, say, the design of the product. If that were not true, the consumer could be deceived or confused sufficiently for an opposition under s 43. If, therefore, a line of shoes were to appear under the trade mark, the *Nicole Kidman Footloose* line of shoe, (like the *Elle MacPherson Intimates* line of lingerie), it might well be possible to argue that the mark would lead the customer to believe that Nicole Kidman was not simply endorsing the shoe but was actually involved in the design or production of the shoe and if that were not true, the consumer would arguably have been deceived or confused in precisely the manner which s 43 is designed to redress.

Infringement

Enforcement of a registered trade mark requires that the elements of infringement liability found in s 120 of the *Trade Marks Act 1995* are made out. Each of the sub-sections of s 120 requires that the defendant be found to have used the plaintiff's registered trade mark *as* a trade mark; that is, as a designator of trade source, a badge of trade origin. Descriptive uses of the mark will not suffice. Section 120(1) governs infringement proceedings for a

---

112   *Trade Marks Office Manual of Practice and Procedure*, Pt 29, 4.4.1

113   Re: Opposition by Elvis Presley Enterprises Inc to registration of trade mark application 1100952(36) – ElvisFINANCE – filed in the name of Elvis Jelcic 2008 ATMO 103.

114   *McCorquodale* (2004) 63 IPR 582 at [59].

defendant's use of a registered trade mark on the same goods for which the plaintiff's mark is registered:

> A person infringes a registered trade mark if the person uses as a trade mark a sign that is substantially identical with, or deceptively similar to, the trade mark in relation to goods or services in respect of which the trade mark is registered.

So, if a trader in perfume managed to trade mark the word 'Alluring' in respect of perfume, it would not be able to prevent another trader in perfume from describing its perfume as 'alluring,' so long as the other trader was using the word descriptively and not as a badge of origin. The test for whether or not a trade mark is being used as a trade mark is simply stated, but, being consumer perception-based, is difficult to apply. Simply put, the test is whether the defendant 's use of a trade mark would appear to the ultimate consumer as a badge of origin being used to indicate a trade connection between the good and the owner of the trade mark. If not, there is no liability for trade mark infringement.[115]

It gets more difficult for trade mark owners to enforce their trade marks when the registration is in relation to classes of goods like publications, posters and CDs. In *Musidor BV v Tansing*, the term 'Rolling Stones' had been registered in relation to sound recordings. The defendant released a CD recording of an early live performance by the Rolling Stones with the words 'Rolling Stones' on the front. A trade mark infringement action by the owner of the mark was rejected on the basis that the defendant's use was not use of the mark as a mark and did not indicate the trade origin, the commercial source of the recording, It was used descriptively and the court said:[116]

> [T]he words 'The Rolling Stones' ... are used here to identify a recording made many years ago of a live performance by those persons in the United States, which has been reproduced and embodied in the discs manufactured by the respondent. That is not a trade mark use by the respondent ... If it matters, there is force also in the further submission that, as a practical matter, there is no other way in which identification readily can be made of the group, a sound recording of whose performance is embodied in the discs.
>
> This is an attempt to gain a monopoly over words used to describe a lawful product. Consistently with the plaintiff s argument, the maker of a film on the Rolling Stones entitled 'The Story Of The Rolling Stones' would be infringing a mark. The producer of a CD called 'John Farnham sings the music of the Rolling Stones' would suffer a like fate.

---

115   *Pepsico Aust Pty Ltd v Kettle Chip Co Pty Ltd* (1996) 33 IPR 161 at 182. Words like 'alluring', which are inherently descriptive of qualities of a product like perfume, are of course at considerably greater risk of not being viewed by consumers as being used as trade marks than are other more fanciful terms. This is one good reason for traders not to attempt to own such words through the process of trade mark registration. Even if registration is achieved, enforcement can be difficult and the trade mark is therefore weak.

116   *Musidor BV v Tansing* (1994) 123 ALR 593 at 606.

Similarly, in *Bravado Merchandising Services Ltd v Mainstream Publishing (Edinburgh) Ltd*,[117] a band called 'Wet Wet Wet' had been able to get its band name registered as a trade mark in respect of publications including books, but could not prevent the publication of a book about the band, with their name on the book cover.

Even if the name Elvis Presley, for example, were to be registered for sound recordings or stage productions, that registration could not function to prohibit descriptive uses of the Presley name, like a CD with a picture of Elvis and the words 'The Songs of Elvis Presley' on the cover.

To return to the fact situation with which this chapter began, namely, the claim by the family of Martin Luther King Jr against the purveyors of badges and T-shirts bearing the likeness of King along with that of Barack Obama. The family's claim, were it to be made in Australia on the basis of trade mark law, might very well not be successful. If the name or likeness of Martin Luther King were to be registered by the King family as a trade mark in respect of badges and T-shirts and the items in question were for sale in markets here, the defendant is likely to be found to have been using the trade mark expressively and as the subject matter of, say, the T-shirt. It would be a T-shirt of Martin Luther King, *not* a 'Martin Luther King' T-shirt. The King trade mark would not have been used by the defendant as a trade mark as is required under s 120 of the *Trade Marks Act* and the infringement action would accordingly fail.

Conclusion

This chapter has traced two dominant legal responses to the problem of providing protection to the celebrity interest in controlling the commercial use of their identities, that is, the *misrepresentation* model as exemplified by the passing-off action in the United Kingdom and Australia and the *misappropriation model* as exemplified by the right of publicity action in the United States. Both models exist within legal orders which also embody a public interest in communicative and competitive freedom and both models accordingly represent a balance between full celebrity control over commercial use of their identities and unimpeded public access to those identities for purposes of trade or comment of various kinds. While the right of publicity action takes its form in the legal context of the First Amendment, the constitutional guarantee of freedom of speech in the United States, the tort of passing-off preserves the public interest by its fundamental requirement that a misrepresentation to the public must exist before the unauthorised commercial use of celebrity identity can be legally inhibited.

---

117   [1996] FSR 205. See also *R v Johnstone* [2003] 1 WLR 1736, where the names of bands printed on the covers of bootleg CDs were found by the House of Lords to be descriptive of the contents of the CDs. They were, importantly, found not to be indicators of the CDs trade origins.

Chapters 3 and 4 will address the celebrity's interests in privacy and reputation, interests which, like the celebrity interest in control over commercial use of their identity, must compete with general legal and social principles which value public communicative and competitive freedom.

Chapter 3
DEFAMING CELEBRITIES

Introduction

> [E]ach man kills the thing he loves...

This ironic observation, resonant of fame itself, was penned by Oscar Wilde as part of his last poem *The Ballad of Reading Gaol*, written after his release from imprisonment for gross indecency which followed the disastrous end to his criminal libel[1] action against the Marquess of Queensbury. Oscar Wilde paid the ultimate price for a defamation action: the truth came out amid great public scandal, his livelihood, family life and reputation were ruined, his finances in tatters.

This celebrated defamation case shows the very high personal risks of a defamation action. A court will hear in public – and the press or media will report – not just the exact words used by the defendant but also what they *mean*. It will examine not just their literal meaning – which might be bad enough – but also all the imputations and innuendos hidden in the words. The claimant's counsel will often articulate the very worst interpretation:

> When Jane Makim, sister of the Sarah Ferguson, the Duchess of York, sued for defamation for articles published in newspapers owned by Nationwide News Pty Ltd which, inter alia, alleged that she had been having an adulterous affair with an Argentinean polo player, her counsel, the sharp and redoubtable Tom Hughes QC, told the jury:
>
> > 'This article suggests she is a promiscuous adulteress ... It suggests she is a slut, a multiple adulteress. Can you imagine anything more shocking than to say that falsely about a decent woman?'

---

1   Traditionally 'libel' was used to describe defamation in some permanent form such as writing or pictures, and was actionable *per se*, whereas 'slander' described merely spoken defamation and was harder to sue upon, requiring proof of actual damage. See Mitchell, P, 'The Foundations of Australian Defamation Law' (2006) 28 *Sydney Law Review* 477 at 478. Under the uniform Australian defamation laws, the distinction is abolished: for example, *Defamation Act 2005* (NSW), s 7. In England media statements are treated as libel, for example, see *Broadcasting Act 1990* (as amended) but there are still instances where the old distinction may be important: Milno, P and Rogers, WHV, *Gatley on Libel and Slander* (Sweet and Maxwell, 11th edn, 2008) at 3.6ff (*Gatley*). 'Libel' and 'defamation' are used interchangeably in this chapter.

Counsel for the newspapers, Ian Callinan QC, protested that her counsel had used much stronger language than any newspaper report:

> 'You might think that indicates how far Mrs Makim is prepared to go … when expressions of that kind are used on her behalf … expressions themselves far more sensational, far more damaging than anything that has been said by my client, and which themselves are likely to gain a great deal of publicity.'

While she was awarded $300,000 damages by the jury after only an hour's deliberation, Makim then had to endure reports of the case and of the pleaded 'slut' imputation on the front pages of national newspapers and wire services like Reuters News around the world. Outside the court, Makim is reported to have said that her reputation had been 'totally vindicated'.[2]

The defence case too might be 'ten times worse than the original libel'.[3] It will try to prove the truth of the slur or to rely on a reasonable belief in the truth of what was said. Or the defence will argue that near enough is good enough, in the sense that substantial truth[4] or contextual truth[5] will do: even if every detail is not correct, overall there is truth in the 'common sting' of the libel or in other meanings not pleaded by the claimant but implicit in the statement. Then they will set to a detailed examination of the broader reputation and history of the claimant. He or she must weather the gratuitous comments which inevitably flow from the reports of the proceedings and endure relentless and often hurtful and insulting cross-examination in open court :

Counsel for the defendant: Do you often get angry?

Judy Davis: No.

Counsel: Do you have a problem with anger management?

Davis: No.

Counsel: Did your spouse once take out an apprehended violence order against you?

Davis: No.[6]

---

2   Anabel Dean, 'Fergie's sister humiliated by "slut" attack' and 'Fergie's sister awarded $300,000 for "slut" reports', *Sydney Morning Herald*, 27 and 28 November 1990. See also 'Duchess of York's sister wins huge damages for defamation', 27 November 1990, Reuters News. Makim also sued the publisher of *The Sydney Morning Herald: Makim v John Fairfax & Sons Ltd* (1990) 5 BR 196.

3   Henry Brougham, MP in a speech to the House of Commons 8 May 1816, quoted by Mitchell, above n 1 at 480.

4   For example, *Grobbelaar v News Group Newspapers Ltd* [2002] 1 WLR 3025 (HL(E)) in which the claimant, a well-known premiership goalkeeper, had his damages reduced to £1. It could not be proven that he had deliberately let in goals but he had been proven to enter into corrupt agreements to do so. 'His reputation as a sportsman has been destroyed by his corrupt dealings. To award him anything more would be an affront to sport, public justice and public policy' at 3040 [36], per Lord Steyn.

5   See below under 'Defences'.

6   *Davis v Nationwide News Pty Ltd* [2008] NSWSC 693 at [31].

Judy Davis, Oscar nominee, Emmy and Golden Globe winner, whose fame was launched by her starring role in iconic Australian film *My Brilliant Career,* was successful in a defamation action against News Ltd, the publishers of *The Daily Telegraph,* over reports of her attendance and alleged demeanour at a meeting to discuss lighting at a local oval during children's soccer training. She complained that the articles, one of which was headed 'My brilliant dummy spit', portrayed her as 'hard-hearted' and a 'child-hating', petulant person. In fact she had spoken out in support of making the ground safer for children, including her own, and did not object to the lights.

'I live a very quiet life,' Davis said. 'I have not encouraged that celebrity cult at all. I am not really that well known at all. I just do my work and go home to my family. I am not sprawled across magazines and I think The Daily Telegraph knows that.'[7]

She was awarded damages of $140,000, including aggravated damages justified by the line of unfounded allegations in the cross-examination, above.

The claimant must endure a stream of interlocutory applications before the trial and appeals after the initial judgment. As Oscar Wilde found to his cost, he must be very sure of his case, or at least of the paucity of the defendant's.

Oscar Wilde brought proceedings against the Marquess of Queensbury for criminal libel after the Marquess had left an open[8] calling card for Wilde with the porter at Wilde's club, the Albermarle Club, inscribed with 'For Oscar Wilde posing as somdomite [sic]'. The Marquess had long pursued Wilde to try to stop his loving association with the Marquess' estranged son 'Bosie', Lord Alfred Douglas, and Bosie, in turn, urged Wilde to protest.

The proceedings became a public spectacle, with crowds in the public gallery and outside the court. They were reported widely in the press, even in New York and Paris. Queensbury was represented by Wilde's school friend Edward Carson QC, who at first reluctant to take the case, had been persuaded that it was his duty to do so by the Lord Chancellor. Carson, in a skilful cross-examination, laid traps for the determinedly witty and surprisingly naïve Wilde. It started badly from the very first question when Carson challenged Wilde's statement that he was only 39, when he was in fact over 40. When it was clear that the defence team would be calling certain boys as witnesses to prove their defence, Wilde dropped the prosecution, but by then the police were hard on his heels and he was immediately arrested and charged with gross indecency. Bosie and others fled to France to wait out the trial. Wilde was examined relentlessly about his conduct, morals and writings.

After two trials – the jury was unable to reach a verdict in the first – Wilde was convicted and served two years' imprisonment, ending at Reading Goal. Penniless, he died only three years after his release, aged 46, in Paris

---

7   Kennedy, L, 'I live a quiet life, actor tells court', *Sydney Morning Herald*, 7 May 2008.

8   The fact that the card was open, not sealed, satisfied the essential element of a defamation case that the statement was 'published' or communicated to a third party.

in 1900, in a small hotel in the Rue des Beaux Arts. Today called L'Hotel, it commemorates his death by lining the same room with letters written by him there.[9] We do not know if they have changed the wallpaper of which he famously said, 'My wallpaper and I are fighting a duel to the death. One or other of us has got to go.'

Wilde's grandson Merlin Holland comments:

> If I could ask my grandfather a single question, it would have to be, 'why on earth did you do it?'… But there is no simple explanation for his conduct. Arrogance born of social and literary success, and the belief that he was in some way immune from the law unquestionably played a part, as did a desire to please young Douglas. I am certain too that there was a perverse element of wanting to play out in court a theatrical piece whose prologue he felt he had written, but whose outcome was known only to the Fates: 'The danger,' as he later said of his demi-monde life, 'the danger was half the excitement.'[10]

John Mortimer QC, renowned advocate, playwright and author, described Wilde's sentence as a shameful day for British justice and put forward another view:

> Or was he, as I believe, a confused and kindly man who did not think, as we would not think nowadays, that he had done anything wrong and that he could rely on his irresistible charms, and his talent for finding clever answers to tricky questions to see him through? If this was so, he was horribly mistaken.[11]

Oscar Wilde's experience may well have rung in the ears of prominent Sydney solicitor John Marsden, a former president of the NSW Law Society, former member of the police board, with powerful friends (and detractors) in politics and the commercial world, who fought the longest running defamation case ever brought in Australia against Channel Seven after it broadcast allegations that he had had sex with under-age boys. But the media defendant also learnt the cost and risks of having to rely on unreliable, unconvincing or just plain seedy witnesses to back up its claims. After 18 months of hearings, 229 hearing days, over $10 million in costs, 113 witnesses just for the defence,[12] over 150 judgments on interlocutory issues,[13] the judge rejected Channel Seven's defences of truth and qualified privilege and awarded damages of $525,000. After the Court of Appeal awarded a new trial on damages, the parties reached a settlement.

In England, it seemed to be pride or folly rather than naiveté that preceded the fall of Lord Jeffrey Archer when in 1987 he brought an action for libel and recovered hundreds of thousands of pounds in damages. His false witness

---

9   <http://www.l-hotel.com>.

10   Holland, M, *The Real Trial of Oscar Wilde* (Fourth Estate, 2003), p xxxiv.

11   Ibid at p xiii.

12   Dempster, Q, 'Defamation case has ruined my life and reputation: Marsden', *The 7.30 Report,* 20 July 2000 <www.abc.net.au/7.30/stories/s154345.htm>. See also the transcript of the program on 27 June 2001 after the verdict <www.abc.net.au/7.30/content/2001/ s320016.htm>. See also highlighted quote from Marsden on p 68.

13   <www.austlii.edu.au/au/cases/nsw/supreme_ct/toc-M.html>.

in that trial eventually led to his imprisonment for perjury and perverting the course of justice, and to the end of his considerable political influence in the United Kingdom. Jonathan Aitken, a former Conservative Cabinet Minister was also brought down by a libel action involving 'not only dubious but elaborate and perjured' evidence.[14] Kate Moss successfully sued various newspapers for allegations related to cocaine use, only months before related newspapers revealed the truth about her addiction with photographs. She lost valuable promotional contracts but her earning power quickly bounced back.[15] Other claimants are devastated by the loss of their actions.

Defamation is a contentious field of law because of the critical impact it has on the freedom of the media to report, inform, comment, entertain and scrutinise public lives and affairs. Until recently, the media were given no

---

14   David Hooper, *Reputations under fire* (Warner Books, 2000), p 94.

15   'She now officially embodies all kinds of newsworthy qualities: danger, sleaze-edged glamour, decadence, sex, corrupted youth and ineffable beauty, addiction, money and fashion': P Vernon, 'The fall and rise of Kate Moss', *The Observer*, 14 May 2006.

special privileges over and above the ordinary citizen to intrude, comment or report on the conduct of others. That position is slowly changing with courts explicitly recognising, by concepts such as 'responsible journalism' discussed below, the significant role of and public interest in a free press.[16]

> 'The press discharges vital functions as a bloodhound as well as a watchdog'.
> *Lord Nicholls in Reynolds v Times Newspapers*

It is a field that, like many other legal fields, has two tiers for study: the micro sphere, that is, the detailed legal principles and rules within defamation law, and the macro sphere, the institutional or social impact that defamation litigation exerts both on the immediate players involved and on the broader community. Statutory reform has tended to be directed at procedural and court rules, always with the objective, often not attained, of bettering an imperfect system or of redressing an unfair balance of the competing interests of personal reputation and freedom of speech. The principles and rules are exceedingly complex. Reading a defamation judgment, one can become mired in such baffling procedural complexity that it often appears that the key issues have been lost in a sea of detail. As the litigants in *Marsden v Amalgamated Television Services Pty Ltd* discovered, a litigant can lose many interlocutory skirmishes but win the case. Yet even then, the win may be pyrrhic.

The complexity has a critical impact on the macro effect of defamation law. Cases are often so complex, the rights and wrongs of the facts so finely balanced, the attitude of the jury so unpredictable, that the outcome will be uncertain and the costs necessarily large or even prohibitive. Tactics and bluff become everything. Meritorious claimants might be deterred from individual claims by the spectre of a long personal ordeal and high financial cost, but the media see active defamation laws as crippling their overall operations and function.[17] At best, media defendants argue that, post-publication, they are forced to settle doubtful or even clearly unmeritorious claims to avoid wasting irrecoverable legal fees, opportunity costs and human resources in defending the claims. Often these factors

> 'It's probably ruined my life and my health. It's certainly ruined me financially. I've lost a lot of friends'. *John Marsden, lawyer*

will be exacerbated by local rules about the general conduct of litigation: the UK media are currently complaining bitterly about the inappropriate use by wealthy celebrity litigants, such as Naomi Campbell[18] and Cherie Blair,[19] of 'conditional fee

---

16 *Highlight*: Lord Nicholls in *Reynolds v Times Newspapers* [2001] 2 AC 127 at 205.

17 Barendt, E, Lustgarten, L, Norrie, K and Stephenson, H, *Libel and the Media The Chilling Effect* (Clarendon Press Oxford, 1997); Kenyon, A, *Defamation Comparative Law and Practice* (UCL Press, 2006).

18 Campbell's recoverable costs were doubled by virtue of a success fee under a conditional fee agreement.

19 Cherie Blair, herself a high-earning barrister and public speaker, relied on a conditional fee agreement in 2008 when she sued *News of the World* over an article that suggested

arrangements' intended to assist the impecunious to seek justice under reforms introduced in 2000. At worst, the so-called 'chilling effect' of defamation laws has a pre-publication impact, constraining the open reporting of facts, the robust expression of opinion and the uncovering of corruption and abuse.[20]

There are many excellent, detailed and informative studies both of general defamation law[21] and of its effect on the media and freedom of speech.[22] In this chapter, we show how celebrities use defamation law to protect their images and reputations. Mostly, those cases will be against media defendants, rather than private citizens, both because of their deeper pockets and because they have the greatest capacity to publish their revelations and comments far and wide. With the Internet and its interface to mobile phones, involving digital images, 'Twitter' and the like, the media have lost that monopoly and anyone can now publish to the world – and be liable in defamation[23] – but nevertheless the mainstream media maintain their predominance as defamation defendants.[24]

Celebrities rank prominently as claimants in defamation cases. A few examples illustrate how celebrities have used defamation actions to control their reputation, status, marketability, profitability, privacy and image.

- Shirley Temple was an early litigant, in 1938 suing *Night and Day* magazine and its distributors in respect of an article about a film *Wee Willie Winkie* based on Rudyard Kipling's story. The article was written by co-defendant Graham Greene who wisely did not appear before the Lord Chief Justice, as the libel was said to be too shocking to read out in open court. Damages of £2000 pounds were paid to Shirley Temple and £1000 to Twentieth Century Fox Corporation. Counsel for the magazine apologised that 'There was no justification for the criticism of the film, which, his clients instructed him was one to see which anybody could take their children [sic]'.[25] More details can be found in a modern biography[26] of Graham Greene than in the contemporaneous Times law report: *Night and Day* was launched only a year earlier with a party at

---

she had a secret feud with Sarah Brown, wife of the then Chancellor of the Exchequer and now Prime Minister. Pierce, A, 'Cherie Blair uses no win, no fee to pursue defamation claim', 18 April 2008, <www.telegraph.co.uk/news/uknews/1584676>.

20   Barendt et al, above n 17.

21   *Gatley*, above n 1; Balkin, RP and Davis, JLR *Law of Torts*, (LexisNexis Butterworths, 4th edn, 2009); Butler, D and Rodrick, S, *Media Law in Australia*, (LawBook Co, 3rd edn, 2007); George, P, *Defamation Law in Australia* (Cambridge University Press, 2006).

22   Barendt, E, *Freedom of Speech* (Oxford, 2nd edn, 2005); Weaver, R, Kenyon, A, Partlett, D and Walker, C, *The Right To Speak Ill: Defamation, Reputation & Free Speech* (Carolina Academic Press, 2006); and Barendt et al, n 17 above; Chesterman, M, *Freedom of Speech in Australian Law: A Delicate Plant* (Ashgate 2000).

23   See, for example, *Applause Store Productions Limited and Matthew Firsht v Raphael* [2008] EWHC 1781 (QB) concerning a posting on a Facebook site.

24   Barendt et al, above n 17, p 1.

25   Law Report March 22, Kings Bench Division, *The Times* 23 March 1938.

26   Sheldon, M, *Graham Greene: The Man Within*, (Heinemann, 1994) p 225ff.

the Dorchester; it was to be a magazine about good writing and entertainment, not politics: it was to be the English *New Yorker* for sophisticated
readers, with the likes of Evelyn Waugh and Anthony Powell contribut-
ing. But its main distributor, WH Smith, refused to sell the issue with the
article, which had been advertised with a poster 'Sex and Shirley Temple.'
Greene's attack on Shirley Temple was a disaster and by the time of the
case, the magazine had folded.

- Nicole Kidman sued *The Daily Telegraph* in Britain for falsely reporting
  in its gossip column, Spy, that Kidman carried and used a bottle of Jo
  Malone 's White Jasmine and Mint perfume while filming *The Golden
  Compass*, claiming it as her favourite perfume, in breach of her (highly
  publicised and lucrative) contract to promote Chanel No 5. *The Daily
  Telegraph* paid her substantial damages for embarrassment and distress.[27]

- Andrew Ettingshausen, a well known Rugby League player at the time
  and member of the national 'Kangaroos' team, sued the publishers of
  'HQ' magazine after they published a photograph of him in the showers
  after a game with two other players. The photograph was overwritten
  with the title of the article 'Hunks Gratuitous nudity, bad language and
  some fine pectorals ... On tour with the Kangaroos (the footballers, not
  the marsupials)'. The photograph was described by the judge 'as grainy
  in quality and the scene appears to have been lit only from the top and
  behind. Nevertheless, below the printing there is a shape between the
  plaintiff's legs which... is certainly capable of being interpreted as his
  penis.' Ettingshausen relied on a 1936 American case, *Burton v Crowell
  Pub Co* in which a widely known steeplechaser had been photographed in
  such a way that part of his horse's saddle appeared to be a 'fantastic and
  lewd deformity' with the effect described by famous Judge Learned Hand
  as 'grotesque, monstrous and obscene'. Hunt J held the 'HQ' photograph
  supported either the imputation that Ettingshausen had deliberately let
  his genitals be exposed to a widespread readership or that simply his
  genitals had been so exposed. Even the latter could, in a jury's eyes, hold
  him up to more than a trivial degree of ridicule. After a stubborn[28] and
  unsuccessful defence of the action by 'HQ', a jury awarded Ettingshausen
  damages of $350,000. The New South Wales Court of Appeal ordered a
  new trial on damages and a second jury on this issue awarded $100,000
  damages. For Ettingshausen, the action was necessary to protect his
  reputation as to his morality, which was in turn critical to his career as a
  schools and junior development officer with the Rugby League.[29]

---

27 'Telegraph pays out to Kidman', <http://guardian.co.uk/media/2007/dec/14/medialaw.
dailytelegraph>.

28 The magazine maintained that the photograph did not reveal his penis. Tom Hughes
QC asked of the New Zealand editor 'Is it a duck?': Rolph, D, *Reputation Celebrity and
Defamation Law*, (Ashgate 2008), p 151.

29 This case is extensively discussed in Rolph, above n 28, p 148ff. Other actions by rugby
league players include that of *Boyd v Mirror Newspapers Ltd* [1980] 2 NSWLR 449
in which player Les Boyd sued in respect of an article headed 'Boyd is fat slow and

- Nicholas Cage won a libel action against the *Daily Mirror* who had repeated allegations by actor Kathleen Turner that he had twice been arrested for drink driving and had stolen a dog. His solicitors commented that the result 'sets the record straight since he has never been arrested for drunk-driving, dog theft or anything else ... As an actor who stars in many family-friendly films and who has a young child and teenager of his own, Mr Cage was understandably upset at having been wrongly depicted as condoning that sort of reckless, dangerous and criminal behaviour.'[30]

- Stephen Berkoff, who we hasten to say we think is good looking, was obviously deeply aggrieved when 'femme terrible' journalist Julie Burchill described a film character called *The Creature* as 'scarred and primeval ... a lot like Stephen Berkoff, only marginally better looking'. A majority of the Court of Appeal held that his pleading that she imputed that he was hideously ugly was capable of being held defamatory by a jury because such an imputation would expose him to ridicule and affect his standing as an actor.[31] He had argued that as an actor and a person in the public eye, the words would reduce the respect with which he was regarded. The words complained of might affect his standing among the public, theatre goers and among casting directors. Neill LJ in the majority referred[32] to *Zbyszko v New York American*[33] where a wrestler had complained about the caption of a photograph describing him as 'not fundamentally different from the gorilla in physique' next to a photograph of a mounted specimen of the Great Kivu gorilla in Lord Rothschild's museum. The New York Appellate Division had allowed his action to proceed on the basis that it put him up to ridicule and contempt. In *Berkoff* Neill LJ concluded that the jury might decide that the remarks gave the impression that Berkoff was 'actually repulsive'. In contrast Millet LJ in the minority emphasised that defamation is an attack on reputation and standing and continued:

  > It is a common experience that ugly people have satisfactory lives – Boris Karloff is not known to have been a recluse – and it is a popular belief the truth of which I am unable to vouch that ugly men are particularly attractive to women ... It is one thing to ridicule a man; it is another to expose him to ridicule. Miss Burchill made a cheap joke at Mr Berkoff's expense; she may thereby have demeaned herself, but I do not believe that she has defamed Mr Berkoff.[34]

---

predictable' and describing him as 'waddling' onto the field. This was capable of holding him up to ridicule. The article also implied that he was partly to blame for his overweight unfit condition, by implying that he had let a 'silvertail' lifestyle get the better of him: this was clearly capable of being held defamatory.

30   Holmwood, L, 'Cage wins libel battle over 'stolen dog',<www.guardian.co.uk/media/2008/apr/04/dailymail.medialaw>.

31   [1996] 4 All ER 1008.

32   Ibid at 1018.

33   228 NY App Div 277 (1930).

34   [1996] 4 All ER 1008 at 1019-1020.

• Roman Polanski sued Conde Nast Publications Limited for its publication of *Vanity Fair* in England. The July 2002 *Vanity Fair* included an article about Polanski which alleged that he met Mia Farrow at a restaurant frequented by celebrities in New York after the murder of his wife, actress Sharon Tate. The article included a quote of someone saying 'The only time I ever saw people gasp in Elaine's was when Roman Polanski walked in just after his wife Sharon Tate had been viciously murdered by the Manson clan …' The quote then went on to allege that Polanski had begun to touch and attempt to seduce a beautiful Swedish girl at another table, promising 'And I will make another Sharon Tate out of you.' Polanski commenced proceedings in England but did not wish to give evidence in England because he would then face extradition to the US for sentencing on charges of unlawful sexual intercourse with a 13-year-old girl of which he had been convicted before fleeing the United States to France (from where he could not be extradited to the United States). He applied to give evidence by video link: Eady J would allow this, the Court of Appeal would not and the House of Lords by a majority of 3:2 restored Eady J's order. A jury eventually awarded him £50,000 damages. The editor of *Vanity Fair*, Graydon Carter, expressed incredulity at this result.[35]

• Elton John sued the publisher of the *Sunday Mirror* for an article claiming that he had been observed spitting chewed food into a napkin, thus indicating an eating disorder. The jury found this defamatory and awarded £75,000 pound compensatory damages and £275,000 exemplary damages, later reduced on appeal to £25,000 and £50,000.[36]

• Max Mosley, head of the peak Formula One motor racing body, FIA, commenced defamation proceedings following the success of his breach of privacy claim against the *News of the World* discussed in Chapter 4 below, after it published a surreptitiously filmed video of his engaging in what they claimed were Nazi-themed sex games, and so described them in its paper.

The tables were turned in *Jamie Fawcett v John Fairfax Publications Pty Ltd* in 2008 when the paparazzo photographer sued the *Sun Herald's* publishers for imputing in a gossip column that he had intruded on and scared Nicole Kidman and had placed a listening device to record her private conversations. The action backfired. Nicole Kidman came straight from the set of *Australia*, setting off another media scrum outside the court, to give evidence for the defence. Although the article was defamatory, the defendants successfully defended the publication on the grounds of justification or truth, substantial truth and/or comment, with any element of public interest satisfied by Fawcett's acknowledgement that 'he made it his business to obtain, even by subterfuge or more aggressive tactics, photographs of celebrities, in particular Ms Kidman'.[37]

---

35   <http://news.bbc.co.uk/2/hi/entertainment/4706619.stm>.

36   *John v MGN Ltd* [1997] QB 586 (CA).

37   *Fawcett v John Fairfax Publications Pty Ltd* [2008] NSWSC 139 at [15].

Defamation, 'public figures', public interest and political speech

In many respects, the defamation law relating to the celebrity claimant will be no different to that which applies to the ordinary citizen: the fundamental principles about identifying the meaning of the publication, what is defamatory, identification of the claimant, publication, many of the defences, and the principles relating to damages and other remedies. The defences of justification or substantial truth, for example, and its related form of contextual truth are the same regardless of the status of the claimant. But sometimes a celebrity may come within the definition of a 'public figure' or be a subject of 'public interest' in its legal sense and for that reason may have to meet stronger grounds of defence.

Much depends on the nature of, and reasons for, their fame. Political celebrities raise particular issues in defamation law, as those who volunteer to occupy public or professional positions or who are involved in government, public affairs, public corporations, or public financial dealings are naturally subject to greater scrutiny and comment than a private citizen. Sporting, aristocratic, fashion or entertainment celebrities may also face different arguments – they may, for example, be touted as 'role models' in order to legitimise comments on their private behaviour. Those who seek or choose the limelight may find it harder to complain when their conduct is subject to criticism or comment. Reluctant celebrities thrust by circumstance into the public eye are another matter again: the family of victims of crime, like the McCanns, whose daughter Madeleine disappeared in Portugal, are clearly in such a category.[38]

The United States

The case of *New York Times v Sullivan* in 1964 was the landmark case – 'one of the most dramatic and far-reaching decisions in American constitutional law'[39] – that changed the path of libel law in the United States for 'public figures'. Sullivan was an elected senior public official in an Alabama city, in charge of police. He claimed to have been personally defamed by a full page advertisement in the *New York Times* headed 'Heed Their Rising Voices' in which it was stated that southern African-American students and leaders like Dr Martin Luther King Jr were subjected to a wave of terror by police in violation of their constitutional rights. The advertisement contained some factual inaccuracies which would prevent the use of the defence of truth under Alabama law. The defendants appealed against the jury's verdict of maximum

---

38   The McCanns accepted £550,000 and an apology in open court in settlement of claims over articles published by Express Newspapers in the months after Madeleine's disappearance, suggesting inter alia that they were responsible for her disappearance, that they had engaged in wife-swapping, and that they had disposed of her body <www.guardian.co.uk/media/2008/mar/19/pressandpublishing.medialaw>.

39   Anderson, D, 'Defamation and privacy: An American perspective' ch 23, in Deakin, Johnston and Markesinis (eds), *Markesinis and Deakin's Tort Law* (Clarendon Press, 6th edn 2007), p 869.

$500,000 damages. The Supreme Court in a single opinion delivered by Justice Brennan reversed the decision and articulated the constitutional protection of debate on public issues:

> The constitutional guarantees require, we think, a federal rule that prohibits a public official from recovering damages for a defamatory falsehood relating to his official conduct unless he proves that the statement was made with actual malice – that is, with knowledge that it was false or with reckless disregard of whether it was false or not.[40]

The constitutional standard demands proof 'with convincing clarity'.[41] Although the rule was articulated by reference to the claimant as a public 'official', the judgment was founded upon a broader basis of 'debate on public issues':

> a profound national commitment to the principle that debate on public issues should be uninhibited, robust and wide-open and that it may well include vehement, caustic and sometimes unpleasantly sharp attacks on government and public officials ... The question is whether it forfeits that protection by the falsity of some of its factual statements and by its alleged defamation of respondent. Authoritative interpretations of the First Amendment guarantees have consistently refused to recognise an exception for any test of truth ... and especially one that outs the burden of proving truth on the speaker ... The constitutional protection does not turn upon the 'truth, popularity, or social utility of the ideas and beliefs which are offered.[42]

The *New York Times v Sullivan* rule was extended beyond public officials to 'public figures' three years later[43], but went no further after a majority of the Supreme Court in *Gertz v Robert Welch Inc*[44] in 1974 contrasted two essential differences between public figures and private claimants: first, public figures have greater access to channels of communication and secondly, they have generally voluntarily run the risk of or invited closer public scrutiny by stepping forward.

> Hypothetically, it may be possible for someone to become a public figure through no purposeful action of his own, but the instances of truly involuntary public figures must be exceedingly rare ... Commonly those classed as public figures have thrust themselves to the forefront of particular public controversies in order to influence the resolution of the issues involved.[45]

Thirty years on, the classifications of particular claimants in the United States remain unpredictable. Undoubtedly some people are now regarded as public figures for all or virtually all purposes. With Internet revelations and expansion of the gossip press, involuntary celebrities are increasingly common, but

---

40   376 US 254 at 279-280 (1964).

41   Ibid at 285-286.

42   Ibid at 270-271.

43   *Butts v Curtis Pub Co* and *Walker v Associated Press*, heard together, 388 US 130, 87 SCT 1975 (1967).

44   418 US 323 (1974).

45   Ibid at 344.

their complaint is more likely to be one of breach of privacy than defamation. Anderson notes that a sports writer, television entertainer and a woman Navy combat pilot have been treated as public figures without much attention to their involvement in public issues, but not a prominent civil liberties lawyer, not a socialite in a divorce case, nor a publicly-funded research scientist.[46]

Australia and England

Australian and English courts do not recognise an equivalent privilege to speak so freely about public figures without fear of a libel suit. Whereas in the United States, a public figure can only succeed in his action by discharging the heavy onus of clearly proving malice on the part of the publisher, in Australia and the United Kingdom the privilege to speak more freely about public figures is a matter of defence: the public figure need only show that the publication was defamatory and then the onus passes to the defendant to prove its defence. Nor is the concept of 'public figure' as predominant or defined as widely in Anglo-Australian law as it is in the United States. In Australia, the emphasis for greater freedom of speech is on the subject matter rather than the person, and that subject matter is closely confined to political speech. Reconsidering a wider constitutional defence formulated only three years previously,[47] the High Court in *Lange v Australian Broadcasting Corporation*[48] significantly narrowed the formulation and format of the defence: the implied freedom was to be considered as part of the qualified[49] privilege to speak freely on government and political matters (which includes the conduct of persons in or candidates for public office), with the onus on the defendant to show that it had a reasonable belief in the truth of the publication and had taken reasonable steps to verify accuracy including, where practicable, attempting to obtain a response from the subject. This tends to be an unpredictable burden to discharge.[50]

In England, the House of Lords has taken a different approach, preferring an evaluation of a number of factors, including the extent to which the matter is one of public concern, to what is described as the narrower 'category-based'[51] approach of the High Court of Australia which was tied to particular types of subject matter. In *Reynolds v Times Newspapers Ltd*, Lord Nicholls enumerated a non-exhaustive list of criteria of variable weight that would be relevant to the judge's 'reasoned judgment' of whether a privilege to publish

---

46 Anderson, above n 39, p 873.

47 *Theophanous v Herald & Weekly Times Ltd* (1994) 182 CLR 104. See Barendt, above n 22, p 72.

48 (1997) 189 CLR 520.

49 With lack of reasonableness becoming the disqualifying factor: *Roberts v Bass* (2002) 212 CLR 1 at [5]; *Jameel (Mohammed) v Wall Street Journal Europe SPRL* [2007] 1 AC 359 at [46] per Lord Hoffmann. See *Gatley*, n 1 above at 15.8.

50 *John Fairfax Publications Pty Ltd v Zunter* [2006] NSWCA 227.

51 Fenwick, H and Phillipson, G, *Media Freedom under the Human Rights Act* (OUP, 2006) pp 1-79.

would be recognised.[52] For several years, the broader privilege formulated in *Reynolds* was not as useful as the press had hoped, but in 2007 it was explained further by the House of Lords, and thereby strengthened, in *Jameel (Mohammed) v Wall Street Journal Europe SPRL.*[53] Lord Nicholls' criteria were not to be seen as hurdles, and the issue of public interest was rather to be approached in a practical and flexible manner.

Lord Hoffmann:

> The Reynolds defence was developed from the traditional form of privilege by a generalisation that in matters of public interest, there can be said to be a professional duty on the part of journalists to impart the information and an interest in the public in receiving it. The House having made this generalisation, it should in my opinion be regarded as a proposition of law ...[54]

Baroness Hale:

> In truth it is a defence of publication in the public interest.[55]

Despite this, the defence has become known as one of 'responsible journalism'. The authors of *Gatley on Libel and Slander* explain that this is because the majority of defendants relying on it are members of the news media engaged in investigative reporting, and the term is a 'convenient shorthand description of its requirements'.[56] It is not, however, only available to journalists.

In 2009, the Supreme Court of Canada applied a defence of 'responsible communication of matters of public interest' to a case about the professional misdeeds of those entrusts by the state with protecting public safety.[57]

The new uniform *Defamation Acts* in the Australian States now include a statutory form of qualified privilege[58] setting out a non-exhaustive list, similar to that set out by Lords Nicholls in *Reynolds,* as factors relevant to the 'responsible journalism' defence, including the business environment in which the defendant operates[59] and the extent to which the publications makes distinctions between suspicions, allegations and proven facts.[60] An important factor is whether a journalist has an honest belief in the truth of what is published or other reasonable grounds for publishing the story. Another factor is the care taken to give the claimant a chance to respond. Again, proven malice will defeat the defence.[61]

---

52   [2001] 2 AC 127 at 205.

53   [2007] 1 AC 359.

54   Ibid at 382.

55   Ibid at 408.

56   *Gatley,* n 1 above at 15.7.

57   *Quan v Cusson* (2009) SCC concerning a police constable who was alleged by a newspaper to have misrepresented himself at rescue efforts at Ground Zero in New York after September 11, 2001.

58   For example, *Defamation Act 2005* (NSW), s 30, partly modelled on the former *Defamation Act 1974* (NSW), s 22.

59   Cf *Rogers v Nationwide News Pty Ltd* (2003) 216 CLR 327.

60   *Defamation Act 2005* (NSW), s 30(3)(d) and (f). On malice, see *Roberts v Bass* (2002) 212 CLR 1.

61   *Defamation Act 2005* (NSW), s 30(4).

The concept of the public figure and even the narrower concept of 'political speech' shows how far the modern law of defamation has come from its early origins, and how closely it reflects fundamental aspects and ideals of the social system which is its context. The earliest defamation actions arose out of the offence of *scandalum magnatum* created in 1275 – the scandalising of magnates, arguably the political celebrities of their day. Power was insecure. These rulers of the closed, feudal system – the magnates – could not countenance any undermining of their power by scandal, rumour and criticism among the more numerous and downtrodden middle or working classes. Seditious libel was a criminal offence. Then, to discourage duelling, and also in response to the greater communication of libels by way of the printing press, the Star Chamber began to accepted civil libel claims. By the 16th century, the common law courts had also recognised slander actions and defamation law was no longer only a weapon for the powerful. Defences on the basis of political reporting and comment remained severely limited for hundreds of years until the very recent protection of 'political speech'. For a brief time, even the fledgling United States of America enacted the *Alien and Sedition Acts* 1798, under the second President, John Adams, but this was anathema to many of the founders of that nation. The third president Thomas Jefferson revoked it as soon as he was appointed, with the 1791 Bill Of Rights containing the First Amendment to the Constitution setting the United States on a path of unparalleled freedom of speech.[62]

Now, in the United States, Canada, England and Australia alike, political and other public 'magnates' must expect scrutiny rather than protection from it. One recent event in Australia illustrates how a public or political celebrity does indeed have greater access to the media than the ordinary citizen and thus a readier means of replying to false or unfair slurs:

> Prominent ex-politician and leader of the former right-wing One Nation Party, and recently a candidate in the state of Queensland elections, Pauline Hanson quickly called a well attended and well-publicised press conference to set the record straight when bogus photographs were published in *The Sunday Telegraph* of 'a young Pauline Hanson' in a revealing, semi-pornographic pose. She quickly denounced them, with proof. Less than a week later she failed to be elected as an independent candidate to the Queensland parliament. If she brought a defamation action she would no doubt argue that she was entitled to substantial damages, even though the falsity was quickly disproved, the whole affair provoked some public sympathy[63] and goodwill towards her, and it was the editor of the paper whose reputation was left in tatters for falling so readily for such a scam. The real subject of the photographs has not yet been identified, and whether she in turn would have an action for breach of confidence or privacy would depend on whether the photographs were taken for publication or private purposes.

---

62   Friedman, LM, *Guarding Life's Dark Secrets* (Stanford, 2007).

63   The fact that a publication can provoke feelings of pity is a ground for it to be treated as defamatory, because it may make others shun and avoid the subject. Sympathy on the other hand may be a less alienating sentiment.

Comment on matters of public interest

It is not just revelations of fact that a public figure or person of 'public interest' must expect and tolerate under the extended qualified privilege to speak freely. Such a person is also fair game for anyone to criticise or comment upon. The defence of comment is probably the most powerful defence that celebrities have to face. It protects freedom of speech in its most defensible form, that is, the freedom of anyone, media[64] or private citizen, to express their honestly held opinions[65] on matters of public interest.

Those in the public eye have always had to endure criticism and reviews of their conduct and work, often in the form of satire. Now, with Internet-connected mobile phones and the phenomenon of Twitter, the review may be instant, sharp and cruel. No doubt these critiques are often devastating to their confidence, self-esteem and morale, but whether the critique is actionable depends on whether it goes beyond the blurred boundaries of 'fair comment' and alleges defamatory facts. The satirist must hope that the subject, and the court, will get the joke.[66] The artist has a right to defend and answer criticism and the critic must allow his victims the same privilege of comment on his critique[67] as he exacted on their work. Comment is now largely a statutory defence in Australia, with uniform defamation laws providing that the expression of honest opinion, based on true or privileged material, on a matter of public interest is protected.[68] Straightforward as that may seem, the defence remains something of a legal minefield for defendants, and one of the most complex to traverse in court.

It is quite clear that mere public curiosity will not satisfy the requirement of an 'interest' or of 'public interest'. '[The defence] does not protect gossip which the public considers entertaining.'[69] Rather, to be a matter of public

---

64   *Silkin v Beaverbrook Newspapers Ltd* [1958] 2 All ER 516 at 517 per Diplock LJ. The media do not have any special privilege as to comment, but they are protected for example where they publish a commentator's comments; *Defamation Act 2005* (NSW), s 31(3).

65   Subject to other legal restraints, such as found in the law relating to censorship of violence and pornography, security, sedition, anti-discrimination, or anti-racism in particular jurisdictions.

66   But compare the very different attitudes to literal but satirical meaning in *Australian Broadcasting Corporation v Hanson* (unreported, Queensland Court of Appeal, 28 September 1998) and the landmark US case *Hustler Magazine v Falwell* 797 F 2d 1270 (4th Cir, 1986). See further Barendt, above n 22, p 228, and Magnusson, R, 'Freedom of Speech in Australian Defamation Law: Ridicule, Satire and other challenges', (2001) 9 *Torts Law Journal* 269 at 282ff, and references therein.

67   *Turner (otherwise Robertson) v Metro-Goldwyn-Mayer Pictures Ltd* [1950] 1 All ER 449 (HL).

68   *Defamation Act 2005* (NSW), s 31, although s 24 preserves common law defences, as to which see Butler and Rodrick, above n 21, pp 85 and 90. Terry Tobin QC has commented that 'In practice, the common law defences may prove as welcome as a phantom limb when it comes to putting a case to a jury', already confounded by the complexity of a defamation case: 'Pitfalls of the Defamation Act 2005', Bar Association of New South Wales Seminar, 24 June 2008.

69   Barendt, above n 22, p 160.

interest at law, the issue must have some relevance to or be a matter of concern for the public.

> In [the doctrine of fair comment], a subject of public interest meant the actions or omissions of a person or institution engaged in activities that either inherently, expressly or inferentially invited public criticism or discussion.[70]

Much will depend on the reason for the celebrity's fame. We have already noted the obvious position of those who hold public office or who are engaged in public life, but a contentious and blurred boundary remains between legitimate scrutiny of their public roles and irrelevant or unjustified revelations of their private life, an issue discussed further in Chapter 4.

A broader category of matters of public interest is that which covers all aspects of artistic, literary, dramatic, and creative work revealed in public and thus calling for public appraisal.[71] Architects, for example, are taken to submit their designs for public comment, as architects from John Soane to Harry Seidler[72] have found out. The celebrity chef is a newer example. What about the celebrity who courts public attention by behaviour on a particular occasion?

> Sydney socialite, and former mistress of the late multi-millionaire Richard Pratt, Shari-Lea Hitchcock brought an action against the *Sun Herald* for its defamatory reporting of her alleged conduct of 'dirty dancing' and putting on 'a nauseating display' at a launch of a television program. The Court of Appeal of New South Wales held, contrary to the judge at first instance on an application to strike out the defence of comment, that the defendant publisher had an arguable case that by courting public attention she had acted in a way which inherently, expressly or inferentially invited public criticism or discussion. The Court of Appeal said that whether the activities of a particular individual are a matter of public interest is a question of fact that turns on the evidence at trial.

Defamation claims today

While the constitutional protection of freedom of speech has reduced defamation litigation in the United States to 'practical insignificance'[73] when compared with the frequency of such litigation in England, nevertheless even in England and Australia there has been a marked downturn in defamation claims by politicians, celebrities and other public figures.

---

70   Dawson, McHugh and Gummow JJ in *Bellino v Australian Broadcasting Corporation* (1996) 185 CLR 183 at 214-215.

71   Heerey, P, 'The Biter Bit – Literary criticism and the law of defamation' (1992) *Univ Tasmania Law Review* 17.

72   *Soane v Knight* (1827) Mood & M 74; 173 ER 1086; *Harry Seidler and Associates Pty Ltd v John Fairfax & Sons Pty Ltd* [1986] Aust Torts Reports ¶80-002 (Cartoonist Patrick Cook successfully defended cartoon as comment on Seidler's architecture).

73   Anderson, above n 39, p 865.

In the United Kingdom this has been largely due to the increased recognition of broad privacy rights under the *Human Rights Act 1998* which have supplanted a sometime indirect benefit of defamation actions, but also partly due to development of a 'responsible journalism' defence on matters of legitimate public interest. Some have even said that 'libel is dead' and although reports of its death appear to be premature, it does look decidedly reduced. It has been reported that in contrast to 1997 when 452 libel writs were issued, in the year to May 2007, only 64 were issued. Claims by celebrities accounted for 30 per cent of *reported* defamation cases in 2006–2007.[74] Some commentators say that this is because society or media celebrities have realised that employing PR driven positive spin is better than risking the vicissitudes of litigation which might take years and still be lost, although their place in the libel court may have been taken by global business magnates.[75]

In Australia, there are now various factors at work which reduce the protection provided to celebrities by defamation law: the recognition of a free speech right under the constitution has discouraged (but not eliminated) claims by political celebrities or public figures, who were previously ready claimants;[76] the reform of differing state defamation laws in 2005 has restored the common law position that the truth of a statement is a complete defence to a defamation claim without the need to show public interest; and there is a slowly evolving recognition and acceptance of a right to prevent disclosures of private information *per se*, as discussed in Chapter 4.

Comparative defamation laws and 'Libel Tourism'

As in the other fields that we discuss in this book – appropriation rights in Chapter 2 and privacy rights in Chapter 4 – defamation law has developed differently in different countries, even those sharing an English common law ancestry. As we have seen, some of this divergence is rooted in fundamental constitutional enactments. Other divergence is relatively recent, due to local legislative reform, changing constitutional contexts, new ways of interpreting old laws or shifting societal and legal attitudes to both facts and matters of principle. There are now some significant differences between the principles of defamation law in the United States, the United Kingdom, and Australia, as well as more marked differences in European civil law countries.[77]

---

74   Tsang, L, 'Is libel dead?' *Times Online*, 29 November 2007, <http://business.timesonline. co.uk/tol/business/law/columnits/article2961486>.

75   Stephens, M, 'New celebrities of the libel courts' 18 July 2006, TimesOnLine <http:// business.timesonline.co.uk/tol/business/law/columnits/article687881>, where he also notes that business men are the new celebrities of the libel bar.

76   Edgeworth, B and Newcity, M, 'Politicians, Defamation law and the 'Public figure 'defence', (1992) 10 *Law in Context* 39. Andrew Kenyon surveys existing empirical work as a background to that set out in his book, which examines the role of meaning and the defence of qualified privilege in defamation law and practice: above n 17.

77   For a comparative view see Zweigert, K and Kotz, H, *An Introduction to Comparative Law*, (Oxford University Press, 3rd edn, 1998), ch 43; and Barendt, above n 22, ch VI.

As well as developing the public figure principles, the Supreme Court of the United States also overturned other entrenched advantages for a claimant where the matter was one of public concern. In *Gertz v Robert Welch,* the US Supreme Court held that even private citizens must show some fault, that is at least negligence,[78] and must prove actual damage where the publication was about a matter of public concern. By *Philadelphia Newspapers Inc v Hepps*,[79] the common law presumption that a defamatory publication was false was also overturned in relation to matters of public concern. Thus in public interest cases, the claimant in the United States is at a considerable disadvantage compared with counterparts in Australia or England, who can still rely on strict liability and the presumption of damage and who do not have the burden of proving falsity.

While the First Amendment to the Constitution of the United States sets that country apart in its paramount protection of free speech, the *European Convention on Human Rights* incorporates freedom of speech as a primary value in Article 10, but expressly as one that must be balanced against other protected interests such as national security, prevention of crime or disorder, or the reputation and rights of others. The United Kingdom has no explicit constitutional or legislative protection of free speech other than, now, protection by way of the *Human Rights Act 1998*, which requires courts to give effect to the provisions of the European Convention. Australia has had to rely on the limited freedom of expression, discussed above and found only recently by the High Court to be implied in the federal Constitution, and now also explicit in some state or territory enactments.[80]

In the United States, each party to litigation pays its own costs regardless of whether it wins or loses the case, unless the case is judged frivolous.[81] Coupled with contingency fees, this system is usually seen as benefiting claimants because they know that even if they lose their case, they will not be required to cough up for their own and their opponent's legal fees. But in the defamation context it also allows media defendants to defend actions through the courts without the spectre of having to carry the claimant's high contingency fee arrangement with his or her lawyers if their defence fails. As explained above, the opposite situation prevails in England, where the general rule is that the unsuccessful party pays the other party's costs and where this may now extend to costs payable under a conditional fee arrangement between the claimant and his or her lawyers. In Australia, contingency fee

---

78   On constitutional grounds, the Supreme Court in *Gertz* only outlawed strict liability: it did not prescribe the required level of fault. Some States require more than negligence, such as 'gross irresponsibility' in New York: Anderson, above n 39, p 876.

79   497 US 1, 110 SCt 2695 (1990). Anderson, above n 39 at 878 points out that that case nicely illustrates how difficult a claimant's burden of proving falsity can be: how was the claimant to prove that he did not, as alleged, have ties to organised crime?

80   *Human Rights Act 2004* (ACT), *Charter of Human Rights and Responsibilities 2006* (Vic). See further Byrnes A, Charlesworth H and McKinnon G, *Bills of Rights in Australia; history, politics and law* (UNSW Press, 2009).

81   Anderson, above n 39, p 881.

arrangements are common for claimants but fees will be chargeable only on a time/service basis without a success fee. Nevertheless, they can be considerable.

Jurisdictional divergence is particularly important in global defamation law because of the principle that a claimant has a cause of action in defamation whenever and wherever the defamatory article is 'published' to a third party. For choice of law in tort, the general Australian rule is that the substantive law of the place where the tort is committed is the governing law to be applied by the forum.[82] Reputations may be global, the more so in the case of celebrities, who often rely on international promotions, sales, business or influence. Multi-jurisdictional publication, for example, by international distribution of books and magazines, by national and international newspapers, by television and radio broadcasts, films, audio and visual recordings, and now by the Internet, means that victims of defamation have a choice of where to bring their actions. Clearly, they will wish to sue in the jurisdiction that is most favourable in terms of legal principles and legal system and most generous in terms of remedies. When they sue in a jurisdiction with which they have little connection, or obviously to avoid restrictions in the law or legal system of their own place of residence, they are pejoratively referred to as 'libel tourists' or as forum 'shoppers'. But even if they choose a forum where they have close links and a reputation to protect, the *defendant* may not be based in the jurisdiction and may argue that it should be governed by its home jurisdiction.

Applying the place of publication rule stills begs the question as to where publication takes place when an item is physically uploaded or 'posted' on a site in, say, the United States and downloaded in Australia. Such was the issue in *Dow Jones & Co Inc v Gutnick*.[83]

> Joseph Gutnick, a gold and diamond miner and financier resident in Melbourne in the state of Victoria, sued Dow Jones, which is based in New Jersey, for what he alleged was a defamatory article in *Barron's Online,* an Internet magazine. He was represented by Geoffrey Robertson QC. The magazine had hundreds of paid subscribers in Victoria, and more in other States on Australia, where Gutnick is well known. The High Court of Australia applied conventional choice of law rules in tort that the appropriate law is the law of the place where the tort is committed and held that, as in any defamation case since *Duke of Brunswick v Hamer*[84] in 1849, a tort was committed each time and wherever the defamatory statement was published to a third party. Third parties had and could download the Barron's article in Victoria that was where publication to them took place: Victorian law applied. As Dow Jones is an American corporation

---

82   *John Pfeiffer Pty Ltd v Rogerson* (2000) 203 CLR 503, *Regie Nationale ses Usines Renault SA v Zhang* (2002) 210 CLR 491.

83   (2002) 210 CLR 575.

84   (1849) 14 QB 185, 117 ER 75.

and Gutnick 'indubitably a public figure',[85] Dow Jones would obviously have preferred to be governed by United States law which would require Gutnick and probably most of the subjects of its publications, to prove some malice on its part, an almost impossible task.

The implications of the Dow Jones case for Internet publishers has caused great consternation in the United States, and certainly it brings into sharp relief the prospect of American publishers being unable to hide behind the First Amendment throughout the world. But it is not a new problem: any international journalist or commentator or filmmaker who strayed outside his or her borders for persons of interest or subject matter faced the prospect of defamation proceedings according to the relevant foreign laws if the publication occurred in the subject's country. These could be crippling and restrictive, as publishers in Singapore have found out, particularly if they even allegedly defamed the premier political family, the Lees.[86]

Recent examples of where a subject sues not in his or her own place of residence but in another jurisdiction where the law or system is more favourable have abounded in England: Saudi billionaire Khalid bin Mahfouz successfully sued American author Rachel Ehrenfeld in Britain after about 20 people in Britain ordered her book online and had it delivered to them there. In her book she alleged that he had financed terrorist attacks. In another case he sued Cambridge University Press rather than the American authors. American professors Broyde and Lipstadt have argued for legislation preventing any American court from enforcing any English defamation judgment against an American.[87] California, Illinois and New York have all enacted such statutes. The New York statute has the curious name, *The Libel Terrorism Protection Act*, passed in response to Rachel Ehrenfeld's failure to obtain declaratory relief against Mahfonz in the US Federal Court.[88] At the federal level, the issue is currently before Congress.[89] However, Partlett argues that the fears that foreign laws would have a chilling effect on US media and that foreign judgments could be readily enforced in the United States were probably unfounded.[90]

Nevertheless, English courts remain the forum of choice for many foreign nationals who have been defamed and who can find even a small number of publications in Britain to base their actions. Lord Hoffmann noted in a case brought in England by prominent Russian businessman and politician Boris Berezovsky and another against the American *Forbes* magazine that the

---

85 David F Partlett, 'The Libel tourist and the ugly American: free speech in an era of modern global communications' (2009) 47 *U Louisville L Review*.

86 Ellis, E, 'Singapore libel case a test of Murdoch's bona fides', *Sydney Morning Herald*, 7 January 2008, p 12.

87 Broyde, MJ and Lipstadt, DE, 'Home Court Advantage' *The New York Times*, 11 October 2007. Pfanner, E, 'A Fight to Protect Americans from English Libel Law', *New York Times*, 25 May 2009, p B3.

88 *Ehrenfeld v Mahfonz*, 518 F3d 102 (2d Circ NY 2008).

89 *The Free Speech Protection Act Bill* 111 HR 1304; 111 S 449, 2009.

90 Above n 85.

claimants were 'forum shopper in the most literal sense', and implied that he was a careful and astute shopper:

> They have weighed up the advantages to them of the various jurisdictions that might be available and decided that England is the best place in which to vindicate their international reputations. They want English law, English judicial integrity and the international publicity which would attend success in an English libel action.[91]

Despite this judicial equanimity, British politicians are increasingly uneasy about the impact of libel claims and costs on the media (perhaps more so now that politicians are so rarely the beneficiaries of a libel claim since *Reynolds*). The House of Commons set up an enquiry which released its report, on libel, tourism and other matters, in March 2010 and the Lord Chancellor has also set up a working party on libel.[92] Some claimants have preferred France as a forum, because of its more streamlined criminal procedures, and remedy of a prompt retraction.[93]

Until recently, Australia had different defamation laws in all States and Territories, making forum shopping a problem for national media, as claimants would select as forum the State with the most restrictive and difficult defences, and the most generous procedures for conduct of litigation and assessment of damages. Countless attempts at achieving consensus and uniformity in reform failed until in 2004 the Federal Attorney General threatened to use constitutional powers to enact federal defamation laws. This threat goaded the States and Territories into action, although it might also be commented that politicians and senior public servants became more interested in reigning in claimant-friendly defamation laws and verdicts when greater constitutional protection of freedom of speech on political matters rendered them less frequent beneficiaries. National uniform defamation laws came into effect in 2006. These statutes have the effect that the common law of defamation applies except to the extent moderated by very similar statutes in each jurisdiction. But most importantly, to prevent litigants forum shopping or bringing multiple proceedings, they make express provision for appropriate choice of law in relation to multi-jurisdictional publications within Australia: the law to be applied is the law with which the harm occasioned by the publication has its closest connection, taking into account the claimant's place of residence or business, the extent of the publication and the harm suffered in each jurisdiction.[94]

---

91   *Berezovsky v Michaels* [2000] 1 WLR 1004 (HL) at 1023-24, quoted by Partlett, above n 85 at 18. See also Lord Hoffman's lecture, 'The Libel Tourism Myth', the Fifth Dame Ebsworth Memorial Lecture, Inner Temple, London, 2 February 2010. An edited version is available at <www.indexoncensorship.org/2010/02/the-libel-tourism-myth>.

92   'Press standards, privacy and libel – Culture, Media and Sport Committee Report <www.publications.parliament.uk/pa/cm200910/cmselect/cmcumeds/362/36206.htm#n.192>.

93   Evans, M and Soulier, J-L, 'French connection to libel', about an action by the owners of the Telegraph against *The Times*. *The Guardian*, 15 April 2005.

94   For example, *Defamation Act 2005* (NSW), s 11. See further Rolph, D, 'A Critique of the national, uniform defamation laws', (2008) 16 *Torts Law Journal* 207 at 210.

Protecting reputations

While defamation *law* as a whole is about balancing the respective interests of reputation and public interest in free speech, the *action* in defamation is simply about protecting reputation, that is, the opinion that others have of a person, either generally or as to a specific attribute, skill or quality. It is an actionable defamation to publish to a third party a statement or representation about another living person which would lower his or her reputation, that is, which would make others (as reasonable people) think less of him or her.

Defamation is an ancient tort, and this long history, in contrast to more recent protections such as that afforded to privacy, immediately provokes the question of why such an intangible interest should have been afforded priority and protection.

In the 20th century, protection of reputation earned a place in two great international and 'universal' declarations and covenants: *The International Covenant on Civil and Political Rights* and the *European Convention on Human Rights*.

The rationale lies in the role that reputation plays in a person's place and status within the organisation of society. Leading torts scholar John Fleming described reputation as '*the* most dearly loved attribute of civilised man' (emphasis added).[95] Strong words. Shakespearean characters famously bemoan damage to reputation – 'Reputation, reputation, reputation! O, I ha' lost my reputation'[96] and contrast the high value of reputation with mere money – reputations are invaluable, entirely personal and not 'negotiable'. Counsel for plaintiffs routinely quote these characters[97] to justify their clients' taking legal action (before going on to argue that only money will undo the slurs.)

Reputation, like character, is made up of many common attributes or aspects: honesty, morality, diligence, intelligence, professionalism, energy, skill (as an actor, doctor, writer, lawyer, sportsman, driver, parent), kindness, consideration for others, carefulness, generosity, modesty, civility, lawfulness. For both there is, of course, a hierarchy of importance. Character is what one actually is or actually has. Reputation is what other people *think* one is or has: it is made up of a mass of opinions about these attributes, both actual and presumed. It may be damaged overall or just in respect of a particular attribute. To a certain extent, everyone begins with a clean slate on the basics – confidence in the human ideal means that everyone is presumed to

---

95   Fleming, J, *The Law of Torts*, (LBC, 9th edn 1998) p 580.

96   Cassio in *Othello*, Act 11, Part III.

97   For example, Iago in *Othello* Act III, Part III, lines 160-66: 'he that filches from me my good name ... makes me poor indeed' but they do not often quote his dismissive rejoinder to Cassio in the previous Act at part iii line xxx: 'Reputation is an idle and most false imposition, off got without merit and lost without deserving', *Gatley on Libel and Slander*, above n 1 at 3. Also often quoted is 'The purest treasure mortal times afford is spotless reputation ... mine honour is my life ...'. Thomas Mowbray in *Richard II* at Act I, part i, 177-182.

be honest and good until shown otherwise. Good reputations do not have to be deserved in order to be protected by defamation law. The careful reader of this chapter will note that many of the successful claimants in defamation proceedings later turn out to be as 'bad' as the defendant suspected yet was unable to prove.[98]

Beyond the basic attributes, a reputation will depend on *public* achievements and conduct. The generous but anonymous millionaire donor will be unknown as a philanthropist, although they may give as much as those who set up eponymous charitable foundations. Thus a reputation can be built and broadened by personal effort and publicity.

Post identified the concept of reputation as having three forms or roles: reputation as property, reputation as honour and reputation as dignity. Reputation may be regarded as an asset, similar to the goodwill of a business, which is earned or acquired through effort and labour and which, like other capital assets, may produce income. To damage this asset is to cause loss in value or a decrease in income. The evaluation of a person leads to a market price:

> The purpose of the law of defamation is to protect individuals within the market by ensuring that their reputation is not wrongfully deprived of its proper market value.[99]

Such an analysis explains why 'commercial' celebrities – that is, celebrities who benefit financially from their status as celebrities – find it worth the considerable financial and personal cost to take action for defamation. For many celebrities, their reputation is integral not just, as with anyone, to their status in society but to their status and market power *as a celebrity*. Nevertheless, celebrity can survive a downfall, as Rolph points out:

> [E]ven with the exposure of his undeserved victory in his libel proceedings against the Sun, and more importantly, the dishonour of his criminal conviction, [Jeffrey] Archer still retained the capacity to rebuild his reputation and to finesse his celebrity – Archer published three volumes of his prison memoirs during his sentence … Thus, whilst Archer's reputation as honour may have diminished, his reputation as a form of property and celebrity, or more accurately, notoriety, still subsists.[100]

Clearly a good reputation opens doors to opportunities while a fall from grace may close them. Not all of these doors are business doors, many will rather be social. Friedman shows how in earlier times, American defamation cases reflected the respective status and ideals of men and women in American

---

98 Even John Profumo collected damages for libel after it was alleged that he was dallying with prostitute Christine Keeler. He later admitted the truth of this liaison which was fatal to his career as Minister for War. *Robertson and Nicol on Media Law* (Thomson, 5th edn, 2007) p 97.

99 Post, RC, 'Social Foundations of Defamation Law: Reputation and the Constitution' (1986) 74 *California Law Review* 691 at 695.

100 Rolph, D, above n 28, p 121. See also McNamara, L, *Reputation and Defamation* (Oxford University Press, 2007); and Solove, DJ, *The Future of Reputation: gossip, rumor and privacy on the Internet* (Yale UP, 2007).

society.[101] Men sued for publications which disparaged them in their business; women sued for publications which doubted their virtue. In modern times, at least from the pattern of defamation cases, it appears the 'virtues' of men and women are becoming more similar.

Not everyone sees reputation in material terms. Windeyer J in *Uren v John Fairfax & Sons Pty Ltd*:

> A man's good reputation, his good name, the estimation in which he is held in the opinion of others, is not a possession of his as a chattel is. Damage to it cannot be measured as harm to a tangible thing is measured. Apart from special damages strictly so called and damages for a loss of clients or customers, money and reputation are not commensurables.[102]

Brennan J in *Carson v John Fairfax & Sons Ltd* also contradicts the notion that defamation damages compensate for decrease in value of an asset:

> Although damages are awarded to vindicate the plaintiff's reputation, damages are not awarded as compensation for the loss in value of a plaintiff's reputation as though that reputation were itself a tangible asset or a physical attribute which once damaged, is worth less than it was before. In order to achieve the purpose of vindicating reputation, damages for defamation are quantified by reference, inter alia, to what is needed to achieve that purpose: those damages are not quantified by reference to a depreciation in the value of a plaintiff's reputation.[103]

So, we can only take the asset metaphor or concept so far. The remedy for defamation – an award of damages – is intended not to compensate for loss of value of a reputation (except where actual loss of income can be proved) but to vindicate or restore reputation. The notion of vindication is at best impracticable and vague, yet it is accepted as a key purpose of the monetary remedy of damages in both trespass[104] and defamation, particularly where the circumstances of the tort were egregious and the plaintiff is unable to point to any special monetary loss for which precise reparation can be given. It reflects the recognition that rights in his person, property or reputation have a value even if never exploited by the plaintiff in money terms.

> Vindication looks to the attitude of others to the appellant: the sum awarded must be at least the minimum necessary to signal to the public the vindication of the appellant's reputation. 'The gravity of the libel, social standing of the parties and the availability of alternative remedies are all relevant to assessing the quantum of damages necessary to vindicate the appellant'.[105]

The idea of vindication is much more closely aligned with the second of Post's roles for reputation – that of reflecting honour in the community. Post sees reputation as the touchstone by which a person's place or rank in society is measured. Society is seen as a hierarchy of ideals with individuals bestowed with various social roles in that hierarchy. Society determines the moral

101   Friedman, above n 62, p 49.
102   (1966) 117 CLR 118 at 150.
103   (1993) 178 CLR 44 at 70.
104   For example, *Plenty v Dillon* (1991) 171 CLR 635.
105   *Carson* (1993) 178 CLR 44 at 61 quoting Fleming, above n 95, p 595.

standards and attributes of each ideal (the good 'royal', the good mother and wife, the good person behind the actor) and accords privileges, esteem and protection to those who live up to these ideals. Reputation becomes then *a* most dearly prized attribute of a civilised person because it reflects the extent to which he or she fulfils society's ideals.

The other purpose of defamation damages is solace or consolation[106] to the plaintiff for the personal distress and hurt caused by the defamation, with damages equally difficult to predict and compare in financial terms. Clearly the idea of 'hurt' fits most closely with Post's notion of reputation as dignity, while damages for embarrassment appear closely related to perceptions of status and honour. It would be presumptuous to assume that a celebrity is different from any ordinary person in the extent to which he or she values honour and standing in society and the esteem in which he or she is held on a personal rather than a commercial basis. We *expect* them to be more thick-skinned but that may be far from reality.

For commercial celebrities, a good reputation is critical. In Chapter 2 we have seen how celebrities have the potential to exploit the commercial value of their identities far beyond the stage in which they achieve their status. Models are expected to be famed and used and photographed for their beauty. But Ricky Ponting and Kiri Te Kanawa endorse luxury watches, George Clooney endorses coffee makers, Nicole Kidman endorses perfume or soft drinks (in advertisements directed by Baz Luhrmann or Ridley Scott). For both men and women, model or actor or sportsman, lucrative celebrity endorsements may be revoked if they or someone close to them is tarred by some rumour of moral indiscretion, personal weakness or substance abuse. If false, they have everything to fight for and a defamation action may be their best attack.

Truth

But what if the defamatory allegation is true? While the defence of justification in all its forms is often complex and difficult of proof,[107] nevertheless, if the defendant can prove substantial truth or the contextual truth of all the imputations sued upon, that will now be a complete defence of 'justification' in all Australian jurisdictions.[108]

---

106   Ibid at 60-61.

107   Butler and Rodrick, above n 21, p 52ff; Balkin and Davis, above n 21, 538ff.

108   As it always was at common law, and still is in England. Another version of the defence of justification is the defence of 'contextual truth': *Defamation Act 2005* (NSW), s 26. Under this defence, a defendant will rely on the substantial truth of defamatory imputations not sued upon by the claimant but made or implicit in the publication, and prove that because *they* are true, the imputations sued upon do not cause any further harm to the claimant's reputation. At common law, a defendant might rely on the so-called *Polly Peck* defence (from *Polly Peck (Holdings) plc v Trelford* [1986] QB 1000) that although each imputation might not be exactly true the imputations had a 'common sting' that could be proved true. See Butler and Rodrick, above n 21 at 54.

Truth alone was not always a complete defence. New South Wales, often described as the defamation capital of Australia because of its pro-claimant laws, required a defendant not only to prove truth but also to prove that the publication was in the public interest. Views differ as to the rationale for this requirement.[109] Undoubtedly, the requirement assisted people to put past misdeeds behind them and to rehabilitate themselves back into society, so that it was particularly suited to a former convict colony. This may explain why in 1847 New South Wales adopted with alacrity an 1843 reform of the common law which was proposed but not adopted in England. But it was not only convicts who want to keep secrets or skeletons in the closet: there was a concern for 'anyone with a past to hide'.[110]

The abandonment of the element of public interest in the defence of justification was a sticking point between the States for decades in previous attempts at uniformity of defamation laws, and was one of the most controversial aspects of the new legislation, with even sections of the media bemoaning its loss and fearing that it would only encourage further intrusions into people's private lives to root out true personal secrets.[111] In practice however, it was probably the less onerous element of the justification defence.

Protection of privacy was only ever an incidental, albeit important, benefit of defamation law. It is clearly now more desirable that the law develop specific protection of privacy, as discussed in Chapter 4 with explicit development of defences appropriate to that interest.

---

109   Mitchell, above n 1 at 494 and the previous pages on the English Bill.
110   Ibid.
111   For example, journalist Monica Attard, *Media Watch*, ABC, April 2006, quoted in Rolph, D, 'Preparing for a full scale invasion? Truth, Privacy and Defamation' (2007) 25 *Communications Law Bulletin* 5.

Chapter 4
CELEBRITIES: PRIVACY AND CONFIDENCES

'There is only one thing worse than being talked about and that is not being talked about'.
Oscar Wilde

The press is overstepping in every direction the obvious bounds of propriety and of decency. Gossip is no longer the resource of the idle and of the vicious, but has become a trade, which is pursued with industry as well as effrontery ...To satisfy the indolent, column upon column is filled with idle gossip, which can only be procured by intrusion upon the domestic circle.[1]

Introduction

We have seen in Chapter 1 how an intrinsic and essential element of what makes a person a celebrity is the *public* nature of his or her life. Without *publicity*, there can be no fame, no celebrity.

From a legal perspective publicity raises many questions of critical importance to the celebrity herself, to her family and associates, to those who employ or deal with her, and to the media engaged in news, information and entertainment. In this chapter, we look at questions which relate to the *private sphere* of a celebrity and *the limits of publicity*. In particular, we will outline the difficulty of identifying the precise point at which intrusion and publicity can no longer be justified by broad notions or specific instances of public interest.

Celebrities of one kind or another have played a key role since the 19th century in carving out the legal protection of privacy around the Western world. From Europe to the United States, we find the names of princes and princesses, presidents, generals, prime ministers and politicians, actors and actresses, poets, writers, playwrights, and fashion models in the leading cases.

This is not surprising. Celebrities of all kinds attract attention, sometimes short-lived, sometimes for their whole lives. Given the role of the media in informing the public and reflecting on events of the times, as well as the financial rewards which flow to those who tempt and satisfy the perennial interest and curiosity of 'members of the public' in the lives of celebrities, it

---

1   Warren SD and Brandeis LD, 'The Right to Privacy' (1890-91) 4 *Harvard Law Review* 193.

is to be expected that the activities of the latter will be widely reported. The media and others will seek out and publish what they can and their intrusions and disclosures will eventually go so far that they provoke challenge.

Lord Byron, Prince Albert and Queen Victoria, Diana Princess of Wales, Prince Charles, General Von Bismarck, Princess Caroline of Hannover, Lord Spencer, Presidents of the United States and France, Naomi Campbell, Jacqueline Kennedy Onassis, Bette Midler, Bette Davis, Marlene Dietrich, Michael Douglas and Catherine Zeta-Jones have all played roles in shaping the legal protection of privacy in the United States, Germany, France, the United Kingdom and indirectly in other countries such as Australia.

For celebrities, every case is a test case. A case by an ordinary member of the public will generally arise from some isolated incident or be brought as a matter of principle. For celebrities, in contrast, every case on privacy becomes a test case of where the boundaries between public and private life lie, for that particular type of person, in a particular society, at a particular time. The one incident is one of many; the 'intruder' or publisher one of many, poised to intrude or report further.

It may be, however, that the boundary thus set lasts only for a time. As mores differ from society to society and time to time, so the outcomes of the test cases become outdated or inappropriate and are themselves subject to new challenges. What is intolerable in one age may be soon be thought tolerable or insignificant.[2] Retiring Chief Justice of the High Court of Australia, Murray Gleeson recently said he had begun to wonder whether what he had considered in 2001 to be 'self-evidently private' was still so in 2008:

> When you look at the kind of information that people publish about themselves it makes you wonder. I used to think that a telephone conversation was normally private but you can't walk down the street without hearing a number of telephone conversations.[3]

The ordinary citizen should not begrudge the legal attention devoted to celebrities. On the one hand it is often argued that celebrity cases distort the law and impinge on legitimate freedoms, because the media are forced to settle unmeritorious claims rather than risk large costs orders.[4] On the other hand, often it is the celebrity who has the means and the interest to pursue a case and take on powerful media players who to others would be daunting opponents. In a recent case brought by Canadian folksinger

---

2   And vice versa. For example, consider, in the Internet age, with ever easier access for those engaged with child pornography, the increased tendency towards censorship amid heightened concern relating to photographic images of under-age models and the 'sexualisation' of children.

3   Speech to the National Press Club, August 2008, reported by Berkovic, N, 'Why privacy just isn't what it used to be', *The Australian*, 22 August 2008, p 17.

4   Particularly, in the United Kingdom, the conditional fee agreements (CFAs) which may even allow a doubling of lawyer-client legal fees if the party is successful.

Loreena McKennitt,[5] the claimant had to contend not only with the author and publisher of a revealing book, but also with the applications to intervene and submissions of a representative range of media organisations, including Times Newspapers Ltd, the (UK) Press Association and the BBC, which were alarmed at the nature of the arguments in the case and the possible precedents it could set. New protections may benefit ordinary individuals as well – if a particular incident transgresses the broader boundaries established around a celebrity, how much more easily will it be judged a transgression around an ordinary citizen. The law relating to celebrities' privacy and confidences consists of many of the same principles as that relating to the ordinary person, except that the balancing process is harder when assessing the legitimate demands of society in relation to 'public figures' or matters of 'public interest'.

A leading English text comments:

> the development of rules of compensation which will achieve a reasonable level [of] recompense and avoid gold-digging still remains to be completed. For while we do wish to see [celebrities] protected from a rapacious press, at the same time neither do we wish to encourage rapacity in these celebrities.[6]

Despite contemporary comments that the law of privacy is in a state of controversy,[7] what is striking about the development of privacy protection is that it long predates the late 20th century explosion of media that many commentators see as inexplicably linked with the notion of 'celebrity'. The quote at the commencement of this chapter was written in 1890,[8] provoked by continual reporting by the local press of a family's social activities. That was irritating enough, it seems, to galvanise the two eminent authors to make a public and heartfelt complaint. To the 'victims' of an intrusion or a public disclosure, it may make little difference if private information so obtained is spread around not just their circle, their street, their village, their workplace, their city, their region but also nationally or internationally. Either way, their peace has been invaded and their private information is no longer private. It may be just as galling and upsetting whether it is broadcast to the few with whom they come into contact from day to day or to the whole world.

Writing in *The Telegraph* in January 2008, William Langley from Los Angeles wrote of Britney Spears' nervous relapse, 'The notorious photos of her emerging knickerless from a car, tearfully shaving her head, and falling around in a Los Angeles strip club would, even a decade ago, never have reached the public arena. That they can now be distributed in seconds and be seen by the entire world not only further fuels the interest, but tests the celebrity's resistance'.[9] But does it really make a difference to Britney

---

5   *McKennitt v Ash* [2006] EWCA 1714; [2007] 3 WLR 194.
6   Deakin, S, Johnston, A and Markesinis, B, *Markesinis and Deakin's Tort Law* (Clarendon Press, 6th edn, 2008) p 861.
7   See, for example, Buxton LJ in *McKennitt v Ash* [2007] 2 WLR 197 at 199 [8].
8   Warren and Brandeis, above n 1.
9   Langley, W, 'Crash and burn: the Spears descent into hell', *The Telegraph*, London, reprinted in *The Sydney Morning Herald*, 8 January 2008, p 9.

Spear's *feelings* if unflattering pictures of her are broadcast not just in Los Angeles and Chicago and New York and her small hometown of Kentwood, Louisiana, but also in Sydney or Moscow?

What is undoubtedly different is the nature of 'the world'. In the 1890s, local papers were hot off the presses and into the streets. News travelled fast by word of mouth around a society but waited for the mail – by horse, by train, or by ship – to spread further. Telegraphic, telephonic, motorised, radio and then television/televisual communications followed decade by decade. However, the late 20th century and early 21st century have seen two developments that together have revolutionised communications – digital technology and the world wide web/Internet. Armed with a digital camera or mobile telephone and the Internet, every single person can be a publisher. Whatever the eye can see, any person can record and publish, to the world.

While it may cause little additional hurt to victims of privacy intrusions that the people who see the product are across the world as well as next door, the world market for images and information does have two important ramifications for the victims. First, while new societies and worlds might once have provided escape – a chance to get away from past reputations and to start afresh without scandal or shame attached – this avenue may now be closed. Information can both precede and follow its subject to all corners of the earth. Britney Spears cannot start a new life as an unknown in New Zealand or Peru. She is recognisable everywhere from the barrage of photographs posted daily on the Internet, in gossip magazines and even serious broadsheets. The objectionable photograph or story, if allowed to go unchallenged, may reappear at regular intervals anywhere.

Remember Julia Roberts' character in *Notting Hill*, Anna Scott, bemoaning the press hordes finding her in a man's shirt as she opened the front door of the shy and self-effacing bookseller's Notting Hill terrace house?

WILLIAM

I mean – today's newspapers will be lining tomorrow's waste paper bins.

ANNA

Excuse me?

WILLIAM

Well, you know – it's just one day. Today's papers will all have been thrown away tomorrow.

ANNA

You really don't get it. This story gets filed. Every time anyone writes anything about me – they'll dig up these photos. Newspapers last forever. I'll regret this forever.[10]

---

10   *Notting Hill* (1999), screenplay by Richard Curtis, accessed at <http://home.online. no/~bhundlan/scripts/NottingHill.htm>.

Old files and old controversies raise another issue: that is, the extent to which legitimate public interest in a person's conduct from a former time or place extends or survives to justify publication in the present day. This is a perennial issue everywhere and one relevant to both defamation law[11] and privacy protection. In the United States, it is recognised in the Restatement of Torts that lapse of time does not necessarily defeat legitimate public interest in a story.[12] A child prodigy, William Sidis, failed in his action against *The New Yorker* decades later in 1940 when it featured him in a 'Where are they now?' story. The judge commented:

> [E]ven if Sidis had loathed public attention at that time, we think his uncommon achievements and personality would have made the attention permissible. Since then Sidis has cloaked himself in obscurity, but his subsequent history, containing as it did the answer to the question of whether or not he had fulfilled his early promise, was still a matter of public concern.[13]

Paradoxically, the author of the piece, humorist James Thurber, later commented that the court had not discerned his implication that 'the piece would help curb the great American thrusting of talented children into the glare of fame or notoriety'.[14]

In contrast, in *Melvin v Reid* in 1931, the Californian Supreme Court upheld the right to privacy of a former prostitute, who had been acquitted years before of murder, after her story and identity were revealed in the film *The Red Kimono*. She was entitled to protect her efforts to rehabilitate herself.[15] But the standing of *Melvin v Reid* and other cases is questioned in the light of more modern cases which place greater emphasis on the protection of freedom of speech in the First Amendment to the United States Constitution.[16]

Markesinis and others argue that the law should follow the longstanding and more nuanced approach of continental European legal systems in distinguishing between those who seek publicity and those who have publicity thrust upon them. The latter should, it is suggested, be able to 'recede back into anonymity and have their rights of privacy eventually revived'.[17] What was once information in the public domain might no longer be so regarded. The reluctant celebrity might be a relative of a willing celebrity; someone caught up involuntarily in an incident; a convicted criminal or wrongdoer;

---

11   See above p 89.
12   *Restatement (Second) of Torts* # 652D comment k.
13   *Sidis v F-R Publishing Corp* 113 F 2d 806 at 809 (2d Cir 1940).
14   Thurber J, *My Years with Ross* (1959), quoted in Solove, DJ, Rotenberg M and Schwartz PM, *Information Privacy Law*, (Aspen, 2nd edn, 2006) p 6.
15   Solove DJ, Rotenberg M and Schwartz PM, above n 14, p 144.
16   Ibid, p 146. See also on this point and generally on US privacy law, Schwartz, VE, Kelly, K and Partlett, DF, *Prosser, Wade and Schwartz's Torts Cases and Materials* (Foundation Press, 11th edn, 2005) pp 971-72.
17   Markesinis, B, O'Cinneneide, C, Fedtke, J and Hunter-Henin, M, 'Concerns and Ideas about the developing English law of privacy (and how a knowledge of private law might be of help)' (2004) 52 *American Journal of Comparative Law* 133 at 144-146.

the family of a victim of crime.[18] There are clearly many competing interests, public and private, in such cases. Infamous criminals who have had their identity protected to allow them to re-enter society include Jon Venables and Robert Thompson, who at the age of ten, murdered two year old James Bulger in 1993. When they were released on a licence in 2001, a permanent injunction was granted to prevent publication of details about their new identities or whereabouts.[19] Notorious child murderer Mary Bell who killed two boys when she was 11, was protected in 2003 by a similar order to protect the privacy of Bell's own daughter.[20]

The second ramification that derives from the world wide market for photographs and information is that the prices they fetch are commensurately higher, fuelling demand, the growth of freelance paparazzi and more and more intrusion. A photo of Nicole Kidman's so-called 'baby bump' was rumoured to be fetching A$100,000 on the world media market – the frenzied attempts to capture an image continued when the baby was born. Getting a perfect photo of Nicole or some other screen or real princess may yield enough to retire on. And the price goes up when the celebrity is at his or her most vulnerable- as marriages and love affairs fail, as loved ones die, as babies are miscarried or not conceived at all, as new babies wreak havoc to ordered lives, when physical or mental illness overwhelms, when programs are axed or homes are lost. With that sort of money at stake, it is no surprise that there is a media scrum or pack awaiting the celebrity's every move or tender moment.

A second general point to make about the development of privacy protection is that while it has been an explicit issue on the legal agenda now for well over a century, it is nevertheless a relatively modern phenomenon in the armoury of legal protections of citizens' personal rights.

In a legal context, invasions of privacy are civil or private wrongs rather than public or criminal wrongs. There is clearly a broad public policy in the maintenance of personal security and social order – and this has led to the recognition, in the courts of equity, of a public interest in the legal protection of confidences. Nevertheless, the protection of privacy comes within the broad field of 'tort law' which developed to provide redress for 'torts' or wrongs,[21] suffered by one citizen at the hands of another.

---

18   In *R v Broadcasting Complaints Commission, Ex parte Granada Television Ltd*, 16 December 1994, *Times Law Reports*, the Court of Appeal upheld a complaint in respect of a Granada television program entitled 'How safe are our children?' showing a photograph of the complainant's child who had been murdered only two years before. The father saw the footage while at a pub. The Broadcasting Complaints Tribunal upheld the complaint that the program was an unwarranted infringement of the parents' privacy.

19   *Jon Venables v News Group Newspapers* [2001] 1 All ER 908. In early March 2010, Venables was recalled into custody following a breach of his licence conditions. The injunction remains in place.

20   Melville-Brown, A, 'It takes more than a few rare cases to make a privacy law', *The Times*, 8 June 2004, <http://business.timesonline.co.uk/tol/business/law/public_law/article41979>.

21   The English word 'tort', meaning wrong, derives from the same French word, which in turn derives from the Latin word 'tortus' meaning 'twisted, wrung' (*Shorter Oxford*

Early tort law in England arose in the 13th century when courts began to allow civil suits between citizens for harm arising out of criminal wrong-doing or 'breach of the peace'. The public authorities could not possibly prosecute for every invasion of another's rights. The common law was chiefly concerned with the primary interest of personal safety and, in a society where power depended on property ownership, that of security and protection of property. As we will see, protection provided by fundamental tort law was usually concerned with *physical* intrusions. Trespass to the person, land and goods occurred by direct contact and invasions, although a *threat* of physical intrusion was also enough to attract a remedy, with a threat of violence amounting to the tort of assault. Incidentally, then, trespass provided some privacy protection. Nuisance, too, protecting the rights of land occupiers to quiet enjoyment of their land, encompassed conduct that did not involve a direct intrusion and provided a remedy that could take into account most of the intangible benefits of undisturbed occupation. But its protection of privacy as such was also incidental to its protection of occupation rights.

It seems, then, that the notion of privacy as an interest worthy or deserv-ing of the law's protection was secondary to these primary interests, and that it tends to attract society's attention only once the people's fundamental needs are met and their fundamental protections well entrenched in its legal system. In societies still battling to ensure basic human rights, such as fair trials and representation or freedom of the press to report on political corruption and government abuses, privacy protection is less likely to be high on the agenda.

The origins of the modern law of privacy

Modern attention to privacy protection has been in two surges. The first was in the late 19th century. It may be no coincidence that at the same time that two Harvard Law school graduates, Warren and Brandeis, were writing their famous and influential article in the *Harvard Law Review* in 1890, reassessing existing protections in the law to reveal 'The Right to Privacy',[22] German legislators were drawing up changes to German copyright laws to provide a new measure of protection for the subjects of photographs. On both sides of the Atlantic, the actors were motivated by what they saw as unreasonable intrusions into private life. What was the social development that had provoked this activity? Gossip and scandal had, after all, been around for centuries.[23]

> In April 1830 *The Times* of London cleared its front page of classified adver-tisements to publish in detail the scandalous affairs of Lady Jane Digby, Lady Ellenborough, which were revealed in divorce proceedings by her

---

English Dictionary 3rd edn, 1944.) Civil law countries still however often refer to a wrong by the Latin term 'delict'.

22   Warren and Brandeis, above n 1.

23   See above Ch 1, and Wilkes R, *Scandal: a scurrilous history of gossip* (Atlantic Books, 2002).

Celebrity adventuress Lady Jane Digby

husband in the House of Lords and then the House of Commons.[24] The transcript of evidence – some 21 witnesses – was sometimes repeated word for word.

For weeks the name of Lady Ellenborough was in every newspaper and Jane's misdemeanours became the breakfast tittle-tattle of the entire country, causing her name to become a byword for scandalous behaviour for generations. Indeed, for decades small news items continued to appear (they were often incorrect) about her adventures ...[25]

Jane Digby went on to give the press plenty of material. As Mary S Lovell described in her fascinating biography, Jane left England after her divorce and travelled steadily east, going on to become confidante, mistress or wife of many prominent men: an Austrian prince, a Bavarian King, a German baron, a Corfiot nobleman, and an Albanian chieftain. She was most famous for her middle-eastern desert travels, which led to her 30-year marriage to a Bedouin chief 20 years her junior, Sheikh Medjuel, and for her palatial home in Damascus which became a mecca for European travellers, keen to meet this extraordinary woman.[26]

The United States recognised the legal concept of privacy decades (perhaps a century) earlier than other countries sharing a British legal ancestry. Not only that, but the concept of privacy has been formulated in the US in much broader terms than elsewhere, encompassing many of the protections which in other jurisdictions come under a different label. It was largely a development of the 'common law', rather than of the legislatures. The United States Constitution and its amendments makes no specific mention of rights to privacy yet it has been held to be implicit in various Amendments.

---

24   Lovell, MS, *A Scandalous Life: The biography of Jane Digby el Mezrab*, (Fourth Estate, 1995), pp 63-70.

25   Ibid, p 63.

26   Ibid. A century later, Jane's descendant Pamela Harriman lived an equally colourful life, but with her undoubted energy, passion and brains put to more political and worldly use: she began as Winston Churchill's daughter-in-law during World War II and many affairs and marriages later, ended her days as the Clinton-appointed Ambassador to France for the United States.

The *Harvard Law Journal* article by Samuel Warren and Louis Brandeis in 1890 was groundbreaking.[27] Not only was this article the first explicit recognition of a freestanding 'Law of Privacy', but the article itself was recognised within a generation as 'having initiated and theoretically outlined a new field of jurisprudence'.[28] The top two Harvard Law school graduates of the class of 1877, Samuel Warren and Louis Brandeis collaborated on the article after Warren was outraged by the press intrusions upon his family's life. Warren had given up his law practice to take over a successful family business and was married to the socialite daughter of a Delaware Senator, whose entertaining was always a subject of interest to the newspapers of Boston. He turned to his classmate and ex-law partner Louis D Brandeis, a future judge of the United States Supreme Court from 1916-1939, to write the article with him.

The two surveyed the law's existing protections of personal rights and property rights and called for the next step to be taken for the necessary protection of the person and for securing to the individual 'the right to be let alone', based on a principle, not of private property, but of 'inviolate personality'.[29]

> In every such case the individual is entitled to decide whether that which is his shall be given to the public. No other has the right to publish his productions in any form, without his consent. This right is wholly independent of the material on which, or the means by which, the thought, sentiment, or emotion is expressed ... The right is lost only when the author himself communicates his production to the public, in other words publishes it. It is entirely independent of the copyright laws ...[30]

While in Germany it was a photographic image that went too far, it does not appear that photographs were the problem experienced by Warren. Rather, the consensus seems to be that it was just a personal abhorrence of gossip, a personal view about low standards of local journalism and irritation at the press's interest – reflected in some 60 articles or mentions over eight years- in his and his wife's family that provoked Warren.[31]

The second surge came with the great international human rights covenants and treaties of the 20th century, in which privacy was recognised and specified as one of the interests which must be protected, but with that

---

27   It is a wonderful example of the obscure distinction between finding the law and making it.

28   Larremore, W, 'The Law of Privacy' (1912) 12 *Columbia Law Review* 694 at 694.

29   Warren and Brandeis, above n 1, p 205.

30   Ibid, p 199.

31   Much has been written about what prompted Warren to write the *Harvard Law Journal* article. Contrary to Prosser's suggestion in his famous 1960 article, n 43 below, p 383, that it was when the press 'had a field day' reporting on Warren's daughter's wedding, others have disproved this possibility. See Gajda A, 'What if Samuel D Warren Hadn't Married A Senator's Daughter?: Uncovering the Press Coverage That Led to *The Right to Privacy' Illinois Public Law and Legal Theory Research Papers Series Research Paper No 07-06*, 1 November 2007 accessed at <http://papers.ssrn.com/abstract=1026680>, for some fascinating sleuth work on the background to the article.

protection balanced with protection of freedom of speech and freedom of the press.

First was the *Universal Declaration of Human Rights* (United Nations General Assembly, Paris,1948) which provides in Art 12:

> No one shall be subjected to arbitrary interference with his privacy, family, home or correspondence, nor to attacks upon his honour and reputation. Everyone has the right to the protection of the law against such interference or attacks.

Later the United Nations *International Covenant on Civil and Political Rights* (1976) provided in Art 17:

> 1. No one shall be subjected to arbitrary or unlawful interference with his privacy, family, home or correspondence, nor to unlawful attacks on his honour and reputation.
> 2. Everyone has the right to the protection of the law against such interference or attacks.

In Europe, the Council of Europe, formed after the Second World War in 1949 by the *Treaty of London*, adopted The *European Convention for the Protection of Human Rights and Fundamental Freedoms* in 1950 which provides in Art 8:

> 1. Everyone has the right to respect for his private and family life, his home and his correspondence.
> 2. There shall be no interference by a public authority with the exercise of this right except such as is in accordance with the law and is necessary in a democratic society in the interests of national security, public safety or the economic well-being of the country, for the prevention of disorder or crime, for the protection of health or morals, or for the protection of the rights and freedoms of others.

The death of the Princess of Wales in a Paris road-tunnel in 1997 triggered a debate in the Parliamentary Assembly of the Council of Europe in 1997 leading to a Resolution[32] on the right to privacy, calling on governments of Europe to ensure that they have in place rules of law or legislation enshrining the effect of Art 8 of the European Convention for the Protection of Human Rights and Fundamental Freedoms 1950[33] which all member states, including the United Kingdom and Germany, had ratified.

Despite the seemingly universal recognition of some right to privacy, the significant differences in the origin, extent, manner and content of the legal protection of privacy around the world make for interesting comparisons. Not all countries would come to the same answer on a particular dispute and, even if they did, they may have arrived there by a different legal route. Even within the European Union, there is a significant 'margin of appreciation' between member states on their individual laws. Writing about two recent breakthrough cases in England, Professor David Anderson, a leading

---

32   Resolution 1165 of 1998.
33   Rome, 4 November 1950; TS 71 (1953); Cmd 8969.

American academic on tort and media law, has stated that they would have been decided differently in the United States, commenting that:

> Rarely do we see stronger proof of the principle that what matters is what the law does, not what it says ... English judges have found ways to protect privacy without elaborating much of a tort framework; in the United States, the law rarely protects privacy despite an elaborate doctrinal framework.[34]

In an earlier work, he had said:

> But privacy is not the only cherished American value. We also cherish information, and candour, and freedom of speech. We expect to be free to discover and discuss the secrets of our neighbours, celebrities, and public officials. We expect government to conduct its business publicly, even if that infringes the privacy of those caught up in the matter. Most of all, we expect the media to uncover the truth and report it – not merely the truth about government and public affairs, but the truth about people.

The law protects these expectations too – and when they collide with expectations of privacy, privacy almost always loses. Privacy law in the United States delivers far less than it promises, because it resolves virtually all these conflicts in favour of information, candour, and free speech. The sweeping language of privacy law serves largely to mask the fact that the law provides almost no protection against privacy-invading disclosures.[35]

Comparisons of legal protections of privacy in different countries in relation to disclosure illustrate how closely it is linked to local constitutional enactments and rights, and local interpretation. The dominance of the 'Free Speech' First Amendment to the United States Constitution in the jurisprudence of that country probably has no equal in other Western countries, despite the presence of similar constitutional guarantees or similar articles in the international covenants. The ultimate impact of major international covenants depends a great deal on their local legislative expression and the power of local courts to enforce them. In a country like Australia, with no express constitutional protection for freedom of speech and no federal statute explicitly protecting human rights, the case law of the United States, United Kingdom and European countries is influential but not directly applicable or analogous. One of our nearest neighbours, New Zealand, despite a shared heritage of English law, has taken a markedly different course to that taken in the United Kingdom.

We will highlight the comparative aspects of particular issues as we meet them but below we will also make the occasional excursus to study a country's treatment in greater depth.

---

34   Anderson, DA, 'Defamation and Privacy: An American Perspective' in Deakin, S, Johnston, A and Markesinis, B, above n 6, p 883.

35   Anderson, DA, 'The Failure of American Privacy Law' in Markesinis, B (ed), *Protecting Privacy* (Oxford University Press, 1999), pp 139-140, quoted by Gummow and Hayne JJ in *Australian Broadcasting Corporation v Lenah Game Meats* (2001) 208 CLR 199 at 253.

'Privacy'

At the outset it is necessary to define what we mean by 'privacy' in this discussion. The term 'privacy' has come to mean many things. In its most day-to-day sense it refers to the state of being private, that is, not exposed to social or public or general view.

In a legal sense, the term 'privacy' has come to encompass a number of aspects of the state of being private or of keeping one's life, personality, property and activities free from interference by others. Many of these, however, have no special relevance to celebrities or public figures. For example, there is a large body of legislation, some named 'Privacy' Acts,[36] and jurisprudence, dealing with 'information privacy' or 'data protection', concerned with the right of citizens to know and control what personal information about them is recorded, stored, used or communicated to others by other people, governments and public and private organisations.[37] The still-controversial landmark decision of the US Supreme Court *Roe v Wade*, striking down State laws against abortion, was based on an implicit constitutional right of privacy against government interference.[38] The Supreme Court noted that while the Constitution did not include any explicit reference to any right of

---

36   For example, *Privacy Act 1988* (Cth); *Data Protection Act 1998* (UK); *Privacy Act 1993* (NZ); *Privacy and Personal Information Act 1998* (NSW): *Privacy Act 1974* 5 USC (552a) (US).

37   Journalists and media organisations are given varying exemptions from the limitations under these statutes on collection, storage and dissemination of information. See Butler, D and Rodrick, S, *Australian Media Law* (Lawbook Co, 3rd edn, 2007), para 10.20 ff. See below, pp 165-166.

38   410 US 113, 93 SCt 705 (1973). See Anderson, DA, above n 34, p 883. In *Roe v Wade* 410 US 113 at 152-53, the court held, 'The Constitution does not explicitly mention any right of privacy. In a line of decisions, however, going back perhaps as far as *Union Pacific R Co v Botsford* 141 US 250 at 251 (1891), the court has recognized that a right of personal privacy, or a guarantee of certain areas or zones of privacy, does exist under the Constitution. In varying contexts, the court or individual justices have, indeed, found at least the roots of that right in the First Amendment, *Stanley v Georgia* 394 US 557 at 564 (1969); in the Fourth and Fifth Amendments, *Terry v Ohio* 392 US 1 at 8-9 (1968), *Katz v United States* 389 US 347 at 350 (1967), *Boyd v United States* 116 US 616 (1886), see *Olmstead v United States* 277 US 438 at 478 (1928) (Brandeis, J, dissenting); in the penumbras of the Bill of Rights, *Griswold v Connecticut* 381 US, at 484-485; in the Ninth Amendment, id, at 486 (Goldberg, J, concurring); or in the concept of liberty guaranteed by the first section of the Fourteenth Amendment, see *Meyer v Nebraska*, 262 US 390, 399 (1923). These decisions make it clear that only personal rights that can be deemed "fundamental" or "implicit in the concept of ordered liberty," *Palko v Connecticut* 302 US 319 at 325 (1937), are included in this guarantee of personal privacy. They also make it clear that the right has some extension to activities relating to marriage, *Loving v Virginia* 388 US 1 at 12 (1967); procreation, *Skinner v Oklahoma* 316 US 535 at 541-542 (1942); contraception, *Eisenstadt v Baird* 405 US, at 453-454; id, at 460, 463-465 [410 US 113 at 153] (White, J, concurring in result); family relationships, *Prince v Massachusetts* 321 US 158 at 166 (1944); and child rearing and education, *Pierce v Society of Sisters* 268 US 510 at 535 (1925), *Meyer v Nebraska*, supra. This right of privacy, whether it be founded in the Fourteenth Amendment's concept of personal liberty and restrictions upon state action, as we feel it is, or, as the District Court determined, in the Ninth Amendment's reservation of rights to the people, is broad enough to encompass a woman's decision whether or not to terminate her pregnancy'.

privacy, it was nevertheless a fundamental right which had roots in many constitutional provisions. There is an extraordinary body of debate and writing in US jurisprudence, dealing with the various aspects and embodiments of the privacy right,[39] and with the voluminous case law in the one hundred or so years since Warren and Brandeis wrote their famous article in the *Harvard Law Journal*. Much of the writing is concerned with defining and analysing the concept of privacy, with the multiple and overlapping layers of interests, rights and values challenging and confounding those seeking some clear delineation and order.[40]

Daniel J Solove, writing in 2002, argues for a pragmatic approach to conceptualising privacy, based on actual problems with similar but not identical characteristics,[41] in preference to attempts to define it by reference to some essence or common denominator or unifying concept. He notes that

> The word 'privacy' is currently used to describe a myriad of different things: freedom of thought; control over personal information, freedom from surveillance, protection of one's reputation, protection from invasions into one's home, the ability to prevent disclosure of facts about oneself, and an almost endless series of other things.[42]

In this chapter, we will use descriptions based on those coined by Professor William Prosser, the famous US torts scholar, in a seminal law review article in 1960,[43] to discuss what we see as the two key aspects of privacy that relate to celebrities. One is the protection of a person from unwanted or unreasonable physical intrusions and surveillance (which we call 'Intrusion'), the other is the protection against disclosure of private information ('Disclosure').[44] Often the issues overlap, since many cases deal not just with an initial intrusion, but also with the resulting disclosure or publication of the information so obtained.

Prosser identified four privacy torts in all.[45] The third was appropriation of another's name and likeness for the defendant's own benefit or advantage.

---

39   See Solove DJ, 'Conceptualizing Privacy' (2002) 90 *California Law Review* 1087.

40   'Privacy is a value so complex, so entangled in competing and contradictory dimensions, so engorged with various and distinct meanings, that I sometimes despair whether it can be usefully addressed at all'; Post RC, *Three Concepts of Privacy*, (2001) 89 *Georgetown Law Journal* 2087 at 2087, quoted by Solove, above n 39 at 1089.

41   Solove draws on the ideas of Austrian philosopher Ludwig Wittgenstein (1889-1951) in this approach. Solove, above n 39 at 1096ff.

42   Ibid at 1095.

43   Prosser, W, 'Privacy' (1960) 48 *California Law Review* 383.

44   Prosser actually referred to 'public disclosure of embarrassing private facts about another' but we think that modern privacy law is not or should not be limited to protection of *embarrassing* facts. Defamation law already provides limited protection against disclosure of embarrassing private facts or images (eg, because the publication might hold the plaintiff up to ridicule, *Youssoupoff v Metro-Goldwyn Mayer Publications Ltd* (1934) 50 TLR 581; *Ettingshausen v Australian Consolidated Press* Ltd, unreported, NSWCA, 13 October 1993, discussed in Ch 3. Privacy protection must hinge on the private nature of the facts, not necessarily on their potential for embarrassing their subject.

45   'It is not one tort, but a complex of four', Prosser, above n 43 at 389.

In an Anglo-Australian context, appropriation of identity or image in a commercial setting will comprise the tort of 'passing off' and has already been dealt with, along with other protections against wrongful *exploitation* of a person's identity or personality, in Chapter 2. Yet recent cases such as *Douglas v Hello! (No 3)*[46] show that there is often a blurred line between protection of privacy and protection of commercial interests where celebrities are concerned.

The fourth was 'publicity that places another in a false light before the public'. It is obvious that the essence of the wrong here is the *falsity* of the information, rather than its embarrassing,[47] defamatory or private quality. If the false information is also defamatory, the subject will generally have a successful claim for *defamation*, as the falsity will prevent the defence of truth being raised, unless the defendant can claim some form of limited privilege which allows him or her to get things wrong in certain contexts, so long as he or she does not do it maliciously.[48] If on the other hand the publicity was false but not defamatory (because the false fact would not lower the person's reputation amongst ordinary reasonable people), the law of defamation could provide no remedy. The tort of *injurious falsehood* might be made out, but only if the speaker knew of the falsity and was thus in law treated as 'malicious', and only if the subject suffered actual loss, such as loss of business. Injurious falsehood was not concerned with protection of feelings. The tort thus provided only limited protection against disclosure of false information. Like defamation, its protection of privacy *per se* was incidental. Prosser argued therefore for the law of 'privacy' to provide a remedy for 'false publicity', and a series of cases in the United States does so, said to derive from a case in which Lord Byron complained of the circulation of a bad poem falsely attributed to his pen.[49] In other jurisdictions, remedies against false but otherwise harmless publicity tend, if anything, to be through industry or public channels, such as the Australian Press Council and the Press Complaints Commission in the United Kingdom.

Here we will concentrate on intrusion and disclosure. Intrusion tends to be concerned most closely with the subject's physical sphere, while disclosure is concerned with information, whether in oral, written or visual form. Both physical sphere and information may, of course, have the quality of being private or public, so the question then becomes how to define what is private and what are the elements or signifiers of privacy.

---

46   [2007] 2 WLR 920, discussed below.

47   The adjective 'embarrassing' does not add much to the legal issues. The critical question for defamation purposes will be, not the embarrassment of the victim, but whether the information tends to lower a person in the eyes of *others*.

48   The defence of 'qualified privilege' discussed in Ch 3. There are also instances of 'absolute privilege' enjoyed by parliamentarians and those involved in court proceedings, where the only recrimination for abuse is the entity's own proceedings for contempt of its processes.

49   *Lord Byron v Johnston* (1816) 2 Mer 29, 35 Eng Rep 851. See further Schwartz, Kelly and Partlett, above n 16 at pp 973-978, noting that at least 20 States recognise false light invasion of privacy, while eight States reject it.

Implicit in the definition of privacy as the state of being private or 'not public' is that there are, in fact, grades of privacy, depending on the degree of exposure outside the strictly personal sphere. Obviously private are things known only to oneself, but some things may still be private even though and because knowledge or exposure of them is confined to one's partner, family, social circle, business, or association. Privacy then may rest on a *deliberate limitation or confinement*, even if the members of the inner circle are numerous. Just as a party of a hundred invited guests may be private,[50] so a letter or document circulated to a hundred people may still retain its private nature.

> Intrusion tends to be concerned most closely with the subject's physical sphere, while disclosure is concerned with information, whether in oral, written or visual form.

Prince Charles successfully sued to restrain the further publication in the press of his private diaries: they were 'private' even though he usually circulated them amongst a list of 21 close friends,[51] including a member of parliament, and even though the diaries often related to his performance of his official duties.[52] One that had been published related to his attendance at the hand over of Hong Kong to Chinese rule in 1997 and included his frank comments on the process and personalities involved on both sides. The conclusion rested on whether Prince Charles had a reasonable expectation of privacy in relation to the diaries. The court held that he did, from their very nature, and quite apart from the fact that the diaries were circulated to a defined and limited group under an express obligation of confidence. The trial judge held:

> The fact that the Hong Kong journal is not of a highly personal or private nature, in the sense that it does not deal with matters of an intimate or medical nature or about members of his family and that its contents are a very long way from the often salacious celebrity information that sometimes features in privacy claims, does not rob the claimant of a reasonable expectation of privacy in the matters to which in his Hong Kong journal he refers.[53]

The Court of Appeal of England and Wales agreed, noting that:

---

50   And will continue to be considered 'private', even if the participants authorise certain photographs of the event to be published. In *Douglas v Hello Ltd (No 3)*, Michael Douglas and Catherine Zeta-Jones did not lose their rights to complain of the publication of *unauthorised* photographs just because they had *authorised* some photographs (for considerable financial gain: [2005] 3 WLR 881 at 913-14 (CA).

51   Compare *Stephens v Avery* [1988] Ch 449 at 454: 'Information only ceases to be capable of protection as confidential when it is known to a substantial number of people'. See also discussion of *Douglas v Hello! (No 3)* below, p 145 ff.

52   *Prince of Wales v Associated Newspapers Ltd* [2007] 3 WLR 222 at 228 per Blackburne J.

53   *Prince of Wales* [2007] 3 WLR 222 at 251 per Blackburne J.

The journal set out the personal views and impressions of Prince Charles ... While most of the events described in the journal were in the public domain, what were not in the public domain were Prince Charles's comments about them, and it was these that were the essence of the publication in The Mail on Sunday'[54]

The Prince of Wales' case was one which concerned disclosure of private information. It illustrates that privacy in that context may rest not just on physical containment or deliberate restriction of audience. It may also rest on an *obligation of confidence* imposed upon the audience or recipients. An obligation or duty or relationship of confidence has long been recognised as a basis for preventing unauthorised disclosure by one of its members. The traditional law of breach of confidence is discussed below. A major development in modern law has been that the protection for privacy may rest on the nature of *the subject matter* itself. This development is discussed under the heading 'Disclosure of Private Facts' below (p 117).

We will see that both the intrusion and the disclosure cases have to grapple with the delineation of the public and the private spheres. It is partly because of the widespread use of this spatial metaphor in several different contexts that the case law is sometimes hard to categorise. It is easy enough to envisage a private sphere where this is delineated by physical boundaries, such as the private home or office. More difficult is it to delineate when one is talking about public spaces such as streets and parks or shops and restaurants to which the public can freely enter. When we come to the law on Disclosure, we will again come across the notion or concept of the 'public sphere' or 'public domain'. It may be bound up in the argument of legitimate public interest in certain conduct or facts. It may take the form of a physical or now virtual public domain or sphere to which the public has free or unlimited access. The question then arises as to whether anyone can expect privacy in this public sphere, and even if the answer is generally yes, whether celebrities or other 'public figures' must lose that expectation, in whole or in part.

Protection from unreasonable or unwanted Intrusion

Greta Garbo famously wanted to be left alone.

With her low husky voice and playing the part of a Russian ballerina in the Oscar winning movie Grand Hotel in 1932, she said 'I want to be alone'. However, she is said to have commented later, 'I never said, 'I want to be alone'. I only said, 'I want to be let alone'. There is all the difference'.[55]

For the most part she had her way, with only the occasional photograph of her, behind dark glasses, walking in New York.

---

54   *Prince of Wales* [2007] 3 WLR 222 at 277 per Lord Philips of Worth Matravers CJ.
55   <http://en.wikipedia.org/wiki/Greta_Garbo#Private_life>.

We have all read the reports or seen the footage of media pursuing public figures or celebrities along the streets and into shops and cafes, camped outside their homes and hotels with long-range lenses, shoving microphones and flashing cameras in their faces, jostling them in crowds, following them in motorcades, knocking on doors or baldly entering premises with cameras rolling.

We are used to this as a sometimes necessary, sometimes acceptable (but sometimes not) part of investigative journalism or the reporting of news and current events. Serious and responsible journalism, a concept now incorporated into the English law of defamation, often calls for a particularly fine balancing of the democratic protection of freedom of the press with rights of personal security, property and privacy, and for close scrutiny of the precise public interest at stake.[56] But we are also increasingly familiar with media scrums, hordes of paparazzi or just ordinary fans or busybodies laying siege to a reluctant or reclusive or just plain famous person, making their every move a public event, when there is arguably no legitimate *need* for the information and the only thirsts that are being satisfied are public curiosity or public entertainment. How does the law deal with protecting people and celebrities from physical intrusions?

Trespass

The law of trespass provides the most longstanding and important protection against unwanted invasion of the person or intrusion upon the physical space of another. It does this by proscribing *direct* unauthorised interferences with another's person or property. Yet while trespass provides some fundamental protection against intrusion, it only goes so far. In the United Kingdom, actor Gordon Kaye of '*Allo Allo*' fame found out how limited it was in protecting his privacy;[57] in the United States, Jacqueline Onassis had to rely on the more extensive United States 'privacy tort'[58] and in Australia, Nicole Kidman had to resort to criminal proceedings to seek an apprehended violence order from the courts against a photographer.[59] In each case the problem was that the conduct was just outside the protection provided by the law of trespass.

---

56   See below at p 142 where Baroness Hale in *Campbell v MGN Ltd* set out a hierarchy of matters of public interest with 'political speech' at the top of the list.

57   *Kaye v Robertson and Sports Newspapers Ltd* (1991) 18 FSR 62, discussed below.

58   *Galella v Jacqueline Onassis and USA* 487 F 2d 986 (1973) (United States Court of Appeals Second Circuit), dismissing an appeal by a self-styled paparazzo Galella against injunctive relief granted to Jacqueline Onassis. J Joseph Smith Circuit Judge, at 991: 'Galella fancies himself as a paparazzo: (literally a kind of annoying insect, perhaps roughly equivalent to the English … "gadfly".) Paparazzi make themselves as visible to the public and obnoxious to their photographic subjects as possible to aid in the advertisement and wide sale of their works'.

59   The case was settled when it came before a magistrate, with one photographer agreeing not to take photographs within 500 metres of Kidman's Sydney home. <www.theage.com.au/news/National/Paparazzi-pledge-to-Kidman/2005/02/11/110>. See also <www.abc.net.au/news/stories/2005/02/11/1301128.htm>; for the paparrazo's side see *Australian Story*, Australian Broadcasting Corporation television, 28 July 2008.

The form of *trespass to the person* known as battery is committed by a direct unauthorised contact with the person of another. A judge once said that 'the least touching of another in anger is a battery'[60]. There is no need for the claimant to prove that he or she had suffered actual injury, as trespass was always and is still today 'actionable *per se*', that is, simply because the tort has occurred and the claimant's right to be left in peace has been interrupted.[61] Anger is not necessary for the touching to be unlawful – it is wrongful enough simply if it is unauthorised. However, it is clear this judge was right when he emphasised that even the smallest unauthorised touching will be wrongful. Thus the law recognises the ultimate right 'to be left alone' in a bodily sense.

Two issues are key: first, what contact will be regarded as 'authorised'? The grey area for most situations is not that to which the subject has expressly agreed,[62] but that to which she may have impliedly consented. So, let us imagine the case of a famous actress who complains that, as she arrives at the theatre every night, or at an awards ceremony or at court to give evidence, she has to make her way through jostling crowds of people who are waiting to catch a glimpse of her and others. One of the fans or media employees pulls her arm vigorously to get her to turn around for a photograph. Trespass? Perhaps. It would seem to be more than just touching her to attract her attention. Worth suing about? Probably not. What if a fan surprises her by kissing her on the cheek, such as once happened to Prince Charles as he came out of the Bondi surf?

After setting out the fundamental principle that every person's body is inviolate – so that everyone is protected against every form of physical molestation – Lord Goff in the House of Lords referred to the general exception for physical interference with the person's consent. He continued:[63]

> A broader exception has been created to allow for the exigencies of everyday life- jostling in a street or some other crowded place, social contact at parties, and such like. This exception has been said to be founded upon implied consent, since those who go about in public places, or go to parties, may be taken to have impliedly consented to bodily contact of this kind. ... [but it is] more appropriate to regard such cases as falling within the general exception embracing all physical contact which is generally acceptable in the ordinary conduct of everyday life.

In many cases, then, the issue is the extent to which the contact transgressed the exigencies of everyday life. Trampling or unreasonable shoving to the extent of injury might amount to trespass, but not so a little everyday discomfort or physical contact in our crowded world. The standard to test the bounds of implied consent is: what can reasonably be expected in the circumstances

---

60   *Cole v Turner* (1704) 87 ER 907.

61   While the action may still be brought in the absence of damage, yet if there is no actual damage or injury, the claimant will only be entitled to nominal damages unless the circumstances are particularly egregious in which case punitive or exemplary damages may be awarded.

62   An issue most relevant in the context of medical or similar procedures.

63   *In re F* [1990] 2 AC 1 at 72-73.

'I never said, 'I want to be alone'. I only said, 'I want to be let alone'. There is all the difference'.
Greta Garbo, actress

in which the subject has placed himself? The case law on this aspect of trespass has tended to arise out of situations which are sensitive, contentious or adversarial; for example, illegal or overzealous contact in contact sports; or touching or restraints by police or security guards outside those in legitimate exercise of their authority or privilege.

It is arguable that a celebrity or public figure has to accept more in the way of crowds and physical jostling at public events than the ordinary person. After all, how much more crowded must the world be expected to be for one who sells millions of copies of her recordings or who relies on millions of votes to stay at the top of her profession or calling?

Secondly, what comprises 'contact'? There has to be some direct physical interference with the person. Offensive or unreasonable touching, hitting with an airborne bullet or instrument, hosing with water, or tripping are clearly actionable.

When Heath Ledger and Michelle Williams were sprayed with water from a high pressure water pistol by three photographers in Sydney in January 2006 as they walked the red carpet to the premiere of 'Brokeback Mountain',[64] they would undoubtedly have had a legal action for trespass in the form of battery. Damages may not have been large, however, for Ledger: although the photographers, who claimed to be retaliating for Ledger allegedly spitting at them on a previous occasion, would not have been able to claim any defence of provocation, provocation may in some cases reduce punitive or exemplary damages, as the conduct and motives of all parties can be considered. This would not have been an issue though for Michelle Williams.[65]

But taking a photograph of someone involves no physical contact, as we see in Gordon Kaye's case. Gordon Kaye was the star of the long-running television comedy series, *Allo! Allo!* a spoof of the genre of Word War II dramas about resistance groups.[66] After suffering very serious head injuries when his car was hit by flying debris during a storm, Kaye was lying in a hospital bedroom. Despite notices prohibiting entry, a journalist and photographer from the *Sunday Sport* newspaper went in and attempted to interview him, taking photographs of him lying semi-conscious in bed. They intended to publish them with an article which claimed that he had agreed to an exclusive

---

64   Timmons, L, 'Heath Ledger Gets Squirted', 16 January 2006, <http://socialitelife.buzznet.com/2006/01/16/heath_ledger_gets_squirted.php>

65   'Sprayed Heath flies out', AAP, January 14, 2006, <www.smh.com.au/articles/2006/01/14/1137118993564.html?from=rss>.

66   Ironically, the series has come to attention again in a highly publicised privacy law case in England, discussed below – that involving Max Mosley, who was accused by the *News of the World* of partaking in sex games in role plays allegedly reminiscent of the *Allo! Allo!* depiction of German soldiers. See further discussion of Mosley's case below.

interview. An application was made on his behalf for an injunction to stop publication.

The case[67] is historic because it showed how, despite the best efforts of the judges in the case, English law at the time – 1991 – was almost powerless to stop the press from publishing the photographs which were the real cause for complaint. It also shows the very different path of English law to that in Germany, where the publication of photographs of Bismarck lying on his deathbed in 1889 led to an order that the photographs be destroyed, and provoked such outrage that changes were made to copyright legislation to give the subjects of the photographs protection that was far more extensive than that in most other countries. In that case, the destruction of the photographs was ordered on the basis that they had been obtained while trespassing.[68] We will see below that the idea that a trespasser should be prevented from exploiting and profiting from the 'fruits' of a trespass to land is well established and often the basis of injunctions against aggressive media crews to stop them broadcasting their film footage.[69] But trespass to land requires the claimant to prove a right of exclusive possession of the space invaded, and it may be that Kaye's legal advisers were unwilling to argue that he had such a right in a hospital room.

In the end, they hooked the remedy onto the claim by the paper that Kaye had given them an exclusive interview and had allowed them to photograph him: this was false, given that he was clearly in no state to be able to give informed consent, it was malicious (because they knew it was false) and it had caused him material damage (that is, the devaluing of his right to sell his story himself when he wanted to). Thus he had a claim for malicious or injurious falsehood, and as the court felt that damages would not be an adequate remedy (despite the assumed damage being monetary), he was entitled to an injunction.

Even if the newspaper had not explicitly claimed a 'scoop', it is possible that the publication of the photograph may have been taken to *imply* that Kaye had given his permission, thus still forming the basis for an injurious falsehood claim by innuendo,[70] but the success of such a claim would have been much less certain.

In the end it was a satisfactory result for Kaye but not so for the general development of the law – it would have been a landmark case if the court had recognised the wrongfulness of the taking of the photographs in the first place and of any publication of them, based on a right of privacy. But the court held

---

67   *Kaye v Robertson and Sports Newspapers Limited* (1991) 18 FSR 62. See also Markesinis, B, 'Our patchy law of privacy – Time to do something about it' (1990) 53 *Modern Law Review* 802.

68   All information about this case is derived from Zweigert, K and Kotz, H, (trans Tony Weir), *An Introduction to Comparative Law* (Oxford University Press, 3rd edn, 1998), p 688.

69   *Lincoln Hunt Australia Pty Ltd v Willesee* (1986) 4 NSWLR 457.

70   As an innuendo can form the basis of an imputation for defamation purposes, there seems no reason why it should not for injurious falsehood. See *Tolley v JS Fry and Sons Ltd* [1931] AC 333.

back from what they obviously thought would be 'judicial legislation', with Leggatt LJ saying that such a right had been disregarded in England for so long that it could be 'recognised now only by the legislature'.[71]

What the case did do was highlight the inadequacy of the tort action of trespass to the person when it comes to protecting people from non-contact harassment or interference.

Lord Justice Glidewell noted:

> [Counsel] for Mr Kaye could not refer us to any authority in which the taking of a photograph or indeed the flashing of a light has been held to be a battery. Nevertheless, I am prepared to accept that it may well be the case that if a bright light is shone into another person's eyes and injures his sight, or damages him in some other way, this may be in law a battery ... [but] there is no evidence that the taking of the photograph did in fact cause him any damage.[72]

Given that the action for trespass, since its earliest days, has not required proof of any actual damage, the legal reasoning in this statement seems flawed, but it does illustrate that the mere taking of a photograph will not found an action in trespass. The Court of Appeal was only too conscious of the gap in the law. Lord Justice Bingham remarking:

> This case ... highlights yet again, the failure of both the common law of England and statute to protect in an effective way the personal privacy of individual citizen ... If ever a person has a right to be left alone by strangers with no public interest to pursue, it must surely be when he lies in a hospital bed recovering from brain surgery and in no more that partial command of his faculties. It is this invasion of privacy which underlies the plaintiff's complaint. Yet it alone, however gross, does not entitle him to relief in English law ... We cannot give the plaintiff the breadth of protection which I would, for my part, wish.[73]

We shall see below that English law has progressed considerably since *Kaye v Robertson* to improve the legal protections against disclosure and publication of obviously private circumstances or information. The sentiments of Lord Bingham would today provide some security to a person, celebrity or not, lying ill in hospital, and, since the case of *Campbell v MGN,* discussed below, it is unlikely that Kaye would need to rely on the action of injurious falsehood to prevent the *publication* of the photographs.[74] While restricting the potential for publication will undoubtedly negate or reduce the incentive to intrude in the first place, it would be even more comforting if the modern

---

71   (1991) 18 FSR 62 at 71.

72   Ibid at 68-69.

73   Ibid at 76.

74   Even by 1998, the European Court of Human Rights rejected Earl Spencer's argument that English law provided no protection against the publication of surreptitiously taken photographs of his wife in a rehabilitation clinic, on the grounds that he had not exhausted his domestic remedies. *Earl Spencer v United Kingdom* [1998] EHRRCD 105. In *Douglas v Hello! Ltd* [2001] 2 All ER 289 (CA), Keene LJ noted at [167] that it was unlikely that *Kaye v Robertson* would be decided in the same way by then ([2001] QB 967 at 1012).

law were also to provide some redress for the *intrusion* into his hospital room and the act of taking the photographs.[75]

Fruits of the trespass

Where the person threatening disclosure or publication did obtain the footage, photographs or information though a recognised wrong such as trespass onto the claimant's land, the complainant's position is strong. The law upholds and strongly enforces the idea that everyman's home is his 'castle', and that he is entitled to the strongest protection of the law, even or especially against government officials.[76]

As that great legal storyteller Lord Denning, Master of the Rolls,[77] said, in stirring language:

> The poorest man may in his cottage bid defiance to all the forces of the Crown. It may be frail – its roof may shake – the wind may blow through it – the storm may enter – the rain may enter – but the King of England cannot enter – all his force dares not cross the threshold of the ruined tenement'. So be it, unless he has justification by law.[78]

Members of the media, private citizens and government officials (except in circumstances clearly defined by statute or the common law[79]) are all subject to this fundamental limitation. They need the express or implied licence or permission of the occupier to enter, otherwise they will have committed a trespass. An initially lawful entry may become trespassory if the entrant does not leave within a reasonable time after permission is withdrawn.[80] While the courts have generally have found an implied licence (in the absence of an express or implied prohibition) for people to enter the *public part* of residential or business premises for various legitimate purposes, such as to make an enquiry or asking for assistance,[81] they have drawn the line at some of the more aggressive methods of investigative journalism, such as what has been described as 'a foot-in-the-door "walk-in" with cameras rolling and for

---

75   If the conduct was intentional and caused actual mental distress to the subject, it is possible that there would be an action for intentional infliction of emotional distress in the United States. Under Anglo-Australian law, the action might arise if the distress was intended or substantially certain to follow from the defendant's conduct. The law in both jurisdictions has developed from the precedent of *Wilkinson v Downton* [1897] 2 QB 57, but cases allowing recovery are much more prevalent in the US than in the other jurisdictions. See Schwartz, Kelly and Partlett, above n 16, p 50ff.

76   *Plenty v Dillon* (1991) 171 CLR 635 at 655 per McHugh and Gaudron JJ, 'nothing breeds social disorder as quickly as the sense of injustice which is apt to be generated by the unlawful invasion of a person's rights, particularly when the invader is a government official'.

77   The title given to the third most senior judge of England and Wales and chief judge of the Court of Appeal of England and Wales.

78   *Southam v Smout* [1964] 1 QB 308 at 320, adopting a quotation from the Earl of Chatham, quoted by Mason CJ, Brennan and Toohey JJ in *Plenty* (1991) 171 CLR 635 at 639.

79   *Plenty v Dillon* (1991) 171 CLR 635 at 647-648 per McHugh and Gaudron JJ.

80   *Kuru v New South Wales* [2008] HCA 26.

81   *Halliday v Nevill* (1984) 155 CLR 1 at 7.

the purpose of subjecting persons who are on the premises to a harassing interrogation'.[82] Clearly, too, the implied licence to enter even the public parts of premises may have been withdrawn by the occupier, making the entry trespassory from the beginning.[83]

Once a trespass has occurred, the occupier is able to use the full armoury of legal remedies. In addition, he or she – or employees or bodyguards on his or her behalf – may legitimately take some physical steps to remove the trespasser by force. This privilege, like all so-called 'self-help remedies', should of course be exercised with extreme caution, as an *excessive or unreasonable* use of force in removing a trespasser may itself constitute a trespass and give rise to liability.[84]

Damages may be awarded for the intrusion itself and for many foreseeable consequences. But often more important to the victim is preventing the disclosure of the material obtained from the intrusion. A court may issue an injunction[85] to restrain the trespasser from profiting from the 'fruits of the trespass' by broadcasting the footage or publishing the photographs.[86] Thus the court in *Lincoln Hunt Australia Pty Ltd v Willesee*[87] indicated that it would have restrained a television station from broadcasting footage obtained while trespassing if damages had not been an adequate remedy. It is arguable that, quite apart from any issues of privacy and confidentiality, but subject to a public interest test,[88] the courts should provide remedies which act as a general deterrence against and reduce the benefits of intrusions upon basic rights such as the rights of occupiers of private property. In Germany, for example, pictures obtained while trespassing must be destroyed.[89]

---

82   Butler and Rodrick, above n 37, p 408.

83   *Halliday* (1984) 155 CLR 1 at 7.

84   See, for example, *Horkins v North Melbourne Football Club Social Club* [1983] 1 VR 153. However, recent tort 'reform' in some States of Australia reduces the protection given to trespassers in the event of excessive use of force by the occupier; see, for example, *Civil Liability Act 2002* (NSW), s 53, which provides that a person using unreasonable force in self-defence or defence of property only incurs a liability if the circumstances are exceptional and the failure to award damages would be harsh and unjust.

85   Because an injunction is an 'equitable' remedy, it is awarded at the discretion of the court rather than by entitlement for a wrong.

86   *Lincoln Hunt Australia Pty Ltd v Willesee* (1986) 4 NSWLR 457; *Emcorp Pty Ltd v ABC* [1988] 2 Qd R 169. Note because it is thought unconscionable for a trespasser to profit from a trespass, the court may grant the injunction against the trespasser whether or not the information disclosed is confidential, and possibly even if it is a matter of legitimate public interest. See also *Rinsale Pty Ltd v Australian Broadcasting Corporation* [1993] Aust Torts Reports ¶81-231 at 62,380; *Takhar v Animal Liberation SA Inc* [2000] SASC 400. However, in *Australian Broadcasting Corporation v Lenah Game Meats* (2001) 208 CLR 199 at 230-231 Gleeson CJ seemed to support the availability of an injunction against a party to a trespass only where the information so obtained was confidential or private.

87   (1986) 4 NSWLR 457.

88   See *Australian Broadcasting Corporation v Lenah Game Meats* (2001) 208 CLR 199 at [137] and at footnote 151.

89   Zweigert and Kotz, above n 68, p 688, citing the rules of *condictio obiniustam causam* and the decision of (the German Imperial Court, Reichsgericht, 45, 170) in the case brought

More difficult is the case against a third party who came into possession of footage or photographs or information – which the occupier would not have allowed to be filmed or collected – from an unknown source. There is then no certainty that trespass occurred – the information may have been obtained by an insider. The third party is not necessarily implicated in any wrongdoing, so the 'fruits of the trespass' argument will not apply. In this situation, the subject will need to rely on a different, developing and less certain basis for protection – that is the law relating to misuse of confidential or private information. This is discussed in the 'Disclosure of Private Facts' sections below.

Just as contentious is the situation where information or footage was obtained during an initial entry which was unlawful but where permission was given by an employee of the occupier to the trespassers to remain which might be construed as a retrospective licence.

> In a case brought by Channel Seven against the ABC and *The Chaser* 'team',[90] Channel Seven sought an urgent interlocutory injunction to stop the ABC broadcasting footage of Channel Seven's studio and offices taken by the team as they entered to speak to newsreader Anna Coren and allegedly to film a 'stunt' with her co-operation. The judge who heard the urgent application felt that there were serious issues to be tried, including the effect of Ms Coren's invitation to the team into her office, and whether it retrospectively rendered the entry lawful. He made orders to preserve the status quo and prevent the broadcast for a short period to allow the parties to argue the matter more fully. The case was then settled between the parties.

As we have seen, trespass requires actual contact with the person to amount to a battery, threats of physical contact to amount to assault or physical intrusions directly onto property (or into airspace) to amount to a trespass to land. Where the 'intrusion' falls short of this, the subject of attention has to look to other legal bases for protection.

Nuisance

One such basis is the common law of nuisance which has long provided a remedy to supplement those provided by trespass to land. Concerned primarily with protecting the rights of occupiers of land, it has the potential to provide a significant degree of privacy protection for the occupier. Whereas trespass protects an occupier from direct and physical or tangible intrusions

---

against those who had trespassed into Bismarck's room and photographed his corpse. See below.

90   *Seven Network (Operations) Ltd v Australian Broadcasting Corporation* [2007] NSWSC 1289. 'The Chaser' is a satirical newspaper published by the defendant companies and their team who also write, produce and appear in a highly successful satirical television series, 'The Chaser's War on Everything', broadcast by the Australian Broadcasting Corporation.

onto land, the action of private nuisance is made out if a person causes an unreasonable interference, through his or her own unreasonable acts or omissions, with an occupier's use and enjoyment of the land in question. Usually this interference will be indirect as the source of the nuisance will be conduct or a state of affairs occurring *off* the occupier's land. Examples of conduct causing an actionable nuisance are: playing excessively loud music, conducting a business which involves patrons disturbing neighbours unreasonably, carrying out noisy building work at unreasonable hours, causing vibrations and damage by building work, polluting the air with fumes or smoke or insects, starting or not controlling a fire which escapes to damage neighbouring land, causing water to flood into a neighbour.

How does the law of nuisance protect privacy? It does so by protecting an occupier from continued surveillance from outside the land where the surveillance interferes with the rights of enjoyment and occupation of a property. The law of nuisance is, however, known as the law of 'give and take, live and let live'[91] and before surveillance will be actionable it must involve unreasonable conduct on the part of the defendant as well as an unreasonable interference with the plaintiff.

The decision of the High Court of Australia in *Victoria Park Racing and Recreation Grounds Co Ltd v Taylor* in 1937 was treated for many years as authority in Australia that the law of nuisance could provide no protection to an occupier from being overlooked by a neighbour or someone outside the property. Certainly Chief Justice Latham in that case stated categorically that there was then no precedent pointing to a 'general right of privacy'.[92] Evatt J, in a dissenting judgment, agreed with him but continued:

> neither is there an absolute and unrestricted right to spy on or to overlook the property of another person.

Legal developments since 1937 support this aspect of Evatt J's judgment and the plaintiff's lack of success in *Victoria Park Racing v Taylor* is seen as turning very much on the facts, rather than as an authority that nuisance may *never* protect an occupier from calculated and sustained surveillance.

Other claimants have been successful. In *Raciti v Hughes*,[93] the defendants, who lived in suburban Sydney, had installed floodlights and camera surveillance equipment on their own property which were positioned so that they would turn on, illuminate and record their neighbours' movements in the latter's own backyard. Young J held that this 'deliberate attempt to snoop on the privacy of a neighbour and to record that on video tape'[94] was an actionable nuisance. He likened the defendants' conduct to the old offence of 'watching and besetting'.

---

91   *Bamford v Turley* 3 B & S 66 (Ec Ch) at 82-4 per Baron Bramwell.
92   *Victoria Park Racing and Recreation Grounds Co Ltd v Taylor* (1937) 58 CLR 479 at 496.
93   (1995) 7 BPR 14,837.
94   Ibid, at 14,840.

In *Australian Broadcasting Corporation v Lenah Game Meats Pty Ltd,* the High Court of Australia effectively cleared the way for the development or future recognition of a general tort for unjustified invasion of personal privacy by leaving open the question of whether Australia should recognise such a tort. *Victoria Park Racing v Taylor* was seen as a case more about protecting the commercial interests of the occupier than one about privacy. In the case at hand, the claimants, Lenah Game Meats Pty Ltd, a corporate entity, tried to stop the ABC from broadcasting an unauthorised film, which had come into the ABC's possession, of their possum slaughter operations. But even if the law were to recognise a privacy action, Lenah could not rely on it. First, there was nothing 'private' about their operations. Second, privacy is a personal right or interest.

Chief Justice Gleeson noted:

> [T]he foundation of much of what is protected, where rights of privacy, as distinct from rights of property, are acknowledged, is human dignity.[95]

Justices Gummow and Hayne:

> Lenah is endowed with legal personality only as a consequence of the statute law providing for its incorporation. It is 'a statutory person, a *persona ficta* created by law' which renders it a legal entity 'as distinct from the personalities of the natural persons who constitute it' ... Lenah's activities provide it with a goodwill which no doubt has a commercial value. It is that interest for which, as indicated earlier in these reasons, it seeks protection in this litigation. But, of necessity, this artificial legal person lacks the sensibilities, offence and injury to which provide a staple value for any developing law of privacy.[96]

Australian Broadcasting Corporation v Lenah Game Meats was not a case about continued surveillance, harassment or stalking, indirect intrusion, watching or besetting, or the kind of interference that may have a real impact of the 'quiet enjoyment' of an occupier of her property. It was a case about disclosure. But the High Court's affirmation that the 1937 decision of *Victoria Park Racing v Taylor* does not stand in the way of greater protection of privacy – whether by actions of nuisance, breach of confidence or a stand alone privacy tort – was a significant legal development.

Aerial surveillance

The law has long had to deal with aerial intrusions and surveillance. We are all now used to helicopters hovering overhead when a special event is held or when a celebrity is town. But what if the helicopter chooses to hover over or near private property?

Before the advent of flying machines, there was a maxim of the law that would give some protection to an occupier against intrusions into the airspace immediately above her property: *cuius est solum eius est usque ad coelum et usque ad inferos* – whoever owns the surface owns the space up to the sky

---

95   *Australian Broadcasting Corporation v Lenah Game Meats* (2001) 208 CLR 199 at 226, [43].
96   Ibid at 256, [126].

and down to the depths of the earth beneath. While this was useful for fixed or temporary incursions like overhanging signs or awnings or scaffolding or cranes, it is impracticable in the context of modern aviation.

What for example is to stop paparazzi from setting up camp outside Nicole Kidman's, Elton John's or Amy Winehouse's home and waiting for a shot of them leaving or entering?

Lord Bernstein, a prominent media owner (and Chairman of Granada Television), was unable to complain in trespass or nuisance when a commercial photographer took aerial photographs of his country estate from a flight over the property (as the photographer had done of many properties over a period of 17 years in the business), before offering to sell them to him. As occupier, Bernstein's rights only extended to a height necessary for the ordinary use and enjoyment of his land and the structures upon it. The flight hundreds of feet above did not interfere in anyway with his enjoyment of his property. He was not even aware that it had occurred until offered the photographs. The judge, Griffiths J, noted:

> The plaintiff's complaint is not that the aircraft interfered with the use of the land but that a photograph was taken from it. There is, however, no law against taking a photograph, and the mere taking of a photograph cannot turn an act which is not a trespass into the plaintiff's airspace into one that is a trespass.[97]

But, as to a nuisance action, Griffiths J did note:

> Nor would I wish this judgment to be understood as deciding that in no circumstances could a successful action be brought against an aerial photographer to restrain his activities.[98]

As well as the difficulty of bringing claims for aerial interference within common law torts such as trespass, for direct incursions, and nuisance, for indirect interference, the claimant is also restricted by statutory protections of aircraft in many jurisdictions. These, for example, may exempt aircraft from liability for the mere act of flying over property, as long as the height is reasonable and the flight otherwise complies with air navigation regulations.[99]

---

97   *Bernstein of Leigh (Baron) v Skyviews & General Ltd* [1978] QB 479 at 488. Note, however, that in cases of entry onto premises by permission or implied licence, the permission may be subject to conditions such as that no photograph will be taken or the implied licence may not include permission to photograph or film. If the condition is breached or the implied license exceeded, the presence of the photographer on the land is then unlawful and trespassory. See *TCN Channel Nine Pty Ltd v Anning* (2002) 54 NSWLR 333.

98   *Bernstein* [1978] QB 479 at 489.

99   Eg, *Damage by Aircraft Act 1952* (NSW). The English equivalent legislation, the *Civil Aviation Act 1949*, was a further basis on which the plaintiff failed in *Bernstein* [1978] QB 479. Note, however, that if the hovering helicopter dropped a camera onto one of the guests or the occupier's roof, any physical damage would be compensable under the legislation without the need to prove fault: *Damage by Aircraft Act 1952* (NSW); *Damage by Aircraft Act 1999* (Cth).

However, if these statutory conditions are not met, the celebrity whose wedding is disrupted by unreasonably low hovering helicopters over or near his own property, or the owner of the property who runs a business providing a wedding venue and whose business is damaged by the helicopters, could well argue a claim in trespass or nuisance if the flight did in fact intrude at an unreasonable height or interfere with the quiet enjoyment of the property. The difficulty, of course, will be preventing the incursion in the first place, as it is inconvenient to delay the ceremony to rush off to court for an injunction. Hence the most practical weapon is a combination of secrecy and a remote location. No doubt Russell Crowe had this in mind when he got married at his rural property on the north coast of New South Wales.

Statutory restrictions on intrusions

Increasingly, in all jurisdictions, there is legislation dealing with the more flagrant and non-controversial forms of intrusion, harassment and surveillance, whether in the course of investigative journalism or otherwise. Breach amounts to a criminal offence. Legislation prohibiting the use of listening, recording and surveillance devices or the interception of telecommunications[100] is widespread, as is legislation dealing with harassment. These are dealt with in detail in texts on media law.[101]

In the United Kingdom, the *Protection from Harassment Act 1997* gives wide relief against conduct which amounts to harassment. Harassment caught by the Act is a criminal offence and can also be the subject of civil proceedings. A court may issue an injunction or a restraining order. It is a defence if the person alleged to be harassing another is acting reasonably: Geoffrey Robertson QC and Andrew Nicol QC argue that a journalist could show reasonableness by proving compliance with a professional code of conduct.[102] However, as it is likely that the code will use reasonableness as a measure of acceptable conduct, it could be said that this will not provide much guidance to the court.

Disclosure of private facts and protection of confidences

Although there seems to be an unstoppable flood of 'revelations' about celebrities on every newsstand, every television station and countless websites, there is a nevertheless a long history of celebrities, royalty or other public figures taking legal action to restrain or prevent the disclosure or publication of private information, in whatever form it may take: newspaper or journal arti-

---

100   For example, *Listening Devices Act 1984* (NSW), *Criminal Code* (Qld) s 227A(1), *Surveillance Devices Act 1999* (Vic), *Telecommunications (Interception) Act 1979* (Cth).
101   Butler and Rodrick, above n 37, pp 386-98.
102   Robertson, G and Nicol, A, *Robertson and Nicol on Media Law* (Sweet and Maxwell, 5th edn, 2007), p 310. See also Lunney, M and Oliphant, K, *Tort Law Text and Materials*, (Oxford University Press, 3rd edn, 2008), p 72.

cles and photographs, books such as 'tell-all' biographies or autobiographies, pictorial or photographic images, and now Internet images.

In countries whose legal system is based on British law, the most common basis for protection was the action recognised by the courts of equity for breach of confidence. In one of the leading modern cases on this action, the judge referred to a couplet attributed to Sir Thomas More (Lord Chancellor from 1529 until his execution by order of Henry VIII in 1535) that

> Three things are to be helpt in Conscience;
> Fraud, Accident and things of Confidence.[103]

Closely related to the action for breach of fiduciary duties,[104] the action originally depended upon the relevant information having been imparted or collected in a relationship of 'trust and confidence' or under an express or implicit obligation or duty to keep it confidential. We will see later how this requirement has recently been discarded in the United Kingdom, under the influence of the European Convention of Human Rights, so that the legal action has been transformed into one with a much wider reach, resting primarily on the *nature* of the information, rather than the circumstances of its origin and source. The modern action in the United Kingdom is now much closer to the action for disclosure of private facts recognised in the United States and elsewhere.

Despite this development, there remains a place for the traditional form of the action for breach of confidence because it protects, limits and enforces the *relationship* or *duty* as much as the information itself. When the Prince of Wales or a famous singer seeks a remedy against a former employee or friend or other confidante, he is asserting and enforcing the *obligations* of confidence and trust and deterring others from the temptation of breaching those obligations.

It was another prince whose legal action clarified the basis and elements of the equitable action in the 19th century. Queen Victoria used to spend a lot of time alone, and with her consort Prince Albert, drawing and etching

---

103   Megarry J in *Coco v AN Clark (Engineers) Ltd* [1969] RPC 41 at 46; (1968) 1A IPR 587 at 590, quoted by Meagher, RP, Heydon, JD and Leeming, MJ, *Meagher, Gummow and Lehane's Equity: Doctrines and Remedies*, (LexisNexis Butterworths, 4th edn, 2002), p 1114, who define 'Conscience' as a reference to the Court of Chancery, that is, the Chancellor's court which was the source of all equitable principles.

104   Fiduciary duties are duties of loyalty and utmost good faith, recognised originally by the courts of equity, in relationships where the fiduciary is bound to act in the interests of the beneficiary or principal rather than his or her own interests, to avoid conflicts of interest and not to make unauthorized profits from the exercise of the duty. Fiduciary duties relate to property and opportunities related to property or transactions. The most obvious example of a fiduciary is a trustee, but other well recognised examples are directors of companies, partners, agents, and lawyers. If such a relationship is present, it may be the more appropriate basis for protection against the exploitation or appropriation of information or opportunities. But the duty of confidence is useful where the fiduciary duty does not exist, see, for example, *LAC Minerals Ltd v International Corona Resources Ltd* [1989] 2 SCR 574; (1989) 61 DLR (4th) 14. See also Meagher, Gummow and Lehane, above n 103, pp 1116-17, on the similarities and overlap.

portraits and family scenes. She gave many of her drawings to close friends and to members of her entourage and household. Some can now be seen in places like Woburn, where Prince Albert and Queen Victoria visited and stayed the night in 1841,[105] a few years before the case. Prince Albert, who did not always have an easy relationship with the press,[106] brought an action against William Strange to prevent him from publishing a catalogue containing descriptions of etchings drawn and made by the Queen, and advertising an exhibition of unauthorised copies or editions of the etchings. They had come into Strange's possession after an employee of the printer, Brown, to whom Prince Albert had entrusted them for printing, unlawfully made and sold the additional copies to a journalist.[107]

The Lord Chancellor Lord Cottenham first upheld an injunction on the basis of common law property rights in the works in question and then went on:

> But his case by means depends solely on the question of property; for a breach of trust, confidence or contract itself would entitle the Plaintiff to the injunction.[108]

This case illustrates how the action for breach of confidence had a different operation from the other remedies which Prince Albert would have had in these circumstances. He could have sued Brown for the breach of contract committed by Brown or his employees. Perhaps he could have sued him too for the tort of conversion (wrongful dealing) of the etchings. He could probably have prevented the unauthorised publication and exhibition of the etchings themselves as a breach of copyright. But he wanted to prevent any disclosure of information *about* them. He wanted to keep them entirely private.

In *Prince Albert v Strange*, the relevant information was entrusted in the course of a contract between Prince Albert and Brown. In many cases, the obligation of confidence may have been an express or implied term of the contract, and in such cases the obligation and remedy will depend on the interpretation of the contract,[109] but it is clear from other case law that the obligation of confidence does not depend on a contractual relationship between the parties. The obligation and the remedy have their source in the principles of equity: rather than the contractual terms, the equitable obligation has at its heart 'the reposing of confidence and its abuse'.[110] In any event, Strange was a third party to any contract between Prince Albert and Brown, so that a remedy against him would have to rest in the equitable jurisdiction.

---

105   'Queen Victoria's Bedroom', Woburn Abbey official website, at <www.woburnabbey. co.uk/the_abbey/queen_victoras_bedroom.php>.

106   Plunkett, J, *Queen Victoria: first media monarch* (Oxford University Press, 2003).

107   Ibid, p 214 ff.

108   *Prince Albert v Strange* (1850) 1 H&TW 21 at 23; (1849) 2 De G & Sm 652.

109   Meagher, Gummow and Lehane, above n 103 at #41-020.

110   Ibid at #41-020.

Lord Cottenham also referred to an earlier comment by Lord Eldon in the case of *Wyatt v Wilson* in 1820 involving 'an engraving of George III during his illness; in which ... [Lord Eldon] said, 'If one of the late king's physicians had kept a diary of what he had heard and seen, this Court would not in the king's lifetime, have permitted him to print or publish it'.[111]

As developed in cases through the second half of the 20th century, the traditional action for breach of confidence had three requirements, the classic exposition of which was set out by Megarry J in a case about a moped design in 1969:[112]

- the information must be (still[113]) confidential or have the necessary quality of confidence; it must be worthy of protection;
- it must have been imparted in circumstances importing an obligation of confidence;
- there must be an unauthorised use or a real risk[114] of unauthorised use.

Opinions differed as to whether the claimant need also show some loss or detriment or the risk of it. It is now generally accepted that he or she need not do so: the wrong, the abuse of confidence, is also the injury.[115]

While most of the 20th century actions related to trade secrets, development opportunities, commercially sensitive information, state secrets, or information imparted to professional advisors, various celebrities had mixed success using the breach of confidence action to restrain the publication of their intimate or family lives and relationships. Much depended on whether the information was still confidential or already out in the public arena, and on how publicly the celebrity had been in publicising their private life previously. If they had previously been happy to talk about or expose or even use their private lives to promote their fame or image, they could not suddenly ask for protection when their spouse did the same.

---

111   *Prince Albert v Strange* (1850) 1 H&TW 21 at 25.

112   *Coco v AN Clark* [1969] RPC 41 at 47-8; (1968) 1A IPR 587 at 590-591 per Megarry J.

113   Whether or not the information in question, that is, photographs of the Douglas-Zeta-Jones wedding, was still confidential at the time of the alleged breach was an issue in *Douglas v Hello! (No 3)* [2007] 2 WLR 920 at 958-959 [122] per Lord Hoffmann: 'Once information gets into the public domain, it can no longer be the subject of confidence ... But whether this is the case or not depends on the nature of the information. Whether there is still a point in enforcing the obligation of confidence depends on the facts'. If an injunction would be futile, the claimant is left with only compensatory remedies or the remedy of an account of the defendant's profits. In the *Spycatcher* litigation, the British government was unsuccessful in stopping the republication of extracts from the book written by Peter Wright, a former British secret agent, because the once-confidential information was already in the public domain: *Attorney General v Guardian Newspapers Ltd (No 2)* [1990] 1 AC 109. See also *Australian Football League v The Age Company Ltd* (2006) 15 VR 419: gossip and innuendo on Internet discussion sites about the results of players' drug tests did not mean that information subject to a contractual confidentially agreement had lost its confidential nature.

114   *Bolkiah (Prince Jefri) v KPMG* [1999] 2 AC 222 at 237 per Lord Millett.

115   Meagher, Gummow and Lehane, above n 103 at #41-050.

John Lennon was unsuccessful when he brought an action against his former wife Cynthia and *The News of the World* to stop them publishing an article in which Cynthia would reveal 'How Yoko stole my husband …'. Lord Denning, then Master of the Rolls commented:

> John Lennon is a person of some notoriety having been a member of a pop group called The Beatles.[116]

He went on that although the court will protect confidences arising out of marriage:

> That may well be in normal marriages, but I cannot say, looking at this case, that either of these two parties have had much regard for the sanctity of marriage. The story that was published last week was bad enough but, as long ago as 1972, there was a long article in the *News of the World* by a former chauffeur which exposed the immorality and misdeeds of this couple and others in their goings-on … It seems to me as plain as can be that the relationship of these parties has ceased to be their own private affair. They themselves have out it all in the public domain.[117]

The court in *Lennon* distinguished the case of *Argyll v Argyll* in which the Duke of Argyll was prevented by an injunction from revealing the secrets about his former wife's personal life, private affairs and conduct which had been disclosed or known to him during their marriage. The court emphasised the policy of the law to uphold and aid the preservation of marital relationships and to preserve the close confidence and mutual trust between wife and husband. The court rejected several arguments by the Duke that the Duchess had lost the right to this protection by her own behaviour. One of these was that she herself had published some articles in *The Sunday Mirror* the year before in which she had betrayed *his* rights by disclosing that he had been taking 'purple hearts' (drinamyl) tablets, and that he had relied on financial help from others to save his castle. Although she herself had breached the marital confidences, the judge described his revelations as 'of an altogether different order of perfidy'.[118] Her previous disclosures did not disentitle her to the court's protection.

The second element identified by Megarry J, that the information was imparted under a relationship or obligation of confidence, was satisfied in most of the cases. Such an obligation was easily recognisable, whether or not arising out of a contract or just the nature of the relationship, in government, employment, agency, commercial and professional cases, and in the more private sphere, in medical, religious, matrimonial and family circumstances. But there is no closed list of categories of confidential relationships and a party may be able to argue that a particular relationship involves an express or implied obligation of confidence.

---

116   *Lennon v News Group Newspapers Ltd and Twist* [1978] FSR 573.
117   Ibid at 574.
118   *Argyll (Duchess) v Argyll (Duke)* [1967] 1 Ch 302 at 331 per Ungoed-Thomas J.

The Princess of Wales sprints from the gym

For example, when surreptitiously-taken photographs of Diana, Princess of Wales using gym equipment were leaked to the press by the gym manager and published in *The Sunday Mirror*, she was unable to rely on any contractual obligation because she had accepted the gym's offer of free membership. Nevertheless she had been assured by the manager that her visits would be confidential. While the gym was open to anyone else who paid the fees, and she often shared the gym with other members, she would still be able to rely on this *undertaking* of confidence. The gym would have had no defence – it quickly offered to hand over the photographs and profits – but the Princess also sued the paper. The paper was set to argue that it had published the pictures in the public interest, to show how lax her security protection was, and although this was clearly disingenuous, their defence would mean that the Princess would be subject to cross-examination in court on her attitudes to her own and others' privacy. The case settled a few days before the trial.[119] (Geoffrey Robertson, who acted on legal aid for the gym, and Andrew Nicol write that she discontinued the action and that 'she secretly paid the gym owner/defendant a vast sum of money to pretend that he had lost the case'.[120])

In *A v B plc* in 2003, the case involved an unidentified married professional footballer, two women with whom he had had affairs and the media: the judge described it as a situation that is 'popularly called "kiss and tell"'[121] The relationships between the man and the women was held to be such as to give rise to a duty of confidence. The trial judge followed what was said in an earlier case involving a confidential revelation of a lesbian affair with a married third party where the court had said: 'To most people the details of their sexual lives are high on the list of those matters which they regard as confidential'.[122] The obligation of confidence was inherent in any personal relationships of this nature. In Australia, too, 'kiss and tell' information is

---

119   Robertson, G, *The Justice Game* (Chatto & Windus, 1998) p 353.
120   Robertson and Nicol, above n 102, p 267.
121   *A v B plc* [2001] 1 WLR 2341 at 2342 per Jack J.
122   *Stephens v Avery* [1988] Ch 449 at 454 per Browne-Wilkinson VC.

accepted as being obviously confidential or private, and readily restrained by an injunction if sought in time: the problem has been rather what remedy to give *after* a revelation.[123]

Where the information in 'kiss and sell' stories is a mixture of information, the former lover may have less success. In *Browne v Associated Newspapers Ltd*, in 2007, the chief executive of the multinational BP corporation sought injunctions to restrain the publication of his relationship with his former partner, 'C' and information which C had obtained during the relationship. Because he had frequently appeared with C at parties and other public events, the fact of the homosexual relationship was no longer confidential.[124] Eady J also held, applying the principles in *Campbell v MGN* discussed below, that Browne no longer had a reasonable expectation of privacy about the relationship. While he did grant an injunction to prevent disclosure of information revealed to C during the relationship in private conversations, such as Browne's views about his colleagues, about which there was no over-riding public interest, the injunction did not cover allegations of misuse of corporate information and resources or of breaches of corporate confidentiality.

Perhaps the most important development for the potential of the action for breach of confidence to form the basis of privacy protection was the speech of Lord Goff of Chieveley of the House of Lords in *Attorney General v Guardian Newspapers Ltd (No 2)*,[125] in which he questioned the requirement for a pre-existing relationship or obligation of confidence between the parties. The issue arises first when a defendant happens upon confidential information. Lord Goff gave the examples of an 'obviously confidential document ... wafted by an electric fan out of a window into a crowded street' or a 'private diary ... dropped in a public place'.[126] To these we could add numerous examples, the misdirected 'confidential' letter, fax or email; the accidentally overheard confidential conversation. Secondly, it arises when a person deliberately seeks out the information by behaviour which falls short of unlawful intrusion or harassment. Thirdly, it arises when information imparted between two parties is passed on to a third party by one of them in breach of the initial obligation.[127]

123   See *Giller v Procopets* [2008] VSCA 236, discussed below.

124   *Browne v Associated Newspapers Ltd* [2007] EMLR 19, per Eady J. The principle of *Bonnard v Perryman* [1891] 2 Ch 269 became relevant to whether or not to grant an injunction once defamatory material was involved.

125   [1990] 1 AC 109.

126   Ibid at 281.

127   In this last example, there is a clear analogy to be drawn between the position of a third party to a breach of a fiduciary duty (such as that of a trustee to a beneficiary of a trust, or of a lawyer to her client) where the liability of the third party depends on whether or not she had sufficient notice or knowledge of the primary duty to make her participation in the breach or her receipt of the benefits dishonest. See Meagher, Gummow and Lehane, above n 103 at #41-110, #41-035. But as to whether information should be treated as property, see now *Farah Constructions Pty Ltd v Say-Dee Pty Ltd* (2007) 230 CLR 89.

Lord Goff formulated the principle as follows, although subject to certain limitations[128] (such as public interest favouring disclosure):

> [A] duty of confidence arises when confidential information comes to the knowledge of a person ... in circumstances where he has notice, or is held to have agreed, that the information is confidential, with the effect that it would be just in all the circumstances that he should be precluded from disclosing the information to others.[129]

By the time the Earl Spencer, the brother of the late Princess of Wales, brought a petition to the European Court of Human Rights in 1998[130] to complain that British law did not provide a remedy where the press had published a surreptitiously taken photograph of his wife in the garden of a private clinic, the government of the United Kingdom was able to defend the action by pointing to this widening principle. As it now protected the unauthorised disclosure of confidential information as such, it could well afford its citizens a reasonable protection of privacy, if only Earl Spencer had availed himself of the legal action.

In the same year, the United Kingdom passed the *Human Rights Act 1998*. This Act, which effectively required the courts to give effect to the provisions of the rights and freedoms guaranteed under the *European Convention on Human Rights*, quickly had a transformative effect on the law of the United Kingdom in this context, as it was applied in cases before the lower courts.[131]

> The language has changed ... We now talk about the right to respect for private life and the countervailing right to freedom of expression.[132]

The English protection of confidential information and the consequent protection of privacy took a giant leap in 2004 with the House of Lords decision in *Campbell v MGN*. Not only did it give the House of Lords the opportunity to consider squarely the wider principle formulated by Lord Goff and the effect of the *Human Rights Act 1998* in this context, but it was also clear acknowledgement by the highest court in the land that English law must now comply with the conventions to which the United Kingdom as a member of the European Community is a signatory, or risk an embarrassing decision of the European courts that it does not. But as we will see, there is still scope for disagreement and uncertainty as to what degree of privacy protection compliance with the European covenants requires, and in particular how much weight should be given to protection of privacy in the delicate balancing act with freedom of speech and the related freedom of the press.

---

128   [1990] 1 AC 109 at 282.

129   Ibid, at 281. See also *Hellewell v Chief Constable* [1995] 1 WLR 804 at 807, *Venables and Thompson v News Group Newspapers Ltd* [2001] Fam 430.

130   *Earl Spencer v United Kingdom* (1998) 25 EHRR CD 105. See also *A v B plc* [2003] QB 195 at 207.

131   Phillipson, G, 'Transforming Breach of Confidence? Towards a Common Law Right of Privacy under the Human Rights Act' (2003) 66 *Modern Law Review* 726.

132   *Campbell v MGN Ltd* [2004] 2 WLR 1232 at [86] per Lord Hope.

Before we look at these current English developments, we will first survey the some of the European legal scene in this context, and see how varied and with what different constitutional and juridicial origins the protection of privacy has developed in two large and neighbouring European countries, Germany and France.

Marlene Dietrich, Brigitte Bardot, the Aga Kahn, Jean-Marie Le Pen, Charlie Chaplin, and President Mitterrand's family have all taken successful and sometimes lucrative legal actions to protect their privacy.

Protection of disclosure of private matters in European law

In striking contrast to the common law, that is, the law built up over centuries by judicial decisions, of England and countries sharing an English heritage, the civil law of Europe is predominantly codified. In France, it was so in the Code Civil or Code Napoleon first enacted in 1804. In Germany, it is the Civil Code of 1900 or Burgerliches Gesetzbuch known as the 'BGB' and the Constitution or Basic Law (Grundgesetz – 'GG') introduced in 1949.[133]

The leading academic comparative lawyers, Zweigert and Kotz, argue convincingly[134] that the practical differences between judicial methods in common law and civil law countries are greatly exaggerated. Civil law judges do, in fact, look to decisions of other courts and not just to the code, and in most common law countries there has been such an explosion of legislation throughout the 20th century that common lawyers, too, must increasingly interpret and apply the words of a statute. Certainly, the distinction between common and civil law systems is not as important today as it might once have been. This is particularly so in the context of privacy protection where rights tend to derive from legislative instruments such as international conventions, declarations, constitutions, and local legislation, so that courts across many countries see their task as one of *interpretation* rather than of original development of the law.

In both French and German law, celebrities have played a key role in forging and enforcing privacy protection, not just by relying on explicit protections of privacy but also by extending the protection given to 'rights of personality', rights to a 'family life' and so on. Celebrities are often seen as 'figures of contemporary society or 'public figures' and include generals, emperors, presidents, princesses, actors, writers.

The French law of privacy and 'la vie privée'. French celebrities like Catherine Deneuve say they could not live anywhere else but France, and this is not just because of '*formidable*' superiority of French style, French fashion, French manners, French food, French countryside, French wine … French

---

133 Beverley-Smith, H, Ohly, A and Lucas-Schloetter, A, *Privacy, Property and Personality: Civil law perspectives on commercial appropriation*, at 94ff. Italy too has powerful privacy laws including court powers to imprison offenders: see Owen, R, 'Berlusconi beauties add fuel to privacy row', *The Times*, 19 April 2007.

134 Zweigert and Kotz, above n 68, ch 18.

'je ne sais quoi'. It is because they have long been afforded protection for their private lives which has had no equal in other western nations. Princess Caroline of Hannover was readily able to prevent the republication of certain photographs in France, yet she had to take her case through several courts to gain similar protection under German law.

Marlene Dietrich, Brigitte Bardot, the Aga Kahn, Jean-Marie Le Pen, Charlie Chaplin, and President Mitterrand's family have all taken successful and sometimes lucrative legal actions to protect their privacy.

As in Germany, the protection developed out of a 'celebrity deathbed' case, but there was a key difference in that legal response was to develop existing principles rather than to enact a new statutory protection. In the 1858 case known as the *Rachel* case,[135] the sister of Rachel, a famous actress, had commissioned a photographer to photograph her dying sister's last moments, subject to an express undertaking that the photographs were not to be revealed to anyone else. Soon afterwards, a drawing which was obviously based on the photographs, appeared for sale. Rachel's sister successfully sued the photographer and the artist, seeking destruction of all copies and drawings. The court based its order on the fundamental tort protections in the French Civil Code, in which Art 1382 provides for liability based on fault:[136]

> Any act whatever of man, which causes damage to another, obliges the one by whose fault it occurred, to compensate it.[137]

The court held:

> No-one may, without the explicit consent of the family, reproduce and bring to the public eye the image of an individual on her deathbed whatever the celebrity of the person involved ... The right to oppose reproduction is absolute. It finds its foundation in the respect which the suffering of families demands ...[138]

Jeanne Hauch has pointed out[139] that this statement of principle was absolute in its terms, effectively imposing a strict liability for publication without consent rather than one based on fault. Further, it developed the protection of privacy rights as one of a collection of 'personality rights', closely allied to but more extensive than copyright as a property right, which also includes the moral rights of creators, the right to control the use of one's image and

---

135   Judgment of June 16, 1858, Tribunal de Premiere Instance de la Seine, 1858 DP III 62 (Fr) (*affaire Rachel*). Our account is based on the very useful analysis of the case by Hauch, JM, 'Protecting Private Facts in France: The Warren & Brandeis Tort is Alive and Well and Flourishing in Paris' (1994) 68 *Tulane Law Review* 1219 at 1231ff. See also Beverley-Smith, Ohly and Lucas-Schloetter, above n 133, p147 ff.

136   'Fault' in tort law generally consists of intentional wrongdoing, in the sense that the actor subjectively intended the interference or harm, or objectively must be taken to have intended it because it was so likely or obvious that it would follow; or negligence, in the sense that the actor's conduct fell below the standard of a reasonable person.

137   Beverley-Smith, Ohly nd Lucas-Schloetter, above n 133, p 150 fn 17. It had long been recognised that the damage could be intangible damage such as emotional harm.

138   Translated in Hauch, above n 135 at 1233.

139   Ibid at 1234.

the right to protect reputation. The absolute nature of the restriction on publication without consent meant that, in France, a person could prevent publication of facts even if they had previously been made public.[140]

Cases involving celebrities developed the further protection of privacy in France. One of the most famous 20th century cases was that brought by Marlene Dietrich in 1955 against *France Dimanche* for revealing aspects of her sexual and private life in an article, by falsely representing that she herself had revealed them in her own words to a fictitious German journalist. The court of appeal upheld the judge's judgment for Dietrich, saying:

> [T]he recollections of each individual concerning her private life are part of her moral property ... no one may publish them, even without malicious intent, without the express and unequivocal authorization of the person whose life is recounted.[141]

It also upheld Dietrich's cross appeal on damages, increasing the damages awarded by the trial judge from 5000 to a massive 1,200,000 francs. The damage was not just for the intangible aspects of the invasion of her privacy, but also for the pecuniary damage in the impact on her potential to publish and profit from her own memoirs.

While the damages in the *Dietrich* case might have been deterrent enough, the celebrity's right to privacy was further strengthened by the decision ten years later granting the family of a well-known actor, Gerard Philipe, a restraining order to stop the publication of a sympathetic but intrusive article on the illness of his young son, including previously published photographs. The magazine's appeal on constitutional grounds, relying on the established liberty of the press,[142] failed because of the intolerable intrusion into the private life of the family, found by the judge, for a purely commercial goal.[143] The case sparked the perennial controversy over the balancing of the legitimate protection of privacy with that of freedom of the press and of expression, particularly as the former had been developed by courts while the latter was entrenched in legislative instruments.

A similar controversy over the legitimate role of judges is waging in Britain today as we write, after the *Mosley* decision discussed below, although it seems to be forgotten by some commentators that the courts are following

---

140   The extent to which republication of previously revealed information is still caught by privacy protection is controversial, as Hauch discusses later in her article, above n 135 at 1273 ff, in an analysis of the so called *Le Pullover Rouge* case. This case in 1979-1981 was about a film based on a book of that name concerning the murder of an eight year old child. The action was brought by her family to restrain the showing of the film.

141   *Marlene Dietrich* case, Judgment of 16 March 1955, Cour d'appel de Paris, 1955 DS Jur 295 (Fr) Translated by Hauch, above n 135 at 1238. See also Barendt E, *Freedom of Speech* (Oxford University Press, 2nd edn, 2005), p 240.

142   *Law on the Liberty of the Press*, July 29, 1881. Also *The Declaration of the Rights of Man of 1789*, Art 11; *French Constitution* Art 34. See Hauch, above n 135 at 1239.

143   Judgment of July 12, 1966, Cass civ 2e, 1967 DS Jur 181 (Fr). Hauch, above n 135 at 1241.

the written directives given in both a European convention and a local statute to effect some privacy protection.

That balancing act was weighed more heavily in favour of privacy with the legislative addition of new articles to the *Civil Code* in 1970. The new Art 9 states:

(1) Each individual has the right to require respect for his private life.

(2) Without prejudice to compensation for injury suffered, the court may prescribe any measures, such as sequestration, seizure and others, appropriate to prevent or put an end to an invasion of personal privacy; in case of emergency those measures may be provided for by interim order.[144]

The first part of the article really said nothing new. Clearly, the right to damages for a breach of this right was already well entrenched. Nor did it change the law, as already set out in *Rachel* and *Dietrich,* which requires consent for publication of someone's photograph: 'This [still] makes for a lot of black bars and electronic blotting of faces in the press and television'.[145]

It was the second part which has proved the most important, because it appeared to limit the availability of coercive remedies, such as pre-publication restraining orders, to situations where the intrusion was into the – not just private but – *'intimate'* aspects of a person's life. Privacy protection thus became deliberately two-tiered[146] and more nuanced.[147] Intimate aspects of one's life – sexuality, sexual orientation, relationships with partners and children – are effectively *always* private, for public figures and the ordinary person alike,[148] as the Aga Khan argued,[149] and even if previously disclosed, as Gunther Sachs, then husband of Brigitte Bardot, argued in 1971.[150]

> The French Cour de Cassation has adopted a consistent position that 'everyone whatever his rank, birth, fortune, present or future occupation, is entitled to a right to privacy'. However, infringements on someone's privacy may sometimes be held to be legitimate, especially when a public figure is involved ... [but the more nuanced approach] still requires that strong public interest justification be demonstrated where substantial breaches of privacy are at stake.[151]

More recent privacy cases in France dealing with privacy in the context of ill health or death include that brought by French actress Chantal Nobel in 1987

---

144 See <www.legifrance.gouv.fr/html/codes_traduits/code_civil_textA.htm#CHAPTER%20 I %20- %20OF%20THE%20ENJOYMENT>.

145 Campbell, M, 'French attitudes serve the powerful, but not the people', *The Sunday Times,* 27 July 2008, <www.timesonline.co.uk/tol/news/world/europe/article4407236>.

146 Hauch, above n 135 at 1243 quotes the 1970 parliamentary debates on the provision.

147 Markesinis, B, O'Cinneneide C, Fedtke J and Hunter-Henin M, n 17 above at 145.

148 Steiner, E, *The New President, His Wife and the Media: Pushing Away the Limits of Privacy Law's Protection in France?,* vol 13.1 *Electronic Journal of Comparative Law,* (March 2009), <www.ejcl.org/131/art131-4.pdf>.

149 Hauch, above n 135 at 1253, note 174, citing judgment of 23 Oct 1990, Cass civ Ire, 1990, Bull Civ I 158, no 222.

150 Beverley-Smith, H, Ohly A and Lucas-Schloetter A, above n 133, p 152, citing Cass, civ 2.1. 1971, *Gunther Sachs,* D 1971, jur, 263.

151 Markesinis, O'Cinneneide, Fedtke and Hunter-Henin, above n 17, pp 145-46.

over photographs of her leaving hospital after a serious road accident;[152] that brought in 2000 by the family of the Prefect of Corsica over magazine articles showing photographs of his body after his assassination;[153] and importantly, that brought in 1997 by the family of President Francois Mitterrand over a book written by his personal doctor entitled *Le Grand Secret*, in which the doctor revealed that the President had kept secret from his family and the nation for years the fact that he was suffering from cancer. Forty thousand copies of the book had already been sold. The Court of Appeal in Paris, in a controversial judgment, issued a permanent injunction against the further distribution of the book. Markesinis and others comment that the decision was probably motivated by the fact that the disclosure was in breach of the doctor's professional confidence.[154] The publisher successfully petitioned the European Court of Human Rights against the injunction, on the basis of Art 10 of the European Convention protecting freedom of expression. The court held that not only had the confidentiality of the material already been weakened by previous sales of the book and publication of excerpts on the Internet, but the family's interest in protecting President Mitterrand's right to privacy had weakened with the passing of time since his death, while the public interest in debate over his term of office had increased:

> The more time passed the more the public interest in President Mitterrand's two seven-year presidential terms prevailed over the requirements of the protection of his rights with regard to medical confidentiality.[155]

But while dead public figures may quickly lose their privacy protection in France if there is a strong public interest in their lives, the balance is much harder to swing in favour of the press while they are alive. A *Sunday Times* journalist, Matthew Campbell, recently commented that 'even the most innocent questions can provoke indignant protestations that this is la vie privée and therefore off limits. No French politician would tolerate the sort of torture that British officials are submitted to at the hands of [journalists]'.[156] He argues that by not revealing to a wider public what is known to a select coterie in Paris, the French media is an extension of power rather than a check against its abuses. This point is well made if there is indeed legitimate public interest in the relevant information, and he refers to a couple of situations where journalists themselves have not revealed their sometime intimate connections to politicians, thus undermining the objectivity of their reporting or analysis. But it really begs the questions which arise whenever privacy and freedom of the press collide; what matters are legitimate public interest and

---

152   *Chantal Noble* case, Cass civ 1, 6 June 1987, Bull civ I no 191, discussed in Barendt, above n 141, p 238.

153   Ibid, p 239; case reference: Cass civ 1, 20 Dec 2000.

154   Above n 17 in fn 46.

155   *Plon (Société) v France*, App No 58148/00, May 18, 2004, quoted by the European Court of Human Rights in *Von Hannover v Germany* (2005) 40 EHRR 1 at [60]. See also Barendt, above n 141, p 242.

156   Campbell M, above n 145.

to what extent do public figures, particularly political public figures, have a right to privacy? It is at least arguable that the fundamental health of a political leader is a matter of public interest where it has the potential to have an impact on his or her performance of official duties. More controversial is the issue of his or her marital or sexual relationships or sexual preferences if no danger to security is involved. Undoubtedly cultural mores are reflected heavily in the way in which privacy laws are interpreted: the French just tend to shrug their shoulders in disbelief or yawn when anglicised notions of private morality are raised.

In contrast to President Mitterrand, who abhorred intrusions into his private life, President Sarkozy has ceaselessly used and welcomed publicity over his marital affairs, first during the divorce from his reluctant previous wife Cecilie and then during the very public courtship and marriage to his new wife, Carla Bruni. They have already been frequent litigants but not so much with complaints about invasions of privacy. Rather, they have relied on the principles which have their origins in the *Rachel* case to stop the unauthorised use of their *images* in commercial advertisements.

In January 2008 they sued Ryan Air which featured a photograph of the couple, at a public event, in an advertisement for cut price tickets in *Le Parisien* newspaper. It showed a 'bubble' of Carla, an Italian, saying 'Avec Ryanair, toute ma famille peut venir assister a mon mariage' ('With RyanAir, my whole family can come to my wedding'). RyanAir apologised. This claim followed a similar one against Ryan Air by the Swedish Prime Minister Goran Persson in 2007, a similar unlitigated advertisements involving Spanish Prime Minister Zapatero in 2006, and the Polish Prime Minister and a female MP in 2007.[157] Bruni sought damages of €500,000, representing her usual commercial fee, Sarkozy sought a symbolic one euro. The court in Paris granted his claim, and granted Bruni €60,000, significantly less than she had claimed. This was not a case of publication of a previously private photograph but one of a photograph for which the couple had posed at a public event. In such a case republication of their image without consent was not as serious. Ryanair offered to pay more damages to a charity, realising how profitable had been the advertisement, the claim and the resulting publicity.[158]

Commentators say that this and other recent cases in France show an increasingly less sympathetic attitude to celebrities or public figures who complain about revelations of previously revealed information. Examples are the 2002 claim by Princess Stephanie of Monaco over photographs of her with her ex-husband in a coffee shop: the court decided that she had been eager to publicise the divorce, so could not complain about this repetition of public facts. Similarly, Cecilia Sarkozy was unsuccessful in her claim against a journalist, to whom she had confided secrets about her marriage, when they were later published in a book.[159]

---

157   Easton, A, 'Ryanair faces legal row over ad', *BBC Online*, 23 May 2007.
158   'Sarkozy, Bruni win damages over RyanAir ad', *Sydney Morning Herald*, 6 February 2008.
159   Steiner, above n 148.

Nevertheless, the protection of privacy in France[160] is alive and well, as is the notion of 'une vie privée' which is very French, much to many journalists' frustration.

The German Law of Privacy

From Germany comes the most significant modern privacy case in European law, and one which may have far-reaching consequences for the freedom hitherto and recently exercised by the press throughout Europe in reporting the day-to-day life of celebrities: the case of *Von Hannover v Germany*[161] in 2004. In this decision, the European Court of Human Rights reviewed the extent to which the protection afforded by German law, including copyright legislation and the Constitution or 'Basic Law' (*Grundgesetz*) introduced after World War II, complied with Germany's obligations under Art 8 of the *European Convention for the Protection of Human Rights and Fundamental Freedoms 1950*, in the light of Art 10.

Article 8 of the *European Convention for the Protection of Human Rights and Fundamental Freedoms 1950*[162] provides:

1. Everyone has the right to respect for his or her private and family life, his home and his correspondence.
2. There shall be no interference by a public authority with the exercise of this right except such as is in accordance with the law and is necessary in a democratic society in the interests of national security, public safety or the economic well-being of the country, for the prevention of disorder or crime, for the protection of health and morals, or for the protection of the rights and freedoms of others.

Article 10 provides:

1. Everyone has the right to freedom of expression. This right shall include freedom to hold opinions and to receive and impart information and ideas without interference by public authority and regardless of frontiers ...
2. The exercise of these freedoms ... may be subject to such formalities, conditions, restrictions or penalties as are prescribed by law and are necessary in a democratic society for the protection of the reputation or rights of others, for preventing the disclosure of information received in confidence, or for maintaining the authority and impartiality of the judiciary.

The power and potential of Art 8 to provide greater protection for privacy and related interests had been enlisted and reinforced following the haunting and tragic death of Diana, Princess of Wales, in a Paris road-tunnel in

---

160   And in jurisdictions with French ancestry, such as Quebec. See *Aubry v Éditions Vice-Versa* [1998] 1 SCR 591.

161   (2005) 40 EHRR 1, <http://echr.coe.int/echr>. Much of the author's analysis of this case below was written originally for an article published in the *New York Law School Law Review*, following a 2004 forum on defamation and privacy law at that law school. See McDonald, B, 'Privacy, Princesses, and Paparazzi' (2005-2006) 50 *New York Law School Law Review* 205.

162   Rome, 4 November 1950; TS 71 (1953); Cmd 8969.

1997 as she and Dodi Al-Fayed were trying to evade hordes of pursuing paparazzi. Her death and the outcry that followed had triggered a debate in the Parliamentary Assembly of the Council of Europe in 1997 leading to a Resolution[163] on the right to privacy, which called on governments of Europe to ensure that they had in place rules of law or legislation enshrining the effect of Art 8 of the European Convention,[164] which all member states, including the United Kingdom and Germany, had ratified.

Germany had its own Constitutional protection of human dignity and personality.

Article 1(1) of the Basic Law provides:

> The dignity of human beings is inviolable. All public authorities have a duty to respect and protect it.

Article 2(1) provides:

> Everyone shall have the right to the free development of their personality provided that they do not interfere with the rights of others or violate the constitutional order or moral law.

Article 2 (1) of the Basic Law had been invoked some years before by another princess. In 1973, Princess Soraya, the beautiful former Empress of Iran, brought an action over the publication of a fictitious interview in a magazine. This case is regarded as developing the protection of a right of personality given by Art 2(1). The Federal Constitutional Court held that there was no public interest in the dissemination of fictitious stories which would enable the rights of freedom of the press to prevail over her rights of personality, and awarded her damages in the nature of a solatium.[165]

In 1993 Princess Caroline (originally 'of Monaco' although she was later known as 'Caroline von Hannover' after her marriage to Prince Ernst August von Hannover) commenced actions in the German courts to stop the republication of certain photos by German publishing companies Hubert Burda Media and Heinrich Bauer in three popular magazines. The photographs depicted Princess Caroline in various *public places*: alone, or with a male companion, or with her children or husband, engaged in ordinary activities such as dining in a restaurant, shopping, on holidays, playing sport, and swimming at a club. All were accompanied by what were described by the Court as 'anodyne' headlines or descriptions, for example, 'Caroline and the blues' and 'The tenderest romance' and 'A woman returns to life'.[166]

---

163 Resolution 1165 of 1998.
164 Rome, 4 November 1950; TS 71 (1953); Cmd 8969.
165 *Soraya*, 34 BVerfGE 269 (1973)
166 The first series, the subject of first proceedings comprised five photos of Princess Caroline with actor Vincent Lindon at the far end of a restaurant garden in Provence, one photo of Princess Caroline on horseback and one of her on a bicycle, three photos of Princess Caroline with her two children and one of her son, two photos of her shopping, one photo of her with Vincent Lindon in a restaurant. The second series, the subject of second proceedings comprised ten of Princess Caroline on a skiing holiday, seven of Princess Caroline and her husband at a horse show in Provence, four of Princess Caroline leaving

Princess Caroline based her actions on both the breach of s 22 of the *Copyright (Arts Domain) Act*[167] and a breach of her right to protection of her personality rights under s 2(1) and s 1(1) of the Constitution or Basic Law.[168]

The *Copyright (Arts Domain) Act 1907* is a highly unusual way of dealing with privacy problems arising out of photography, and is best explained as an *ad hoc* political response, in the early days of photography, to a public scandal. It derives from an incident involving photos of Bismarck on his deathbed in 1889, taken by photographers stealing by night into his room, and from the scandal and politico-legal debate that followed.[169] The Federal Constitutional Court described it as seeking to strike a fair balance between personality rights and community interest in being informed.[170]

Section 22(1) provides that images can only be disseminated with the express approval of the person concerned, or for ten years after death, with the consent of the deceased person's relatives. Section 23(1) provides for an exemption from seeking the subject's permission where images relate to the domain of contemporary society on the condition, as set out in s 23(2), that publication does not interfere with a legitimate interest of the person concerned.

As discussed in Chapter 2, copyright laws normally protect the rights of the creator of a work, such as the photographer, not the subject. Generally, a person portrayed in a photograph will only have copyright in the photograph by express agreement with or assignment of the rights from the photographer, or where the photograph was commissioned by the subject.

The German law does not give the subject the copyright as such but, by requiring express approval to publication, gives the right to control publication or dissemination.[171]

---

her house in Paris, seven of her with her husband playing tennis or with bicycles. The third series, the subject of the third set of proceedings comprised a sequence of photos shot long range of Princess Caroline in swimsuit and towel tripping over something and falling at the Monte Carlo Beach Club.

167   The KUG (Kunsturhebergesetz – Copyright Act 1907).

168   See Zweigert and Kotz, above n 68, pp 690-691, where the authors note that the issue of whether a court judgment has properly balanced the interests of protection of personality rights and freedom of expression is now dominated by constitutional considerations and by decisions of the Federal Constitutional Court. The interplay between the 'private law' principles in the BGB and the public law articles in the German Constitution, particularly with respect to privacy law and as a predictor of the impact of the then proposed Human Rights legislation in the United Kingdom, is discussed by B Markesinis in 'Privacy, Freedom of Expression and the Human Rights Bill: lessons from Germany' (1999) 115 *Law Quarterly Review* 47.

169   This incident and the case that followed are discussed by H Zweigert and H Kotz, above n 68, p 688. The Reichsgericht upheld a claim by Bismarck's heirs to insist on destruction of the photographs as the defendants had obtained the pictures by trespassing on the property of others. (Reichsgericht 45,170).

170   Paragraph II(1) of Federal Constitutional Court judgment quoted in *Von Hannover* (2004) App No 59320/00 (Eur Ct HR June 24, 2004) at [25].

171   For detailed analysis of s 22 and s 23, see Beverley-Smith H, Ohly A and Lucas-Schloetter A, above n 133, p 105 ff.

The ability of the press to avoid the protection given by this German copyright provision depended on proving that Princess Caroline came within the exception relating to a 'figure of contemporary society'. Such a person does not have the right to control or veto publication.[172] The German courts accepted their argument with alacrity describing her as such a figure 'par excellence'.

In three sets of proceedings, Princess Caroline had only mixed success in the German courts. The first proceedings showed an interesting contrast between German law and the much more settled protection of privacy in neighbouring France, as she was readily able to prevent the further publication of the photographs in France where French law, particularly Art 9 of the French Civil Code, prevailed. But overall, she failed to prevent the republication of most of the photographs in Germany, when in the last appeal to the Federal Constitutional Court, it held that, for a 'figure of contemporary society *par excellence*', protection depended upon some interference with the person's 'private sphere' in a public place. This in turn depended on the place being sufficiently and objectively 'secluded'. A mere desire to be left alone was not relevant, nor was the surreptitious means by which the photo was taken a sufficient factor to render the publication a breach of privacy on its own. Princess Caroline did however succeed in stopping the re-publication of photographs of her out with her children, based on the protection given by s 6 of the Basic Law regarding a person's intimate relations with their children.[173] In a further action launched in the European Court of Human Rights, she argued that the criteria set down by the German courts for determining the boundaries of her 'private sphere' when out in public were so narrow that they failed to provide adequate protection of her privacy as required by Art 8.

Essentially, she argued that:

1. The concept of a 'secluded place' in public was too narrowly defined to be adequate protection.
2. The onus was placed on her to establish every time and often months after the relevant date that she had been in such a place and thus she was a constant target for the paparazzi.
3. The weaker German protection undermined the protection given to her by French law which protected her whenever she was not at an official event.
4. Interest in her was purely for entertainment and profit.

The German government, in defence of the courts and its legislation, argued that they had properly balanced the two competing interests of subject and press. The public had a legitimate interest in knowing how 'a figure of contemporary society *par excellence*' behaved in public. The secluded place

---

172   Whereas in France they still do. Barendt, above n 141, p 243.

173   Paragraph II(1)(c) (dd) of Federal Constitutional Court judgment quoted in *Von Hannover* (2005) 40 EHRR 1 at [25].

concept was not the only factor taken into account in regard to photos taken in public places: the nature of the photograph was also considered. The two magazine publishers and an industry Association also intervened to support the German law, (interestingly, they described it as half-way between French law and United Kingdom law[174]) stressing the wide definition of 'public figure', the blurring of the line between political commentary and entertainment, the fact that Princess Caroline was the official 'First Lady' of the Grimaldi family which had always sought media attention and finally the fact that the publications did not damage her reputation.

Princess Caroline was successful, with the European court holding that the limited protection given by the German court decisions violated Art 8 of the European Convention. However, the court stopped short of granting the monetary remedy sought by Princess Caroline, instead inviting the parties to make further submissions within six months, with a clear hint that by then they might have reached a settlement, which they did.

The decision rested on an sanalysis of the relevant German law, the 1998 Resolution of the Parliamentary Assembly of the Council of Europe and the balancing act required by Arts 8 and 10 of the European Convention of Human Rights, recognised in the Resolution as neither absolute nor in any hierarchical order: 'they are of equal value'.[175] The court also reviewed previous cases such as the *Mitterrand* case, where it had had to balance these interests.

In accepting Princess Caroline's arguments, the court made a number of points:

1. The case did not concern the dissemination of ideas, but of images containing very personal or even intimate information about an individual.
2. The photos showed her in scenes from her daily life, thus engaged in activities of a purely private nature such as practising sport, out walking, leaving a restaurant or on holiday.[176]
3. Princess Caroline does not exercise any function within or behalf of the State of Monaco although she does represent the ruling family of Monaco at certain cultural or charitable events. She was thus to be distinguished from politicians as to whom the public's democratic right to be informed might in special circumstances extend to aspects of their private life.[177] The situation does not come within the sphere of any political or public debate. The court disagreed with the German courts' categorisation of Princess Caroline as a 'figure of contemporary society "par excellence"' within the meaning of the *Copyright (Arts Domain) Act*, describing her rather as a '"private"

---

174   Ibid at [46].
175   Ibid, at para 11 of the Resolution.
176   *Von Hannover* (2005) 40 EHRR 1 at [61].
177   Ibid at [63]-[64].

individual'. In any event, that Act must be interpreted narrowly to ensure that the State complies with its positive obligations to protect privacy.

The court's conclusion was that the sole purpose of the publications was to satisfy the curiosity of a particular readership regarding details of Princess Caroline's private life and could not be deemed to contribute to any debate of public interest to society. Therefore, 'freedom of expression calls for a narrower interpretation … It does not mean that readers are entitled to know everything about public figures'.[178] Further, the fact that the photos were taken without her knowledge and consent and the harassment endured by many public figures in their daily lives cannot be fully disregarded.[179] Increased vigilance in protecting private life, even beyond the private family circle and into the social dimension, is necessary to contend with new communication technologies for taking, storing, transmitting and disseminating photos. The Convention is intended to guarantee practical and effective and not just theoretical or illusory rights.[180] An individual needs to be given precise indications by the law as to when and where they are or are not in a protected sphere.

The European Court of Human Rights considered that the spatial and functional criteria set down by the German courts had been too vague and too difficult to determine in advance to protect an individual's private life effectively: unless she can prove that she is in a secluded place, then as a 'figure of contemporary society "par excellence"' Princess Caroline would be forced to accept that:

> she might be photographed at almost any time, systemically, and that the photos are then very widely disseminated even if they relate exclusively to details of her private life.[181]

Rather,

> the decisive factor in balancing the protection of private life against freedom of expression should lie in the contribution that the published photos and articles make to a debate of general interest. It is clear in the instant case that they make no such contribution since [Princess Caroline] exercises no official function and the photos and articles relate exclusively to details of her private life [emphasis added]'.[182]

There was no legitimate public interest in knowing those details which could override her right to effective protection of her private life. Rather, she had a *legitimate expectation* that it would be protected. The German courts did not strike a fair balance between the competing interests: there had been a breach of Art 8.

---

178 Ibid at [66]-[67].
179 Ibid at [68].
180 Ibid at [71].
181 Ibid at [74].
182 Ibid at [76].

The ruling by the European Court of Justice was a highly significant victory for persons such as Princess Caroline. Professor Eric Barendt states that '[i]t is difficult to exaggerate the importance of this decision'.[183]

First, the case tested the definition of 'public figures': Princess Caroline's position appears to be borderline. She was born to the role rather than choosing it. She did not appear to rely on or benefit financially from publicity in a career. Like many members of families with inherited titles, she plays no governmental role but merely represents the family on public or charitable occasions. That is not necessarily the case with all members of a royal family. Two factors which do not appear to have been explored are first, whether her financial position is entirely independent of any public funds, and secondly, whether a person should be able to retain a title, in itself a publicly endowed title, albeit a remnant of a past age, as an acknowledgement or declaration of some special status in the social hierarchy, while at the same time professing to be a 'private person'. She does, after all, use the title 'Princess' rather than a 'commoner' title such as Madame or Frau or Mrs or Ms.

Secondly, even in the case of public figures, the court's decision indicated a greater respect for the notion that some aspects of their life will remain private and free of intrusion even when they are out in public. The two applicable tests (1) whether the information came within their 'legitimate expectation' of privacy so as to invoke a need to be balanced with the right to freedom of expression, and if so, (2) whether it contributes to a debate of general interest, is a fairly high bar for the media to overcome. A 'debate' implies the existence of a serious ongoing issue of public importance.

Thirdly, by way of comparison it was indicated that politicians may have the least expectation of privacy and there does appear to be a growing body of opinion that some of their conduct in their private domain could reasonably be considered as relevant to their suitability for office.[184] But even then, there will be limits.

Contemporary developments in the United Kingdom

At approximately the same time in 2004 that the European Court of Human Rights was hearing and deciding Princess Caroline's petition, the House of Lords in London was hearing an appeal in the case brought by Naomi Campbell, supermodel, against the owners of the 'Mirror' newspaper.[185]

---

183   Above n 141, p 243. The decision of the European Court was the subject of some criticism in Germany: Zacharias, D, *New tendencies concerning the Right to privacy: the Campbell and Hannover Cases* (Shaker Verlag, 2005)

184   See, for example, Joshua Rozenberg, *Privacy and the Press* (Oxford University Press, 2004), p v of the Preface asking: 'Surely we are entitled to know a little more about those who hold positions of authority in society – if only to decide whether they are fit to remain in office?'

185   *Campbell v MGN Ltd* [2004] 2 All ER 995. Much of the author's analysis of this case below, like that of *Von Hannover v Germany*, was written originally for an article published in the *New York Law School Law Review*, following a 2004 forum on defamation and privacy law at that law school: McDonald, B, above n 161.

Naomi Campbell commenced proceedings in February 2001 on the day that *The Mirror* published an article and photograph showing her leaving Narcotics Anonymous. The article was headed 'Naomi: I am a drug addict' and was accompanied by several photographs, one of her dressed in baseball cap and jeans with the title 'Therapy: Naomi outside meeting' and the other 'Hugs: Naomi, dressed in jeans and baseball hat, arrives for a lunchtime group meeting this week'. The article described her attendance at counselling and group therapy sessions and included, 'This is one of the world's most beautiful women facing up to her drink and drug addiction — and clearly winning'. It also described an incident when she was hospitalised and had her stomach pumped, stating that although she had claimed it was for an allergic reaction, 'those closest to her knew the truth'. It seemed to be accepted that the defendant newspaper had received its information about Naomi Campbell's attendance at Narcotics Anonymous either from one of her entourage or from another person attending the meetings.[186]

A few days after she commenced proceedings, *The Mirror* published two further articles disparaging her for bringing proceedings, republishing one photograph with text such as 'Naomi Campbell whinges about privacy', and an editorial headed 'No hiding Naomi'. She claimed damages for her distress, embarrassment and anxiety, and aggravated damages due to the defendant's later publications and conduct at the trial.

At the trial, Campbell accepted that because of her previous public denials of her drug addiction, the press was entitled to publish the fact of her addiction and the fact that she was seeking treatment.[187] But she claimed that the fact that she was receiving treatment at Narcotics Anonymous, the details of the treatment and her appearance leaving an Narcotics Anonymous meeting were private and confidential matters (' the associated facts'). The trial judge gave judgment for £2,500 compensatory damages and £1000 aggravated damages.[188] The Court of Appeal allowed an appeal by the defendant, holding that attendance at Narcotics Anonymous meetings was distinguishable from usual medical treatment as it was publicly known that drug addicts could benefit from Narcotics Anonymous meetings and that the relevant test as to publication was whether the disclosure would have offended a reasonable reader of ordinary sensibilities.[189]

The House of Lords, by a majority of three to two, allowed Campbell's appeal and restored the judge's order.[190] The publication of the associated facts and the photographs of her leaving and attending the Narcotics Anonymous meetings were an unjustifiable infringement of her right to privacy. One of

---

186   If this was so, it is curious that more was not made of this allegation, as, in either case, the leaking of the information was an obvious breach of a pre-existing confidential obligation.

187   The right to reply publicly or to correct publicly a public statement by the subject has long been seen as the basis of a defence of qualified privilege to a defamation action. *Adam v Ward* [1917] AC 309.

188   [2002] EWHC 499 (QB).

189   [2003] 1 All ER 224.

190   *Campbell v MGN* [2004] 2 All ER 995.

the dissenting judges, Lord Hoffman, noted that despite the dissent by himself and Lord Nicholls as to whether the newspaper went too far in publishing the associated facts in this case, the House was unanimous on the general principles as to the way in which the law should strike a balance between the right to privacy and the right to freedom of expression.

The House held:

- The duty of confidence would arise whenever the person who came under the duty was in a situation where he knew or ought to know that the other person could reasonably expect his or her privacy to be protected.
- The reasonable expectation of the subject was to be assessed by asking whether the publication of the information would be highly offensive to a reasonable person of ordinary sensibilities if they were in the same position as the subject.[191]
- Attendance at Narcotics Anonymous was private information which imported a duty of confidence. The therapy was put at risk by disclosure. The assurance of privacy was an essential part of the exercise of attending the meetings and the attendants owed a duty of confidence to each other.
- The right to privacy and respect for private life had to be balanced against the right of the media to impart information to the public. Neither Art 8 nor Art 10 of the European Convention had pre-eminence over the other.[192] The values enshrined in Arts 8 and 10 are now (and perhaps have always been) part of the common law cause of action for breach of confidence.[193] Any limitation on one right at the expense of another had to be rational, fair, and proportionate to the need.

It seems to be at this point that the majority and minority depart. The majority, Lord Hope, Baroness Hale and Lord Carswell, allowing the appeal, continued:

- Relevant to the balancing exercise was that, in contrast to the undoubted right of the public to know that Campbell had previously mislead them, there were no political or democratic matters at stake and no pressing social need for the public to know about her treatment. The fact that the

---

191   *Campbell v MGN* [2004] 2 All ER 995 at 1004. Lord Nicholls notes at [22] that the test is similar to that set out in the *Second Restatement of Torts in the United States* (1977) Art 652 D, p 394. See also *Australian Broadcasting Corporation v Lenah Game Meats* (2001) 208 CLR 199 at [42] per Gleeson CJ. Lord Nicholls cautioned against using the 'highly offensive test' at the initial stage of deciding whether the information was private. In his view, the offensiveness of the publication was relevant at the later stage of balancing freedom of expression. In his view, '[e]ssentially the touchstone of private life is whether in respect of the disclosed facts the person in question had a reasonable expectation of privacy'at [21].

192   On this point, the House of Lords approved *Douglas v Hello! Ltd* [2001] EMLR 9; [2001] 2 All ER 289. See also *Douglas v Hello! Ltd (No 3)* [2003] 3 All ER 996 at 1043 ff.

193   See also *A v B plc* [2003] QB 195 at 202 [4]. Lord Hoffmann describes the influence of human rights law as more subtle and indirect and appears to question whether Arts 8 and 10 are incorporated in domestic law, but nevertheless describes, at [55], freedom of the press and the right to protection of personal information as 'important civilised values' as though they were always there.

publication had the potential to cause her harm carried a good deal of weight.

- The photographs added greatly to the intrusion which the article as a whole had made into her private life. The taking of photographs in a public street had to be taken as one of the incidents of living in a free community, but the publication was subject to what was offensive. The fact that they were taken deliberately, in secret and with a view to publication in conjunction with the articles was highly relevant to the offensiveness of the publication. (Campbell could not have complained if the photographs had been taken to show the scene in the street by a passer by and later published as street scenes.[194])

In contrast, the minority, Lord Nicholls and Lord Hoffmann, relied on the following factors in deciding that the publication of the associated facts and photographs did *not* unjustifiably infringe her privacy:

- Her public statements. Campbell's public lies when she had gone out of her way to say that unlike many fashion models she did not take drugs, had put her addiction and treatment into the public domain. It was not enough that she was a public figure with a long and symbiotic relationship with the media. A person may attract or even seek publicity about some aspects of his or her life without creating any public interest in the publication of personal information about other matters. Sufficient public interest was created by her public statements. Treatment by attending Narcotics Anonymous meetings is a form of therapy that is well known, widely used and much respected. This additional information was of such an unremarkable and consequential nature that to divide it from the central facts was 'to apply altogether too fine a toothcomb. Human rights are concerned with substance, not with such fine distinctions'.[195]

- Journalistic margins. Lord Nicholls: Even if the associated facts were private, non-publication would have robbed a legitimate and sympathetic newspaper story of detail which added colour and conviction: this information was published, in fairness to her, to demonstrate her commitment to tackling her drug problem. The balance ought not to be held at a point which would preclude a degree of journalistic latitude in respect of information published for this purpose. Greater weight had to be given to the rights of the press at this point. Lord Hoffmann: The test of proportionality is a matter on which people may differ. But judges are not newspaper editors. 'It is harsh to criticise the editor for painting a

---

194   Presumably though in such a case, the plaintiff would consider an action in defamation where one issue would be whether any defence of qualified privilege based on the privilege of reply would excuse the publication of 'associated facts'. But that raises the question, which remains; that is, whether the claimant would have any basis for a defamation action where the central facts are defamatory but justifiable and the associated facts are private but not defamatory.

195   *Campbell v MGN* [2004] 2 All ER 995 at 1005 [26].

somewhat fuller picture in order to show her in a sympathetic light'.[196]. Where the main substance of the story is conceded to have been justified, should the newspaper be held liable whenever a judge considers that it was not necessary to have published some of the personal information? Or should newspapers be allowed some margin of choice? The practical exigencies of journalism demand some latitude must be given. She concedes the truth of the essential. The editor thought it necessary to provide detail and photographs by way of verification. It is unreasonable to expect that newspapers will always get it absolutely right.[197] To do more would inhibit the public interest. From a journalistic point of view, photographs are an essential part of the story. The decision to publish was within the margin of editorial judgment.[198]

- The lack of intrusion or harassment. The fact that the photographs were taken surreptitiously adds nothing to the complaint about publication. The plaintiff made no complaint about being hounded,[199] or about the taking of the photograph. In general, the fact that the pictures were taken without consent is not enough to amount to a wrongful invasion of privacy. There was no intrusion into a private place and nothing humiliating or embarrassing about the picture.[200] Further, while in general pictures contain more information than textual description, in this case, the photographs added no information and showed nothing untoward.

For celebrities seeking to protect their privacy and for media and paparazzi seeking to report on celebrity lives, the significance of the decision of the House of Lords in *Campbell v MGN Ltd* lay in its affirmation that the action for breach of confidence has been freed from its earlier constraints of requiring an initial confidential relationship, the common view of the court on the relevant test for what information would be regarded as confidential or private, and the view of the majority that the photographic images and the surreptitious nature of their taking added greatly to the offensiveness of the publication.

Lord Hoffman points out that the law has changed its emphasis from the fixing, as equity usually did, upon the conscience of the holder of the information arising out of some relationship, to fixing upon the information itself.[201] Further, in doing so, the new approach[202] reflects a shift in the underlying values which the law protects:

> What human rights law has done is to identify private information as something worth protecting as an aspect of human autonomy and dignity ... Instead

---

196   Ibid at 1012 [59].
197   Ibid at 1013 [63].
198   Ibid at 1015 [77].
199   This factor is in marked contrast to the arguments of Princess Caroline in the *Von Hannover* case discussed above, pp 132-37.
200   If there had been, then the plaintiff may have had a defamation action.
201   *Campbell v MGN* [2004] 2 All ER 995 at 1009 [44].
202   See also *Douglas v Hello!* [2001] 2All ER 289 at 320 [128].

of the cause of action being based on the duty of good faith applicable to confidential personal information and trade secrets alike, it focuses upon the protection of human autonomy and dignity – the right to control the dissemination about one's private life and the right to the esteem and respect of other people.[203]

Lord Hope disagreed that the policy of the law had shifted as much as Lord Hoffmann said[204] but it does seem that with the new emphasis on a person's reasonable expectation of privacy, the law of confidential or private information would increasingly fill a gap which the law of defamation has only partially and imperfectly protected.[205] This is reflected in Lord Hoffman's judgment where he juxtaposes the privacy of personal information with the law of defamation as two different limitations on the freedom of the press.[206]

As in *Von Hannover v Germany*, the issue of public interest to support the right of the press to publish information about celebrities and public figures was canvassed in the case. Baroness Hale formulated a hierarchy of matters of public interest.

> Top of the list is political speech. The free exchange of information and ideas on matters relevant to the organisation of the economic, social and political life of the country is crucial to any democracy … Intellectual and educational speech and expression is also important in a democracy … Artistic speech and expression is important in fostering both individual originality and creativity and the free thinking and dynamic society we so much value. No doubt there are other kinds of speech and expression for which similar claims can be made.[207]

The majority clearly felt that the information about Miss Campbell's treatment was much lower on the scale of public interest than the information of her drug addiction. It did not seem to be argued that because she held herself out as a role model for young women, any information on her commitment to treatment would have a strong public benefit in itself.

The transformation of the cause of action for breach of confidence into a cause of action for misuse or wrongful dissemination of private information, widely defined to include one's picture in certain situations, has the capacity to fill a gap which, as *Kaye v Robertson* showed, was gaping in the common law of the United Kingdom and other common law countries without constitutional guarantees of privacy. It still does not equate to the widespread general tort of invasion of privacy known to the United States. Yet it may be more effective and less objectionable on freedom of speech grounds because it is not so wide. Of course, if this transformation is regarded as solely due to the direct or indirect incorporation of the European Convention of

---

203   *Campbell v MGN* [2004] 2 All ER 995 at 1010 [50]-[51].

204   Ibid at 1017 [86].

205   See Robert Post's seminal article on the protection of reputation in terms of property, dignity and honour: Post, RC, 'Social Foundations of Defamation Law: Reputation and the Constitution', (1986) 74 *Californian Law Review* 691.

206   *Campbell v MGN* [2004] 2 All ER 995 at 1010 [56].

207   Ibid at 1036 [148].

Human Rights into the law of the United Kingdom, then other non-European countries such as Australia, have to find another justification for a similar development. The *International Covenant on Civil and Political Rights*, if ratified by a country, may be sufficient justification for a common law development on what is now regarded as a fundamental right in a civilised society. Certainly, the judgment of Gleeson CJ of the Australian High Court decision in *Australian Broadcasting Corporation v Lenah Game Meats Pty Ltd*,[208] in which he adopted the tests for 'private information' set out in the *Restatement (Second) of the Law of Torts* and in the seminal article on 'Privacy' by WL Prosser in 1960,[209] indicates the readiness of courts outside the United States to adopt principles of law which are not exclusively referable to particular provisions or amendments of the United States Constitution, but are of more general application. In *Campbell v MGN Ltd*, the trial judge and the House of Lords in turn applied Gleeson CJ's test, showing the increasing international convergence of the law in this field.

A particular feature of the Naomi Campbell case was that she was, to a certain extent, in some sort of personal distress at the time of the photograph. As we have seen, from George III to Bismarck, from Rachel to Mitterand, to the Countess Spencer, to Kaye, and to Campbell, there is something inherently intrusive in depicting a person when medical issues such as illness or treatment are involved, and if the local law gives any protection to privacy, it is most likely to do so in such circumstances. An exception seems to be in California where, for all the American protection of privacy law, the media hound Britney Spears in and out of medical institutions at every nervous breakdown. But as is pointed out above, American privacy law makes more noise than impact.

What was still uncertain after the *Campbell* case was the extent to which the British courts would protect celebrities from photographs of them in their ordinary everyday life. Back in 2001, a judge had refused permission for judicial review of a decision of the Press Complaints Commission rejecting a complaint by newsreader Anna Ford.[210] She had complained about photographs published in the *Daily Mail* and *OK!* which had been taken of her and her partner on a beach while on holiday, using a long-lens camera. The PCC had held that she did not have a reasonable expectation of privacy on a publicly accessible beach. Would British courts go as far as the *Von Hannover* in restraining publication of some photographs taken in public places, and if not, are they just waiting for a correction by an appeal to the European Court of Human Rights? Would protection be easier when children were involved?

These questions were quickly answered, at least in part, in the flood of celebrity cases which followed *Von Hannover* and *Campbell* in the United

---

208   (2001) 208 CLR 199.

209   Prosser, above n 43 at 396-7, cited by Lord Hope in *Campbell v MGN* [2004] 2 All ER 995 at 1020 [94].

210   *R (on the application of Ford) v Press Complaints Commission* [2002] EMLR 5.

Kingdom. The law is still very much in a state of development, albeit rapid. It is striking that the modern cases continue to be about photography or visual images or footage. The development has generally been very much against the interests of the popular media. While Elton John has been unsuccessful in stopping photographers taking pictures of him in the street,[211] JK Rowling, Ewan McGregor, Elizabeth Hurley and Hugh Grant, Tony and Cherie Blair,[212] Sienna Miller[213] and Max Mosley have been successful – so far. Some celebrities have launched court actions for injunctions or damages, while many others have used the complaints procedures of the Press Complaints Commission. The conclusions of that body have reflected the shifts in the law: in contrast to the result for Anna Ford, the Commission upheld Elle McPherson's privacy complaint over photographs of her and her children on a secluded beach on Mustique.[214]

But before we come to these recent examples, we should look at another interesting development in the way in which celebrities, and those with a commercial connection to them, have been using the laws of confidence, to protect their *commercial* interest in maintaining privacy.

Using breach of confidence to protect commercial interests

As we have seen, one of the features of being a celebrity is that there seems to be an unending fascination with – and thus a market – for their most personal details. Because of this, the line between purely personal information and 'commercial' information is now blurred if not non-existent. But a distinction can still be drawn between the protection of a subject's personal feelings and dignity and the protection of his or her commercial interests in the way in which information is used or exploited or appropriated. We have seen in Chapter 2 how the laws of copyright and trademarks and the tort of passing off, as well as statutory remedies for misleading and deceptive conduct, may protect exploitation rights. But there are gaps in that protection, and the law relating to confidential information has been used to fill them.

While many of the cases, particularly, but not only, those involving royalty, are about purely personal information, there are many instances

---

211   *Elton John v Associated Newspapers* (unreported, June 2006); see Tech, D, 'When uncertainty takes precedence', *The Guardian*, 24 July 2006 <http://mediaguardian.co.uk/mediaguardian/story/0,,1827223,00.html>.

212   The ex British Prime Minister and his wife Cherie settled a substantial damages claim against Associated Newspapers for long lens photographs of the couple and family and friends while on holidays at Sir Cliff Richard's villa in Barbados, donating the proceeds to charities. Dyer, C, 'Mail pays for violating Blair's privacy', *The Guardian*, 23 November 2007 <www.guardian.co.uk/media/2007/nov/23/privacy.dailymail>.

213   British actress Sienna Miller sued a paparazzo and Big Pictures UK Ltd complaining of a campaign of harassment: once the case was set down for trial, settlement involved a substantial payout and an agreement that the photographer would stop following her. 'Miller wins payout' *Sunday Telegraph*, 23 November 2008.

214   Forbes, E, 'PCC finally forced to act on privacy', *MediaGuardian*, *The Guardian*, 12 February 2007.

where parties will be seeking to protect the commercial value of information. The early breach of confidence cases involving trade secrets are clearly such cases, as are those dealing with unpublished (and thus not copyrightable) ideas, customer lists, potential mining and development sites, and so on.

The leading recent case on the protection of the commercial interests in private information is that brought by *OK!* magazine, following the publication by a rival pictorial personality-gossip magazine *Hello!* of unauthorised photographs of wedding of Michael Douglas and Catherine Zeta-Jones at the Plaza Hotel in New York.

After a bidding war for exclusive rights, Douglas and Zeta-Jones had signed a £1 million contract with *OK!* giving it exclusive rights, for nine months, to publish photographs of the wedding and promising to take all reasonable steps to restrict access to the wedding and to prevent those present taking other photographs which might find their way into the hands of rival media. Despite tight security a freelance photographer/ paparazzo, posing as a waiter or guest, surreptitiously gained access and took photographs of the wedding which he sold to *Hello!*[215]

The couple and *OK!* sought an interlocutory (temporary) injunction to restrain publication of the unauthorised photographs. It was initially granted and continued for a few days, but dissolved by the Court of Appeal of England and Wales,[216] at which point *OK!* accelerated its own issue with the authorised pictures for publication the next day, with *Hello!* publishing their magazine a few hours later on the same day. Some national daily newspapers also published some of the unauthorised photographs on that day. The claimants then sought damages from *Hello!* for the losses they said they had suffered as a result of the *Hello!* publication.

The claimants based their claims on two actions – an action for breach of confidence and an action for the tort of causing loss by unlawful means.

Zeta-Jones and Douglas were successful in obtaining what Lord Hoffmann in the House of Lords later described as 'modest damages'.[217] The trial judge awarded them £3750 each for the distress caused to by the publication of the unauthorised photographs, £7000 for them both for the cost and inconvenience of having to make hurried new arrangements with *OK!* as a result of the defendant's conduct, and nominal damages of £50 each for breach of the *Data Protection Act 1998*. The defendant's appeal against this judgment failed. The Court of Appeal applied the principles from *Campbell v MGN*. What is most interesting about the judgment of the Court of Appeal is the further careful consideration of the relative impact of photographs compared with text. In *Campbell v MGN Ltd*, both Lord

---

215 The fact that he was a trespasser may well have entitled the couple to an injunction to prevent *him* from publishing the fruits of the trespass, regardless of imposition of confidence, but their real fight was with rival publisher.

216 [2001] QB 967.

217 *Douglas v Hello! Ltd (No 3)* [2007] 2 WLR 920 at [110].

Hello! magazine's publisher outside the High Court in London

Nicholls of Birkenhead and Baroness Hale had supported the old adage that 'a picture is worth a thousand words'.

In *Douglas v Hello! Ltd (No 3)*, the Court of Appeal commented on the intrusive nature of photography and the recognition of this in case law which had prevented the disclosure of photographs taken without consent, particularly if they concerned the subject's private life and their publication would be humiliating or damaging. One such case was *Theakston v MGN Ltd* concerning unauthorised photographs of the presenter of the television program *Top of the Pops* in a brothel with at least three prostitutes. One of the prostitutes had sold her story and some photographs to *Sunday People* after demanding money from him. The court in that case had restrained the publication of the photographs but not the story.[218] The Court of Appeal in *Douglas* commented:

> This action is about photographs. Special considerations attach to photographs in the field of privacy. They are not merely a[n alternative] method of conveying information ... they enable the person viewing the photograph to act as a spectator, in some circumstances voyeur would be the more appropriate noun, of whatever it is that the photograph depicts. As a means of invading privacy, a photograph is particularly intrusive.[219]

The fact that the relevant information is photographic may have an impact too on the extent to which its 'confidential' or 'private' nature will survive some publication at an earlier time:

> Once intimate personal information about a celebrity's private life has been widely published it may serve no useful purpose to prohibit further publication.

---

218   *Theakston v MGN Ltd* [2002] EMLR 398.
219   *Douglas v Hello! Ltd (No 3)* (CA) [2005] 3 WLR 881 at 908 [84].

The same will not necessarily be true of photographs. In so far as a photograph does more than convey information and intrudes on privacy by enabling the viewer to focus on intimate personal detail, there will be a fresh intrusion of privacy when each additional viewer sees the photograph and even when one who has seen a previous publication of the photograph is confronted by a fresh publication of it.[220]

The Court of Appeal rejected the argument that by authorising *OK!* to publish photographs of their wedding, Douglas and Zeta-Jones were prevented now from claiming that their wedding was a private occasion and as such protected by the law of confidence. However, it would be very relevant when the court is considering the amount of any damages.[221] This point is indeed reflected in the small amount of damages they were awarded compared with the commercial value of the photographs, and the award of damages of £1,033,156 awarded by the trial judge to *OK!* Magazine against *Hello!*.

No appeal was brought from the Court of Appeal's upholding of the couple's claim. The main point of legal interest in the case is in fact not the Douglas/Zeta-Jones claim for breach of confidence, but that of *OK!*. Its claim was relatively unusual – it was not a party who had communicated confidential information in return for a commitment or undertaking of confidence, rather it was suing to protect the commercial value of confidential information *which it had bought*. It had the benefit[222] of an obligation of confidence which others (Douglas and Zeta-Jones) had imposed on their wedding guests. That benefit was worthless if the information was already out.

The House of Lords, by a majority of three to two, agreed with the trial judge that the benefit of the obligation of confidence related to *any* photographs of the wedding, not just the authorised photographs. This makes good sense: if it were otherwise the action would add nothing to an action for breach of copyright. All the elements of an action for breach of confidence were present: the photographs were confidential information as they were not publicly available; the information was obtained when there was an obligation of confidence – the couple had made it clear to attendees that photographs were not to be taken; the defendant had made unauthorised use of the information to the detriment of the claimant.

Lord Hoffmann noted that while the couple's case may have been about protecting their privacy, that of *OK!* was not:

OK! has no claim to privacy under article 8 [of the European Convention of Human Rights] nor can it make a claim which is parasitic upon the Douglases' right of privacy. The fact that the information happens to be about the

220   Ibid at 913 [105].

221   Ibid at 913-14. See Markesinis, O'Cinneide, Fedtke and Hunter-Henin, above n 17 at 23: 'excessive damage claims for commercially-based publicity cases need to be resisted – infringements upon a person's control of their personal image should not be equated with gross intrusions upon personal privacy …'.

222   'OK! Ltd was entitled to sue for breach of an obligation of confidentiality to itself'. [2008] AC 1 at 50 [129] per Lord Hoffmann.

personal life of the Douglases is irrelevant. It could have been information about anything that a newspaper was willing to pay for.[223]

An obligation of confidence was clearly imposed upon the trespassing photographer who knew of the restrictions imposed by the Douglases, not just for their own benefit but also for the benefit of *OK!*.

'*Hello!*', by reason of the circumstances in which they acquired the pictures, were subject to the same obligation.[224]

After affirming the right of *OK!* to use the law of breach of confidence to protect its commercially confidential information, Lord Hoffmann went on:

> Is there any reason of public policy why the law of confidence should not protect information of this form and subject matter? There is in my opinion no question of creating an 'image right' or any other unorthodox form of intellectual property. The information in this case was capable of being protected, not because it concerned the Douglases' image any more than because it concerned their private life, but simply because it was information of commercial value over which the Douglases had sufficient control to enable them to impose an obligation of confidence. Some may view with distaste a world in which information about the events of a wedding, which Warren and Brandeis in their famous article on privacy 'The Right to Privacy' (1890) 4 *Harvard LR* 193 regarded as the paradigm private occasion, should be sold in the market in the same way as information about how to make a better mousetrap. But being a celebrity or publishing a celebrity magazine are lawful trades and I see no reason why they should be outlawed from such protection as the law of confidence may offer.[225]

The majority rejected the argument favoured by the minority, that is, that the information had lost its confidential character, by a few hours, by the time *Hello!* published the photos. While agreeing that once information gets into the public domain, it loses its quality of confidence, Lord Hoffmann drew a fine distinction between mere descriptions of the wedding – information which anyone was entitled to report – and information in the form of photographs:

> The pictures published by *OK!* were put into the public domain and it would have had to rely on the law of copyright, not the law of confidence, to prevent their reproduction. But no other pictures were in the public domain and they did not enter the public domain merely because they resembled other pictures which had.[226]

OK! Ltd was successful then in obtaining substantial damages based on the misuse by *Hello!* of the confidential information.[227]

---

223   *Douglas v Hello! Ltd (No 3)* [2008] AC 1 at 48 [118].

224   Ibid at 48 [121].

225   Ibid at 49 [124].

226   Ibid at 49 [122].

227   Its alternative claim, arguing that *Hello!* had committed the tort of intentionally causing loss by unlawful means, was not. While the majority of the House of Lords upheld the dismissal of this claim, it did so on the basis that *Hello!* had not interfered with the Douglases' ability to deal with *OK!* (the Douglases had already made their contract with *OK!*) or their ability to perform *their* obligations under the contract (there was

Other examples have followed *Douglas v Hello!* of celebrities using the law of confidence and privacy to protect what also amount to their commercial interests in their private sphere. In *Beckham v MGN Ltd*,[228] David and Victoria Beckham were successful before Eady J in obtaining an injunction to restrain the press from publishing photographs of their new home, with Eady J holding that they could control publication of such photographs.

Celebrity families in public places

Von Hannover and *Campbell* both involved photographs of celebrities taken in public spaces, yet the House of Lords in *Campbell* did not go nearly as far as the European Court of Human Rights in *Von Hannover* in the formulation of a concept of a 'private sphere' in a public space. Despite its consideration of other analogous cases, a court of course need only, and must only, make a decision and set out the law on the facts before it. The two complaints were different in many respects. Naomi Campbell's case was a one-off incident, it rested very much on the nature of the information, and the particularly confidential surroundings – that of medical-related treatment at Narcotics Anonymous – and there was not the same element of continual stalking or intrusion that Princess Caroline complained about. Princess Caroline's claim also rested very much on the claim that she was *not* to be considered a 'public figure' when not on official duties, while as Lord Hoffmann (in the minority who would not have upheld her claim) noted, Naomi Campbell 'is a famous fashion model who lives by publicity. What she sells is herself; her personal appearance and her personality'.[229]

One aspect of Princess Caroline's various claims that was not the subject of her petition to the European Court of Human Rights was the claim in respect of photographs of her out and about with her children. Princess Caroline had succeeded in the German Constitutional Court in stopping the republication of photographs of her out in public with her children, based on the protection given by s 6 of the German Basic Law regarding a person's intimate relations with their children.[230] It should be noted that her claim

---

no allegation that the Douglases had by *Hello!'s* actions breached their duty to take reasonable steps to ensure other photographs were not taken or leaked to the press). 'All they did was to make *OK!'s* contractual rights less profitable than they would otherwise have been'. Without an underlying breach of contract or other unlawfulness, there could be no secondary liability for inducing a breach of contract or causing loss by unlawful means.

228 Unreported, 28 June 2001; discussed in Robinson, F, 'How image conscious is English law' (2004) 15(5) *Ent LR* 151 at 154, who also discusses *Attard v General Manchester Newspapers* (unreported, 14-15 June 2001, Fam Div, Bennett J) in which it was held that a surviving conjoined twin had a reasonable expectation of privacy on the public steps of a hospital. Certain newspapers had, however, obtained contractual permission to publish photographs.

229 *Campbell v MGN* [2004] 2 WLR 1232.

230 Paragraph II(1)(c)(dd) of Federal Constitutional Court judgment, quoted in *Von Hannover* (2005) 40 EHRR 1 at [25].

here was in respect of her *own* rights to protection of her relations with her children.

JK Rowling, the extraordinarily successful author of the Harry Potter series, tested the reach of the new privacy protection of English law, when she (as Mrs Joanne Murray) and her husband launched proceedings on behalf of their son David Murray.[231] The couple had been out walking with their infant son in a buggy when the defendant Big Pictures Ltd (presumably through an employee or agent) took a photograph of the family group which was published in the *Sunday Express*. The photograph was taken covertly using a long range lens. The family was unaware of this at the time, but before the publication had made it plain that they objected to any publication of photographs of David. Big Pictures had offered not to further publish or sell images, to make attempts to stop publication by others and had apologised to the family. Litigation against the *Express* was settled, leaving only Big Pictures as defendants. David's claim alleged an infringement of his right to privacy contrary to Art 8 of the European Convention on Human Rights. Big Pictures' move to strike out the claim, arguing that he had no basis for an action, was successful and David then appealed to the Court of Appeal against this strike out order. It is important to note that a strike out order is given where, even if the facts alleged were true, the claimant has no arguable legal basis for a claim. Thus neither the judge's decision nor the Court of Appeal's judgment is a decision as to the merits of the claim, but rather whether it should go to trial.

This was a case of a photograph of a member of a famous family out and about in public as part of their everyday life. It was the sort of photograph that routinely appears on covers and fills the pages of popular magazines about celebrities. It was clearly similar to many of the photographs in Princess Caroline's case. The Court of Appeal noted, however, that it was bound by *Campbell v MGN Ltd* rather than *Von Hannover*,[232] although also noting that neither was a case about a child 'being targeted as David was here'.[233]

The court surveyed the various judgments in *Campbell*, noting, for example, Lord Hoffman's view that the famous and the not so famous who go out in public must accept that they may be observed or photographed without their consent and his citation of Chief Justice Gleeson's comment in *Australian Broadcasting Corporation v Lenah Game Meats Pty Ltd*,[234] that part of the price we pay for living in an organised society is that we are exposed to observation by other people. Applying the principles from *Campbell*, the analysis must ask several questions:

First, where the information is not obviously private, is there in the circumstances a reasonable expectation of privacy, viewed objectively from the perspective of a person of ordinary sensibilities in the same circumstances

---

231   *Murray v Express Newspapers plc* [2009] 1 Ch 481.

232   Ibid at 498 [20].

233   Ibid at 508 [47].

234   (2001) 208 CLR 199 at 226 [13].

JK Rowling who sued for breach of her infant son's privacy

as the claimant? The relevant circumstances include the attributes of the claimant, the nature of the activity involved, the place, the nature and purpose of the intrusion, the absence of consent, the defendant's awareness or lack of awareness of the lack of consent, the effect on the claimant and the circumstances and purposes of the publication.

How should this question be considered when the subject or claimant was a young child? Clearly a very young child is often too young to have awareness or sensitivity, or to give consent. The Court of Appeal agreed with the trial judge that:

> 'The court can attribute to the child reasonable expectations about his private life based on matters such as how it has in fact been conducted by those responsible for his welfare and upbringing' ... Thus, for example, if the parents of a child courted publicity by procuring the publication of photographs of the child in order to promote their own interests, the position would or might be quite different from a case like this, where the parents have taken care to keep their children out of the public gaze.[235]

The court then formulated the question for trial here to be whether young David Murray 'had a reasonable expectation that commercial picture agencies like BPL would not set out to photograph him with a view to selling those photographs for money without his consent, which would of course have to be given through his parents'.[236] Expressed like that, it is hard to see how a court will find other than for the claimant. Later in the judgment, the Court of Appeal stated that the law should protect children from being targeted in

---

235   *Murray v Express Newspapers plc* [2009] 1 Ch 481 at 503 [37]-[38].
236   Ibid at 503 [39].

a public place when the person who took or procured the photograph knew that this would be objected to. This they said, was not a guarantee of privacy, because there is a second step to be considered.

Second, if the first question is answered positively, then a balancing process, taking into account Art 8 and Art 10, must be undertaken by the court. The second question to be asked is one of proportionality, how a balance should be struck between the claimant's right to privacy and the publisher's right to publish.[237]

The Court of Appeal came to a different conclusion from that of the judge. The special position of children who are not themselves famous is recognised in cl 6 of *The Press Complaints Commission Editors' Code of Practice*:

> v) Editors must not use the fame, notoriety or position of the parent or guardian as sole justification for publishing details of a child's private life.

The court expressly disapproved of the reasoning and conclusion of the New Zealand Court of Appeal in a similar case, *Hosking v Runting*, involving the photographing in the street of children of famous parents.[238] In contrast, it felt that its own approach was consistent with that of the European Court of Human Rights in *Von Hannover* and further that, more likely than not, the European court would hold that on the assumed facts, 'the article 8/10 balance would come down in favour of David'.[239] With that glaringly obvious hint that the case should be settled, the case was directed to trial.

The decision had instant effect. One week after the *Murray* decision, Big Pictures Ltd settled a claim by Hugh Grant, Elizabeth Hurley and Arun Nayar for £58,000 plus costs. The claim concerned photographs taken with a long-range camera of the three of them, some showing also Elizabeth's small son playing naked, while holidaying on an island in the Maldives. The photographs had been published in the *News of the World* and the *Mail on Sunday*. In contrast to the unsuccessful complaint by Anna Ford some years earlier, this case had two distinguishing facts – the inclusion of a child in the photograph and the fact that the party were on private land not a public beach.[240]

While each case is decided on its own facts, the decision for the claimant in *Murray* obviously has potentially enormous ramifications for the way in

---

237 Ibid at 504 [40]. It is interesting that the court referred to the right to publish when the claim at hand was a claim against the photographer and distributor, the claim against the publisher having been settled.

238 *Hosking v Runting* [2005] NZLR 1, in which the New Zealand court had applied a stricter test of whether the publication in question would be *highly offensive* to a reasonable person. See also *Rogers v Television New Zealand Limited* [2007] NZSC 91. The approach of the New Zealand courts has been in marked contrast to that of the courts of the United Kingdom: they have recognised a new tort of invasion of privacy. See further Butler and Rodrick, n 37 above, at 10.355-10.395.

239 *Murray v Express Newspapers plc* [2009] 1 Ch 481 at 511 [60].

240 Schillings, 'Hugh Grant, Elizabeth Hurley and Arun Nayar Settle Privacy Claim', 15 May 2008 <www.schillings.co.uk/Display.aspx?MasterId=4fl1caa22-de0e-40a5-8032-d5438f>.

which media operators and photograph agencies conduct their celebrity spotting business where children are involved. Removing the chance to publish takes away a market, at least among the major media outlets. It will also have ramifications for the potential for parents to control and influence the public exposure of their children: it will make their efforts to screen their children if they so wish much more powerful. On the other hand, it seems to open up a free reign to parents to unleash their children's privacy and develop their publicity value. Child prodigies and celebrities can be a great asset: think of Shirley Temple or Bindi Irwin. Whether or not children's legal rights to be protected from exposure to constant publicity *should* depend so much on the willingness of their parents to protect them is another matter. Solove writes that the story of child prodigy William Sidis illustrates the problems for someone who was thrust by his father into the limelight as a child and by being hounded by the media.[241]

Privacy and more sex

We have seen above how a person's sexual relationships and activities are accepted examples of aspects of a person's life that are deserving of protection from unauthorised disclosure. Rarely will disclosure these days be seen as a matter of public interest unless there is some element of criminal behaviour, exploitation, hypocrisy, corruption or risk to security or proper governance and public process. With shifts in what is considered defamatory and with truth now a defence on its own to an action in defamation, the subjects of revelations would these days rarely be brave enough or foolhardy enough to sue on that basis.

The recent case of *Max Mosley v News Group Newspapers Limited* has sparked enormous controversy, for several reasons. First, it is a modern test case on the difference between the legal notion of 'public interest' and the undoubted 'interest', curiosity or fascination, of the public in the unusual sex lives of others. Second, it is a case involving someone who is in the public eye for two aspects of his life – his own sport-related career and his family's history – but not for any 'public' role in democratic or government processes. Third, it has accentuated the role of the courts and individual judges in the legal determination of the limits of privacy and the freedom of the press. The British popular press see it as a challenge to their decades-old practices of reporting on what they call morality; the victim sees it as protecting a private life which is harmless and none of anyone else's business, but the disclosure of which is devastating to his family and public life.

Max Mosley is the son of Sir Oswald Mosley and his second wife Diana. The couple are famous or infamous in living memories. He was the head of the British Union of Fascists before and after World War II. She was one of the Mitford sisters, daughters of Baron Redesdale, whose siblings included Nancy, the famous novelist, wit, columnist and biographer; Jessica, communist and writer; Deborah, who became the Duchess of Devonshire and chatelaine of

---

241   Solove, DJ, Rotenberg M and Schwartz PM, above n 14, p 6.

Max Mosley leaving the High Court in London after his successful action

Chatsworth, one of the most famous English estates; and Unity, a besotted visi-tor and admirer of Hitler (who badly injured herself when attempting suicide after Great Britain declared was on Germany.) Oswald and Diana Mosley were married in 1936 in Berlin at the home of Nazi Propaganda Minister, Joseph Goebbels. When war broke out they were interned in Holloway Prison until 1943. Max was born in 1940. With his parents, who were always of much media interest, he had a somewhat peripatetic life after the war. He was educated in France, Germany and England, studying physics at Oxford University and law at Gray's Inn. He trained as a parachutist in the 'Territorial Army', the volunteer reserve force of the British Army. He was outspoken about his father's right to free speech. He attempted a political career with his father's post-war Union Movement and later with the Conservative Party, but it went nowhere. Meanwhile, while practising as a barrister, he began motor car racing and becoming heavily involved in the sport and the Formula 1 competition. In 1993 he was elected President of the FIA, the 'Federation Internationale de l'Automobile', and is now in the fourth four-year term of what has been a controversial presidency on many issues.

In March 2008, the *News of the World* published an article with a number of photographs, and on its website, the same article and photographs together with video footage. The article was headed 'FI BOSS HAS SICK NAZI ORGY WITH 5 HOOKERS', with a subheading 'Son of Hitler-loving fascist in sex shame'. A further article a few days later referred to an interview with one of the women and was headed 'MY NAZI ORGY WITH F1 BOSS'. The photographs showed Mosley and five women engaged in sexual activities and games involving bondage, domination and sado-masochism. They were taken by one of the women using a concealed camera supplied by a journalist.

Mosley immediately applied for an interim injunction against the *News of the World* to restrain further disclosure of the material, but Eady J refused the application:

> The dam has effectively burst. I have, with some reluctance, come to the conclusion that although this material is intrusive and demeaning, and despite the fact that there is no legitimate public interest in its further publication, the ... order ... would be a merely futile gesture.[242]

Mosley claimed damages on the basis of breach of confidence and/or the breach of his right to privacy under the European convention. The judgment makes it clear that this is but one action in the United Kingdom. Eady J adopted what had been said in *Campbell v MGN Ltd* that the values enshrined in Arts 8 and 10 of the convention 'are now part of the cause of action for breach of confidence'.[243] The accepted new methodology is to ask whether the claimant had a reasonable expectation of privacy in respect to the information and facts and, if so, to balance or weigh the competing Convention rights of privacy and freedom of expression by an intense focus on the particular facts.[244]

The newspaper made two arguments: first that Mosley had no reasonable expectation of privacy and, second, that even if he did, his right to privacy was outweighed by the public interest underpinning the right to freedom of expression. The public had a legitimate interest, it was argued, in knowing of Mosley's activities because they were Nazi-like, because they were illegal or because he was President of the FIA.

Eady J stressed that this was once again a complaint where visual images have a much more intrusive and damaging effect than a mere verbal description. They make every reader a spectator or even a voyeur. This case, unlike many of the other recent leading cases like *Von Hannover* and *Campbell,* concerned photographs on private property of sexual activity: 'it is at the extreme of intimate intrusion'.[245]

Everything turned therefore on the validity of the public interest defence. It is often said that there is 'no confidence in iniquity', in the sense that there is an obvious public interest in the disclosure of crime. But Lord Goff in the *Spycatcher* case had pointed out that this principle did not necessarily require or protect disclosure to the media or the public: a more limited disclosure might be sufficient.[246] The disclosure must be proportionate to the crime – 'even those who have committed serious crime do not become 'outlaws' so far as their own rights, including their rights to personal privacy, are concerned'.[247] In any event criminality here was doubtful and trivial:

---

242   *Mosley v News Group Newspapers Ltd* [2008] EWHC 687 (QB) at [36].
243   Ibid at [9] citing Lord Nicholls in *Campbell v MGN* [2004] 2 WLR 1232 at 1238 [17].
244   Ibid at [9].
245   Ibid at [9].
246   *Attorney General v Guardian Newspapers Ltd (No 2)* [1990] 1 AC 109 at 282.
247   *Mosley* [2008] EWHC 1777 (QB) at [118].

[I]t would hardly be appropriate to clutter the courts with cases of spank-
ing between consenting adults taking place in private property and without
disturbing the neighbours. That would plainly not be in the public interest ...
[nor would it] justify hidden cameras and worldwide coverage.

More problematic was the argument of public interest based on the alleged
Nazi-like style of the sexual activities and games. It was alleged that there
was a clear allusion to domination and abuse in concentration camps. Eady J
held that if there had been such conduct then clearly it would have been in the
public interest to reveal it as it would call into question Mosley's suitability as
head of the FIA. But after an exhaustive analysis of the facts – beatings were
given and received, the women were dressed in horizontally striped pyjamas,
some German accents were used, some dressed in jackets like modern day
Luftwaffe uniforms, heads were 'searched for lice', Mosley's bottom was
shaved, one woman called out 'We are of the Aryan race – blondes' – he
concluded that there was no Nazi or concentration-style conduct involved. It
was just standard 'S & M' or 'BDSM'. With that argument gone, all that was
left was the argument that it was so immoral and depraved that it warranted
disclosure. Eady J rejected this soundly. It is well recognised that a person's
sexual life is private. European states must provide protection for privacy.

> It is not for journalists to undermine human rights or for judges to refuse to
> enforce them merely on grounds of taste or moral disapproval.[248]

Eady J therefore rejected the public interest defence based on his own view of
the material, as he believed the judge is required to do, against increasingly
well recognised criteria.[249] He also considered the argument that there is
a defence of 'responsible journalism' such as has developed in the law of
defamation, so that the question is rather whether a responsible *journalist*
would have perceived that publication is in the public interest. But even if
the newspaper journalists here believed that there was a Nazi element to the
events, there was no rationale basis for that belief.

Eady J's final task was to assess damages. Noting that the policy behind
protection of privacy and confidences was to protect personal dignity,
autonomy and integrity, he held that damages should reflect distress, hurt
feelings and loss of dignity; provide a measure of vindication of rights; be
proportionate with damages for intangible damage given in other contexts
such as personal injury cases; take account of aggravating conduct by the
defendant which 'rubs salt in the wound' such as the persistence of the 'Nazi'
arguments. On the other hand, Mosley was to some extent reckless and
gambling with the risk of exposure. The damage done by disclosure of private
information cannot be undone, so that no amount of money would effectively
compensate him. Eady J concluded by awarding damages of £60,000, the
largest award yet given in an English privacy case.

---

248   Ibid at [127].
249   Ibid at [130].

Not content with that award, Mosley has since gone on to petition the European Court of Human Rights that privacy protection in the United Kingdom does not adequately protect privacy because it does not require that a victim of disclosure be given notice of publication and thus the opportunity to apply for an injunction to *restrain* publication. That case awaits a hearing.

In the meantime, the controversy created by the case has continued. The judge who heard the case, Eady J, has been the subject of stringent criticism by the editor of the *Daily Mail*, Paul Dacre who, in a speech to the Society of Editors in Bristol[250] called his judgments 'arrogant and amoral', and Eady J has himself become the subject of media scrutiny.[251] Members of the tabloid media have used the often-heard complaint about 'unelected and unaccountable judges', and called for the use of juries to decide the issues. Eady J was obviously prepared for this onslaught as he was at pains to point out in *Mosley* that a judge hearing the case was carrying out the function required of him or her by parliament and by the European Convention.

Recent developments in Australia

In contrast to the developments in the United Kingdom in the past ten years, prompted by the *Human Rights Act 1998*, Australian cases have not yet seen the dramatic transformation of the action for breach of confidence into one for breach of privacy. In 2001, the High Court of Australia in *Australian Broadcasting Corporation v Lenah Game Meats Pty Ltd* freed lower courts from the discouraging position stated by majority and minority judges alike in the 1937 High Court decision in *Victoria Park Racing v Taylor* that there was no 'general right of privacy'[252] and implicitly encouraged the development of more common law protection of privacy and private information.

ABC v Lenah Game Meats Pty Ltd was not itself seen as a suitable case for the development of privacy protection: it was a case about a corporation seeking to prevent the public disclosure of unauthorised video footage of its (licensed) possum-slaughtering operations. First, the activities were not 'private' in nature:

---

250   Dacre, P, 'The Threat to our Press', Guardian, 10 November 2008, <www.guardian.co.uk/media/2008/nov/10/paul-dacre-press-threats>.

251   Campbell, D, 'Private man who dislikes bullies and hypocrites', *Guardian*, 11 November 2008, <www.guardian.co.uk/media/2008/nov/11/privacy-law>.

252   *Victoria Park Racing and Recreation Grounds Co Ltd v Taylor* (1937) 58 CLR 479, per Latham CJ at 496 and per Evatt J at 517. Yet in 1973 Professor WL Morison in his *Report on the Law of Privacy* (New South Wales, Parliament, Paper No 170, 1973, para [12].) noted that it was not a case about privacy but about the racecourse's 'pocket book': 'The independent questions of the rights of a plaintiff who is genuinely seeking seclusion from surveillance and communication of what surveillance reveals, it may be argued, should be regarded as open to review in future cases even by courts bound by the decision'. This statement was quoted and described as correct by Gummow and Hayne JJ, with whom Gaudron J agreed, in *Australian Broadcasting Corporation v Lenah Game Meats Pty Ltd* (2001) 208 CLR 199 at 249 [108].

If the activities filmed were private, then the law of breach of confidence is adequate to cover the case. I would regard images and sounds of private activities, recorded by the methods employed in the present case, as confidential. There would be an obligation of confidence upon the persons who obtained them, and upon those into whose possession they came, if they knew, or ought to have known, the manner in which they were obtained.

The problem for the respondent is that the activities secretly observed and filmed were not relevantly private. Of course, the premises on which those activities took place were private in a proprietorial sense ... [Lenah] had the capacity ... to grant or refuse permission to anyone who wanted to observe, and record, its operations. The same can be said of any landowner, but it does not make everything that the owner does on the land a private act. Nor does an act become private simply because the owner would prefer that it were unobserved.[253]

Second, Lenah as a corporation, that is, a mere legal entity, lacked the natural sensibilities which any law of privacy as such[254] would aim to protect.

Yet the High Court gave strong indications of the direction that future common law protection should take. There was a clear preference for the development of existing causes of action, particularly the equitable action of breach of confidence, such as has occurred in the United Kingdom, rather than of a new freestanding tort, such as in New Zealand. One of the reasons for this was the lack of precision of the concept of privacy. We referred to this problem at the beginning of this chapter: 'privacy' has many meanings. It is undoubtedly true that by keeping the actions within the confines of the action for breach of confidence, the court confines the action to one that is about *disclosure or misuse* of information, rather than about the intrusion itself. Of course, confining the use of the fruit so obtained will take away the incentive to intrude, but that is an incidental although important benefit.

The court accepted that the action for breach of confidence no longer requires the information to have been imparted under a pre-existing relationship of trust or confidence (although, as later cases show, this is often the case). Rather, it depends in this context on the information being of an obviously confidential or private nature. Gleeson CJ, drawing on the *Restatement of the Law Second, Torts*[255] in the United States and on the influential 1960 article by leading torts scholar William Prosser on 'Privacy',[256] commented on the kind of information that would be deserving of protection:

Part of the price we pay for living in an organised society is that we are exposed to observation in a variety of ways by other people.

There is no bright line which can be drawn between what is private and what is not. Use of the term 'public' is often a convenient method of contrast, but there is a large area in between what is necessarily public and what is necessarily private. An activity of not private simply because it is not done in

253 *Australian Broadcasting Corporation v Lenah Game Meats Pty Ltd* (2001) 208 CLR 199 at 225-226 [39]-[43] per Gleeson CJ.
254 Although it is clear that a corporation can protect confidential information.
255 Paragraph 652A.
256 Prosser, above n 43.

public ... Certain kinds of information about a person, such as information relating to health, personal relationships, or finances, may be easy to identify as private; as may certain kinds of activity, which a reasonable person, applying contemporary standards of morals and behaviour, would understand to be meant to be unobserved. The requirement that disclosure or observation of information or conduct would be highly offensive to a reasonable person of ordinary sensibilities is in many circumstances a useful practical test of what is private.[257]

Members of the House of Lords in *Campbell v MGN* adopted and commented on this formulation, agreeing that the latter test is not needed when the information is obviously private,[258] and commenting also that care must be taken to distinguish the two relevant issues: the threshold question of whether the information in question is private in nature and the second, whether, in the light of other balancing interests such as public interest, the disclosure is objectionable. Lord Hope described the 'highly offensive' test as potentially stricter than the preferred test of what is private information:

Essentially the touchstone of private life is whether in respect of the disclosed facts the person in question has a reasonable expectation of privacy.[259]

There been several cases since *ABC v Lenah Game Meats Pty Ltd* which relate to private citizens, in which the Australian courts have had to decide novel and important questions of law arising out of the expanded action for breach of confidence, as well as the opening up of the judicial development of further privacy protection made possible by confining or redefining the ratio in *Victoria Park Racing v Taylor*.

The cases have, so far, concerned situations where the claimant had a range of other actions available to recover damages for the wrong suffered. The higher courts have generally shown themselves reluctant to recognise a new freestanding tort of invasion of privacy particularly if other legal avenues are available.[260] There were, however, two decisions in lower courts where relief was given on the basis of a tort of breach of privacy, despite many other actions being made out on the facts. The first, *Grosse v Purvis*,[261] in the Queensland District Court, concerned a former lover stalking the claimant, trespassing into her house and harassing her. In addition to other causes of action, Skoien SJDC identified a general tort of wilful unreasonable intrusion of privacy and awarded a total of $178,000 in compensatory, exemplary or

257 *Australian Broadcasting Corporation v Lenah Game Meats Pty Ltd* (2001) 208 CLR 199 at 226 [41]-[42].
258 *Campbell v MGN* [2004] 2 All ER 995 at 1020 [94] per Lord Hope of Craighead; per Baroness Hale at 1032 [136].
259 *Campbell v MGN* [2004] 2 All ER 995 per Lord Nicholls at 1004 [21]; per Baroness Hale at 1033 [137].
260 For example, *Kalaba v Commonwealth* [2004] FCA 763 at [6] per Heerey J: 'I accept ... that at the moment there is no tort of privacy, although [members of the High Court in *ABC v Lenah Game Meats*] left open that possibility'.
261 [2003] Aust Torts Reports ¶81-706.

The higher courts have generally shown themselves reluctant to recognise a new freestanding tort of invasion of privacy particularly if other legal avenues are available.

punitive, and aggravated damages. The case was settled after an appeal was lodged.

Settlement also followed after the ABC lodged an appeal in *Jane Doe v Australian Broadcasting Corporation*,[262] in which Judge Hampel of the Victorian County Court had awarded more than $200,000 damages to the claimant on the basis of claims of breach of statutory duty, negligence, breach of privacy and breach of confidence in very different but circumstances. The ABC had unlawfully identified the claimant as a victim of a rape when reporting on the criminal proceedings against her assailant. The journalists had pleaded guilty to breach of the *Judicial Reports Act 1958* (Vic), and had apologised to the claimant during those criminal proceedings. There was no evidence that they intended to break the law: the inference was that the fault lay with an inexperienced journalist and sub-editor who were either unaware of the statutory prohibition or did not consider it, and with their employer which may not have given them appropriate training. The claim based on a breach of a statutory duty enacted for the protection of the claimant is arguably the most appropriate action in the circumstances[263] and damages would flow from it. Given the clear statutory breach, it was a highly suitable case for settlement by a media defendant, but it is unfortunate that we now do not have the benefit of an appellate court's review of the first instance judgment. Despite the lengthy analysis of the legal issues by the trial judge, there are a number of troubling aspects of the decision, not least the conclusion:

> that this is an appropriate case to respond, although cautiously, to the invitation held out by the High Court in *Lenah Game Meats* and to hold that the invasion, or breach of privacy alleged here is an actionable wrong which gives right to a right to recover damages according to the ordinary principles governing damages in tort.

To hold that negligent conduct by the media, which does not have as its primary purpose a deliberate intrusion or considered disclosure, gives rise to a tort for breach of privacy would have serious ramifications for the concept of open justice and for the media in reporting court and other public proceedings. It is one thing to say that they should be guilty of a statutory breach and liable for ensuing harm on a strict basis, that is, regardless of fault. The legislature may be taken to have set out that criminal and civil liability in the statute. Arguably, those liabilities should cover the field. It is quite another thing to say that there should be a new tort of *negligent* invasion of privacy, or one of strict liability. It is even questionable whether the action for breach of confidence, where there was no pre-existing relationship or

262   [2007] VCC 281.
263   See also *GS v News Limited* [1998] Aust Torts Reports ¶81-466.

obligation of confidence, should be satisfied by a negligent[264] rather than an intentional breach. Judges often consider all possible arguments in case other conclusions do not survive appellate scrutiny, but in the absence of a clear intent to expose the claimant, the facts that would be problematic for the other actions, for example, the fact that the claimant was identified in public in open court, would be equally or more so for a breach of privacy action. Finally, given that the judge upheld a claim for breach of confidence, it is seriously questionable whether an appeal court would agree that a parallel new tort should be recognised.

The Court of Appeal of the Supreme Court of Victoria has since handed down its judgment in *Giller v Procopets*.[265] It was not a media case nor one involving a public figure, the information involved was obviously private and the claimant was clearly deserving of some protection and some remedy. The information involved was a video of consensual sex between the claimant and her former de facto partner, which he had distributed and threatened to distribute among their family and acquaintances. The information in question had thus been collected during a relationship of trust and confidence, so that protection could rest on this basis alone. The claimant's legal problem was really not whether she could protect the confidence, but the remedy for the clear breach of it. Damages for mental distress consequent on some other damage, such as personal injury or property damage, are not contentious in common law tort claims. But mental distress short of illness is problematic. The court considered whether she had a freestanding cause of action in tort for intentional infliction of emotional distress which fell short of a recognised psychiatric illness[266] – in line with long-standing authority, the majority held that she did not.

---

264 In the sense that the discloser was not actually, but should reasonably have been, aware that the information was private. The New South Wales Law Reform Commission in its 2007 Consultation Paper 1 *Invasion of Privacy*, p 171, argues that in regard to a proposed statutory action, discussed below, including liability for negligent or accidental acts would 'go too far'. There could be an even less culpable type of negligence, that is, where the disclosure itself was inadvertent, such as by dropping a document on the street or sending a fax or email to the wrong address. Again, in the absence of a pre-existing obligation of confidence (which would probably give rise to an action in negligence anyway particularly if the careless person was a professional), it is questionable whether liability for breach of confidence or privacy should ensue.

265 [2008] VSCA 236.

266 Unlike in the United States, the English and Australian courts have long held that there is no freestanding action for mere emotional distress, shock, vexation or grief which falls short of a recognised psychiatric illness, even where the distress in inflicted intentionally. Maxwell P held in *Giller v Procopets* [2008] VSCA 236 that such a claim should be upheld because of the now medically accepted lack of clearly defined boundaries between mental illness and other forms of mental disturbance, and because of the clear, subjective intent to cause distress in this case. But he was in the minority and his bold views are against the weight of authority. Even if he is correct that the requirement of a recognised illness is only, as a matter of strict precedent, confined to cases where intent had to be imputed by the court, such as in the original case of *Wilkinson v Downton* [1897] 2 QB 57, it would nevertheless open the floodgates to recognise a general action for intentional infliction of distress.

A key issue then was the basis for assessment of damages in a non-commercial *equitable* claim for breach of confidence, such as this, where, essentially, the claimant sought damages for the fact of the disclosure and for the distress caused, rather than by reference to the commercial value of the confidential information. In *Campbell v MGN*, Naomi Campbell recovered £3500 in damages for mental distress including aggravated damages[267] with no discussion in the House of Lords on the availability of such damages in a purely equitable claim. Michael Douglas and Catherine Zeta-Jones recovered 'very modest' damages of £3750 for the distress they suffered by the author-ised publication of wedding photographs.[268] Surprisingly, neither Campbell nor the 'Douglases' seem to have sought an account of the defendants' profits from their breaches of confidence.

The extent to which courts of equity may borrow or reflect damages given at common law is highly contentious in Australia and one which is steeped in the history and jurisdiction of the courts of common law and equity.[269] Remedies for breaches of equitable duties generally comprise compensation for loss or an account of the defendant's monetary or material gains arising from the breach. If equitable compensation is now to encompass compensa-tion for mental distress, then this would logically be available for the whole range of equitable wrongs – a novel idea. On the one hand it may be argued to be as inappropriate and without authority as an award in equity of exemplary damages, disapproved in *Harris v Digital Pulse Pty Ltd*.[270] On the other hand, it is argued that not to award such compensation would mean a claimant would have no remedy after a breach:

> An inability to order equitable compensation to a claimant who has suffered distress would mean that a claimant whose confidence was breached before an injunction could be obtained would have no effective remedy.[271]

Noting that there was no Australian authority on the issue, but finding encouragement in the judgments of Gummow and Hayne JJ in *ABC v Lenah Game Meats* that recognised forms of action should be developed and adapted to meet new situations and circumstances, the Court of Appeal unanimously held that damages for mental distress were available in the equitable claim although only a majority agreed on the significant increase in the amount awarded by the trial judge, from a total of $8000 for compensatory damages,

---

267 Usually recoverable at common law only where consequential upon some personal injury or property damage, or, alone, only in actions for trespass (such as battery, assault and false imprisonment) which has always been actionable *per se*, that is, without proof of actual damage.

268 So described by Lord Phillips MR in *Douglas v Hello! Ltd* [2005] 3 WLR 881 at 953 [256], discussed by Neave JA in *Giller v Procopets* [2008] VSCA 236 at [416].

269 In 2003 the New South Wales Court of Appeal overturned an award of exemplary or punitive damages (only till then in Australia awarded in common law tort claims) in an equitable claim for a breach of a fiduciary duty, a claim with many similarities to a claim for breach of confidence: *Harris v Digital Pulse Pty Ltd* (2003) 56 NSWLR 298.

270 (2003) 56 NSWLR 298.

271 *Giller v Procopets* [2008] VSCA 236 at [424] per Neave JA.

including $3000 aggravated damages, to a total of $40,000, including $10,000 aggravated damages. Given her success in this claim and several claims for assault, the court declined to say anything more about a freestanding claim in tort for invasion of privacy[272], with Ashley JA stating that ' a generalised tort of invasion of privacy is not yet recognised in Australia'.[273]

It is noteworthy that the respondent in *Giller v Procopets* was unrepresented by legal counsel. Presumably, if he had been, stronger arguments would have been put to the court on the nature and quantum of the remedy. If not in this case, then surely in another, the issue of the availability and assessment of compensation in equity for mental distress will find its way to the High Court. In the meantime, lower courts and litigants will endeavour to find their way through this difficult and uncertain body of legal principle. Chief Justice Gleeson commented, on his retirement from the High Court that the trial judges in *Grosse v Purvis* and *Doe v Australian Broadcasting Corporation*:

> were pursuing what they regarded as their proper function in following existing authority and taking an opportunity to fill in what they saw as some gaps in the law.[274]

We have not yet in Australia had a civil case which tests the boundaries between what is public and what is private information in relation to a celebrity or public figure. There have been plenty of examples of disclosures which are ones of a) clearly objectionable, or b) legitimate issues for public discussion – for example, of political matters, and so falling within implied rights under the Australian Constitution, or c) lying on the boundaries between these two. Examples are the revelations by the *Sunday Sun-Herald* in 1991 that leading Australian Ballet dancer Kelvin Coe was suffering from AIDS;[275] by journalist Laurie Oakes, who later said that he agonised over the decision to publish, that leading Labor minister Gareth Evans and Australian Democrat leader turned Labor MP Cheryl Kernot were having an affair at the time of her switch;[276] years earlier, about the liaison between Treasurer Jim Cairns and his secretary Junie Morosi;[277] more recently allegations that flam-

---

272   Ibid at [452] per Neave JA.

273   Ibid at [129].

274   Above, n 3.

275   *Sunday Sun-Herald*, 25 August 1991. Mr Coe's partner retaliated by throwing red paint over the journalist Bob Crimeen after allegedly luring him to the Regent Hotel in Sydney.

276   See transcript of *The 7.30 Report*, Australian Broadcasting Corporation, 4 July 2002 <www.abc.net.au/7.30/content/2002/s599023.htm>. 'The man who started this story rolling, Laurie Oakes, is adamant that it is in the public interest. Laurie Oakes, Political Journalist, Channel Nine Interview: The point is that Cheryl Kernot chose to write a book and she chose to write a book purporting to be a political history which was based on a falsehood and as a result of that aspersions were cast on a whole lot of other people, blame was cast for what happened to her when obviously this underlying thing, this steamy affair, was crucial to what happened to her, crucial to her behaviour, crucial to her lapses of judgment. Look, it even decided when Gareth Evans left politics. This was important political influence'.

277   Tiffen, RE, *Scandals, Media, Politics and Corruption in Contemporary Australia* (UNSW Press, 1999), pp 86-87, and on other Australian political scandals, throughout.

> Attitudes to sexual and social mores have changed, so that information which was once treated as defamatory is now not necessarily so.

boyant stockbroker Rene Rivkin was engaged in homosexual relations with his employees. Until recently, public figures of all sorts have tended to use the law of defamation to protect their privacy. But attitudes to sexual and social mores have changed, so that information which was once treated as defamatory is now not necessarily so.[278] Also, in some States such as New South Wales, the defence of truth or justification used to require proof that publication was in the public interest, giving indirect privacy protection, but this has now changed, making defamation less useful in protecting private matters. It is only a matter of time before a celebrity or public figure case will be litigated to test the reach of Australian privacy law and the boundaries of public interest in such cases.

Statutory protection of privacy in Australia

We have seen how the enactment of the *Human Rights Act 1998* in the United Kingdom, requiring courts to give effect to the *European Covenant on the Protection of Human Rights*, has transformed the protection of privacy in that country. Critical to that protection, though, is the balancing exercise that courts must undertake to protect freedom of speech according to the covenant. It is only when there is no legitimate public interest or interest in free speech to be protected that the courts will come down on the side of privacy.

Perhaps in response to such developments elsewhere but also in response to public commentary and concern about media intrusions and the impact of digital, wireless and new electronic technologies, Australian legislatures and government bodies have been giving increasing attention to protection of privacy. During 2008, both the New South Wales Law Reform Commission (NSWLRC) and the Australian Law Reform Commission (ALRC) released consultation papers and reports on a whole range of 'privacy' issues.

The NSWLRC was specifically asked to consider the desirability of introducing a 'statutory tort of privacy' in New South Wales. The NSWLRC, in its consultation paper,[279] recommended a statutory action but that it not be called a 'tort' action, for a number of reasons which show that this is more than just a matter of nomenclature. Calling the action a 'tort' would tie it to the traditional common law and equitable principles and restraints on remedies, whereas the NSWLRC considered that a court should be free to grant the most appropriate remedy in the circumstances. While at first glance this sounds desirably flexible, it does have the disadvantage of being unpredictable, and

---

278 *Rivkin v Amalgamated Television Services Pty Ltd* [2001] NSWSC 432.

279 New South Wales Law Reform Commission, Consultation Paper 1 *Invasion of Privacy,* May 2007. The paper surveys and draws on international developments in the United Kingdom, Canada, Hong Kong, Ireland, New Zealand, the United States, France and Quebec.

there are good reasons why any defendant, but particularly media defendants upon whom society relies for information, should be able to predict what its obligations and liabilities will be if it commits a wrong. In any event, such a broad power would inevitably be construed against the backdrop of developed principles, unless the legislation is specific. Significantly, the NSWLRC envisaged that compensation for mental distress short of psychiatric illness would be available.[280]

> There is no general tort of invasion of privacy, but the courts are now rapidly making up for lost time in developing a body of principles that have the equivalent effect.

Further, creating a statutory tort of invasion of privacy – with the onus on the claimant simply to prove a reasonable expectation of privacy, then passing to the defendant to defend the disclosure – would not give appropriate status and weight to the equally important public interest values such as free speech.

As NSWLRC Commissioner Professor Michael Tilbury explained:

> A preferable approach is to put privacy on a level playing field with these other interests. The public interest then becomes not a defence but an essential consideration in determining whether or not there has been an invasion of privacy in the first place. No interest is presumptively protected at the expense of another.[281]

Such an approach would reflect the methodology seen in the UK case law where courts balance the protections of Arts 8 and 10 of the European code.

Finally, and perhaps surprisingly, the NSWLRC wished to free the statutory privacy protection from the tort based definitions of the term, begun by Warren and Brandeis in their *Harvard Law Review* article in 1890 and much influenced by Professor Prosser in his 1960 *Californian Law Journal* article. Professor Tilbury comments that although the protection from intrusion and disclosure currently lies at the heart of privacy protection, there is no reason to confine the law of privacy to current circumstances. By not defining the term 'privacy', the legislation would leave to the courts the role of developing the concept in future, within defined but broad objectives.[282] So, paradoxically, given the outrage expressed by some that judges have too much power which should be reigned in by legislation, the legislation would give the courts the power to develop the concept beyond its current limits.

The ALRC has also completed a major review of Australia's privacy law, encompassing the concept of 'privacy' in its broadest sense with the major emphasis being on data collection, use, storage and dissemination in a number

---

280   Tilbury, M, 'Invasion of Privacy: A Statutory cause of action, not a tort', *Gazette of Law and Journalism*, 12 May 2008, <www.glj.com.au/392> p 5.

281   Ibid, p 2.

282   Ibid, p 4. Nevertheless, the report, op cit, n 279 above, p 160, gives an example of a non-exhaustive list of the types of invasion that fall within it. One of these is '[using a] person's name, identity, likeness or voice without authority or consent'. Arguably, such an example would significantly extend the range of interests protected in the name of privacy, and come close to 'image rights' seen in France, discussed above.

of contexts such as credit reports, criminal and other investigations and proceedings, and health and social services. In the interests of uniformity, the ALRC has agreed that the NSWLRC would take the primary responsibility for the formulation of proposals for reform.[283] But its report does refer to a number of submissions in favour and against the introduction of a statutory action. Some of these make what may now seem like surprisingly hyperbolic and rapidly outdated assertions about the state of the common law and statutory protections:

> it is unacceptable that people who suffer flagrant invasions of their territorial or bodily privacy or the privacy of their communications have virtually no recourse under existing privacy laws.[284]

It is true that there is no general tort of invasion of privacy, but the courts are now rapidly making up for lost time in developing a body of principles that have the equivalent effect. Protection of disclosure of private facts is now rapidly becoming stronger. The most significant gap in existing law, in our view, is that which deals with the acts of pursuit and surveillance of people, particularly those in the public eye. No doubt Nicole Kidman would agree. But as the notion of a private and family sphere is developed and the law restricts the opportunity to use or exploit the fruits of that surveillance, it will take away much of the market for that conduct. A broad statutory action is not going to solve the most contentious issue of where the boundaries between private and public spheres lie.

Importantly, the ALRC approves a statutory action only in cases of serious invasions of privacy. It would achieve this by requiring a claimant to satisfy *both* tests of what is to be regarded as a sufficiently private to be worthy of protection; the reasonable expectation of privacy test *and* the 'highly offensive to a reasonable person' test, set out by Gleeson CJ in *Australian Broadcasting Corporation v Lenah Game Meats*. But, arguably illustrating the redundancy of a statutory action, the ALRC Report then gives[285] four examples of conduct which would satisfy the serious invasion of privacy test: all of them would undoubtedly warrant protection under existing common law and equitable principles.

The most desirable aspect of the proposed statutory action is its explicit requirement for a balancing of private and public interests, a process which, in the absence of a national Bill of Rights, Human Rights Act or explicit constitutional guarantee, remains uncertain and unpredictable in Australia. The Australian Capital Territory and Victoria introduced a *Human Rights Act* in 2004 and a *Charter of Human Rights and Responsibilities* in 2006

---

283   ALRC Report 108 *Australian Privacy Law and Practice* Vol 3, May 2008 at 2536.

284   ALRC Report 108 *Australian Privacy Law and Practice* Vol 3, May 2008 at 2557, citing submission by the Public Interest Advocacy Centre, Submission PR 548, 26 December 2007.

285   ALRC Report 108 *Australian Privacy Law and Practice* Vol 3, May 2008 at 2570.

respectively, and it will be interesting to see what effect these have on the courts' development of the common law of privacy in these jurisdictions.[286]

The federal government's reaction to the ALRC proposal for a statutory action was lukewarm, especially in the light of other issues given some priority by the Labor government in its first term of office after a long period in Opposition. One of these is the issue of whether Australia should have a Bill of Rights, an issue on which there is continuing debate across the community.

The New South Wales Law Reform Commission released its final report in 2009,[287] recognising the desirability that any action for breach of privacy be uniform across all Australian jurisdictions, and expressing a preference for uniform State and Territory legislation rather than a federal statute. It is a brave proposal in that it is unspecific in defining the precise privacy interest to be protected, or the gaps in the existing law to be remedied, and instead proposes a general action for the invasion of privacy. It also recommends a wide raft of possible remedies, including damages for mental distress, which under existing law are only available in the relatively rare cases where a defendant is judged, subjectively or objectively, to have intended to cause such distress. [288]

There is of course no support in the media for such an action.[289] The media are rightly concerned of the chilling effect that a statutory right may have on the often instant editorial decisions to be made when putting a story on current affairs to print or broadcast[290] and on the media's role in the public scrutiny of misdeeds and abuses of position.[291] As Gleeson CJ noted in the oft-quoted extract from his judgment in *Australian Broadcasting Corporation v Lenah Game Meats:*

> Part of the price we pay for living in an organised society is that we are exposed to observation in a variety of ways by other people.[292]

Reflecting attitudes expressed about a Bill of Rights, many members of the community are also unlikely to support new legislation if it is unclear precisely what conduct will be affected, what interests will be protected and what consequences will flow from breach of the proposed statutory action.

---

286 Neither provides for a cause of action for breach. See generally Byrnes, A, Charlesworth, H and McKinnon, G, *Bills of Rights in Australia; history, politics and law*, (UNSW Press, 2009).

287 'Invasion of Privacy', New South Wales Law Reform Commission, Report 120, April 2009.

288 Under the principle from *Wilkinson v Downton* [1897] 2 QB 57; *Giller v Procopets* [2008] VSCA 236.

289 A proposal to introduce a statutory action in Ireland was dropped after fierce opposition from the media. ALRC Report 108, above n 283 at 2543.

290 David Marr of the *Sydney Morning Herald*, commentary at a seminar, 'Public Interest in Media Law in the United States and Australia', University of Sydney Law Faculty, 31 May 2008.

291 ALRC Report 108, above n 283 at 2555.5-6, citing submissions expressing serious concerns with a proposed statutory action from the Australian Press Council and others.

292 (2001) 208 CLR 199 at 226 [41].

THE TIMES

No. 68631 ■ THURSDAY FEBRUARY 23 2006 ■ NEWSPAPER OF THE YEAR

£40m stolen in biggest cash raid

Armed robbers posing as police officers stole up to £40 million after kidnapping and threatening the wife and young son of a security manager.

The gang struck at a centre in Tonbridge, Kent, run by Securitas, which distributes money to thousands of cash machines. They tied up 14 staff and loaded their haul on to a 7.5 tonne lorry before fleeing. The raid was so big that ministers and Bank of England officials were immediately alerted.
NEWS page 4

Iraq civil war fear

Iraq was facing the threat of civil war after the Golden Mosque in Samarra, one of the holiest Shia shrines, was blown up by insurgents.
NEWS page 3

Bird flu tests on 12

Twelve people, including four children, are in isolation in India awaiting tests results to see if they have contracted the human form of H5N1 bird flu.
NEWS page 2

SAMURAI SU DOKU

Can you solve it in 60min? times2

Why big business is warming to the idea of big government
ANATOLE KALETSKY page 21

COMMENT	18	WEATHER	75
BUSINESS	48	TELEVISION &	
REGISTER	66	RADIO	times2

Buying The Times overseas
Austria €4.30; Belgium €3.29; Canada $4.50; euro zone Toronto $4.91; Canaries €3.25; Cyprus C£1.96; Denmark Dkr 26.00; Finland €6.00; France €3.29; Germany €3.25; Gibraltar £1.80; Greece €3.29; Italy €3.29; Luxembourg €3.29; Malta Lm1.80; Morocco Dh36.03; Netherlands €3.29; Norway Nkr 35.00; Portugal €3.29; €3.29(C); South Africa Rand 29; Spain €3.29; Sweden Skr 32.75; Switzerland Sfr 5.00; Tunisia Dlh 5.25; Turkey YTL4.50; US $5.50. Periodicals Postage Paid at Rahway NJ. Postmaster: Send address corrections to The Times c/o Mercury International 365 Blair Road, Avenel NJ 07001.

www.timesonline.co.uk

The diaries of a dissident Princ

By Andrew Pierce

LAWYERS for the Prince of Wales were yesterday forced to release a private journal that revealed the heir to the throne's wide-ranging thoughts on Tony and Cherie Blair, the demise of the *Royal Yacht Britannia*, and an acerbic view of the Chinese President.

Mr Justice Blackburne ruled that extracts from the 3,000-word manuscript, which is at the centre of a privacy battle between the Prince and *The Mail on Sunday* should be published.

The newspaper's lawyers had argued that the journal contained evidence of "clear political hostility", which the public was entitled to read.

The judge's decision will be seen as an embarrassing setback for the Prince, who had gone to court with the aim of preventing any further publication of his writings.

The journal, written by the Prince as he returned from the handover of Hong Kong to China in the summer of 1997, is scathing about Chinese leadership and both warm and critical of the Prime Minister.

He wrote that Mr Blair had spent only 14 hours in Hong Kong. "They then take decisions based on market research and focus groups, on the papers produced by political advisers and civil servants none of whom will have ever experienced what it is they are taking decisions about."

The Hong Kong journal, one of eight obtained by the newspaper from a former employee of the Prince, was released to the press yesterday by the Prince's lawyers. In bizarre scenes journalists were locked in a room in the High Court and given one hour to copy by hand sections from the document but were forbidden from reproducing it in its entirety.

The Prince is seeking a summary judgment — a ruling without a full trial — over his claim for breaches of confidentiality and copyright against *The Mail on Sunday*. He also wants the journals returned.

The journal described how he landed in Hong Kong and was "delivered" to the *Britannia*, which was on its last overseas engagement. He said that there was a "kind of exasperated sadness experienced by all and sundry" about the decision. "Why is this happening?", he quoted as a comment from Madeleine Albright, the then US Secretary of State.

"The PM and Mrs Blair came on board for an hour and seemed suitably impressed after the whistlestop tour around the ship. If only he could have seen the yacht with the receptions
Continued on page 2, col 3

Reports, pages 6-9
Letters, page 19

SANZ PAULA/EPA

Prince Charles in Hong Kong: attempt to keep diaries private backfired yesterday

ON T CLUB
'It too to rea not fir althou it puz to why seat so uncon

ON TC
'They decisio marke focus papers politic civil se whom experi they a decisio

ON C
'[They irresis tempta intimi local p soldie a glass about their

Conclusion

There have been some notable exposes of celebrity 'privacy' in recent times. Prince Harry's address to a fellow British Army soldier as 'my little Paki friend' was disclosed in the world press and may have taught him a valuable lesson that what might once may have been dismissed as hearsay is now recordable and transmissible from a mobile phone anywhere in the world. Tiger Wood's plaintive plea on his personal website – 'Personal sins should not require press releases and problems within a family shouldn't have to mean public confessions' – was quickly outdated by events. He has come to realise that he had no hope of what he described as a 'right to some simple, human measure of privacy'[293] given his previous willing exposure to the golfing world's adulation and the benefits of lucrative commercial endorsements.

Outside the United States, at least, some celebrities have begun to gain some protected ground, and in doing so, have carved out an increasing recognition of privacy for everyone. Whether such protections against organised media will ultimately be futile in the Internet age, where everyone is a publisher, remains to be seen.

International celebrities continue to push for a convergence of laws from different jurisdictions. Taking advantage of an increasingly greater sympathy for celebrities' privacy under British law, Brad Pitt and Angelina Jolie have now attempted to import into the United Kingdom an American notion of breach of privacy: they argue that the publication of false rumours of a separation and division of assets and children amounts to an invasion of their privacy. Success in such an action where the allegation is neither defamatory nor a disclosure of true private facts, would be a first for the British courts.[294] Nevertheless, as we have seen in this chapter, the law of privacy around the world is in a state of rapid development, and it is fair to say it has taken over from defamation as the key legal battleground between media and celebrities. It also illustrates how celebrities are increasingly using the law of privacy, as well as that of trademarks, passing off, and defamation to manage their images, reputations and public personalities.

---

293   <http://web.tigerwoods.com/news/article/200912027740572/news/>.

294   <www.guardian.co.uk/media/2010/feb/09/angelina-jolie-news-of-the-world-brangelina>. In the past complainants were more likely to take their complaint to the Press Complaints Commission.

TABLE OF CASES

TABLE OF STATUTES

INDEX

European Court of Human Rights, vi, 124, 129, 131, 134, 136, 149, 152, 157

Evans, Gareth, 163

experience of celebrity, 2

'expressive elites', 3

fame, 7-24
    characteristics, 2
    court society, 9-10
    modern form, 8
    state formation, 9-10

Fawcett, Jamie, 72

Féderation Internationale de l'Automobile (FIA), 154

Fleming, John, 85

Ford, Anna, 143, 152

France
    disclosure of private matters, 125-31
        Civil Code, 128
        health context, 128-9
        legitimate public interest and, 129-30
        protection of privacy rights, 126-7
        Rachel case, 126
        two-tier protection, 128

France Dimanche, 127

Franck, Georg, 22

Franklin, Benjamin, 18

freedom of speech, 67-8, 69, 78, 81

Garbo, Greta, 105

Germany
    law of privacy, 125, 131-7
        constitutional protection of human dignity and personality, 132, 134
        Copyright (Arts Domain) Act, 133
        photographs, publication of, 109, 112, 133-4
        Von Hannover v Germany, 131, 132-6, 143, 149, 150

Gleeson, Murray, 91, 115, 143, 150, 158, 166, 167

Goldberg, Whoopi, 30

Grant, Hugh, 144, 152

Greene, Graham, 69

Gurevich, Aaron, 13

Gutnick, Joseph, viii, 82-3

Gwynn, Nell, 8

Habermas, Jurgen, 17